Contemporary Black and Asian Women Playwrights in Britain

This is the first monograph to document and analyse the plays written
by Black and Asian women in Britain. The volume explores how Black
and Asian women playwrights theatricalize their experiences of
migration, displacement, identity, racism, and sexism in Britain. Plays
by writers such as Tanika Gupta, Winsome Pinnock, Maya Chowdhry,
and Amrit Wilson, among others – many of whom have had their work
produced at key British theatre sites – are discussed in some detail.
Other playwrights' work is also briefly explored to suggest the range and
scope of contemporary plays. The volume analyses concerns such as
geographies of un/belonging, reverse migration (in the form of tourism),
sexploitation, arranged marriages, the racialization of sexuality, and
asylum seeking as they emerge in the plays, and argues that Black and
Asian women playwrights have become constitutive subjects of British
theatre.

GABRIELE GRIFFIN is Professor of Gender Studies at the University of
Hull. During the 1990s she edited four volumes of plays with Elaine
Aston. Her recent publications include *HIV/AIDS: Visibility Blue/s*
(2000), *Thinking Differently: A Reader in European Women's Studies*
(with Rosi Braidotti, 2002), and *Who's Who in Lesbian and Gay Writing*
(2002). She is co-editor of the journal *Feminist Theory*.

CAMBRIDGE STUDIES IN MODERN THEATRE

Series editor
David Bradby, *Royal Holloway, University of London*

Advisory board
Martin Banham, *University of Leeds*
Jacky Bratton, *Royal Holloway, University of London*
Tracy Davis, *Northwestern University*
Sir Richard Eyre
Michael Robinson, *University of East Anglia*
Sheila Stowell, *University of Birmingham*

Volumes for Cambridge Studies in Modern Theatre explore the political, social, and cultural functions of theatre while also paying careful attention to detailed performance analysis. The focus of the series is on political approaches to the modern theatre with attention also being paid to theatres of earlier periods and their influence on contemporary drama. Topics in the series are chosen to investigate this relationship and include both playwrights (their aims and intentions set against the effects of their work) and process (with emphasis on rehearsal and production methods, the political structure within theatre companies, and their choice of audiences or performance venues). Further topics will include devised theatre, agitprop, community theatre, para-theatre, and performance art. In all cases the series will be alive to the special cultural and political factors operating in the theatres examined.

Books published
Brian Crow with Chris Banfield, *An Introduction to Post-Colonial Theatre*
Mario DiCenzo, *The Politics of Alternative Theatre in Britain,*
 1968–1990:7:84 (Scotland)
Jo Riley, *Chinese Theatre and the Actor in Performance*
Jonathan Kalb, *The Theatre of Heiner Müller*
Richard Boon and Jane Plastow, eds., *Theatre Matters: Performance and*
 Culture on the World Stage
Claude Schumacher, ed., *Staging the Holocaust: the Shoah in Drama and*
 Performance
Philip Roberts, *The Royal Court Theatre and the Modern Stage*
Nicholas Grene, *The Politics of Irish Drama: Plays in Context from*
 Boucicault to Friel
Anatoly Smeliansky, *The Russian Theatre after Stalin*
Michael Patterson, *Strategies of Political Theatre: Post-War British*
 Playwrights
Elaine Aston, *Feminist Views on the English Stage: Women Playwrights,*
 1990–2000
Gabriele Griffin, *Contemporary Black and Asian Women Playwrights in*
 Britain

Contemporary Black and Asian Women Playwrights in Britain

Gabriele Griffin
University of Hull

CAMBRIDGE
UNIVERSITY PRESS

CAMBRIDGE UNIVERSITY PRESS
Cambridge, New York, Melbourne, Madrid, Cape Town,
Singapore, São Paulo, Delhi, Tokyo, Mexico City

Cambridge University Press
The Edinburgh Building, Cambridge CB2 8RU, UK

Published in the United States of America by Cambridge University Press, New York

www.cambridge.org
Information on this title: www.cambridge.org/9780521174510

© Gabriele Griffin 2003

First published 2003
First paperback edition 2011

A catalogue record for this publication is available from the British Library

Library of Congress Cataloguing in Publication data
Griffin, Gabriele.
Contemporary Black and Asian women playwrights in Britain / Gabriele Griffin.
p.   cm – (Cambridge studies in modern theatre)
Includes bibliographical references and index.
ISBN 0 521 81725 0
1. English drama – 20th century – History and criticism.   2. Feminist drama,
English – History and Criticism.   3. English drama – Women authors – History
and criticism.   4. English drama – Black authors – History and criticism.
5. English drama – Asian authors – History and criticism.   6. English
drama – 20th century – History and criticism.   7. Women, Black – Great
Britain – Intellectual life.   8. Asians – Great Britain – Intellectual life.
9. Feminism and literature – Great Britain.   10. Women and literature – Great
Britain.   11. Woman, Black, in literature.   12. Asians in literature.   1. Title.
11. Series.
PR739.F45G75   2003
822′.914099287 – dc21   2003048991

ISBN 978-0-521-81725-7 Hardback
ISBN 978-0-521-17451-0 Paperback

Contents

Plates

Acknowledgements

I first started thinking about this monograph whilst teaching an MA course on 'Race, Ethnicity and Gender' at Kingston University. My thanks therefore go to the students on that course with whom I had many lively debates about these issues, and in particular Ise Obumhense and Honorine Ranivoharisoa whose views, insights, and experiences informed my thinking on these matters. Thanks also go to former colleagues from Kingston University, in particular Tom Betteridge, who offered much stimulating conversation.

In the spring of 2001, Kingston University granted me a sabbatical which enabled me to progress the research for this volume, and in the autumn of 2001 I benefited from an AHRB grant under their leave scheme which gave me important respite from teaching and other duties when I moved to the University of Hull. A grant from the Faculty Research Committee of the University of Hull enabled me to spend some valuable time at the British Library. I would also like to acknowledge the British Academy whose grant enabled archival research at the Bristol Theatre Collection, the Theatre Museum in London, picture research, and the reproduction of the photos in this volume.

Many Black and Asian women playwrights provided time, scripts, production images, conversation, and information. Among them I'd like to thank most particularly Rukhsana Ahmad from Kali Theatre Company who dug through the company's archives for photos, scripts, and information, gave generously of her time and was a delightful visitor to an undergraduate course on 'Contemporary Women's Theatre' I taught at Kingston University. I'd also like to thank Zindika who provided scripts, as well as much insight into her work and into the experience of those children who were left behind in the West Indies as their parents sought to make a life in Britain, and who pointed me in the right direction regarding production photos. Ketaki Kushari Dyson gave me generously of her time and made me aware of the difficulties of living between two cultures in which one's standing as a writer is not the same. Rani Drew answered my emails promptly and provided me with copies of her playscripts in an act of great generosity – my thanks to her. I'd also like to thank Felix Cross of NITRO, formerly the Black Theatre Co-operative, who gave me time and looked through their archives for relevant material and images.

Professor Peter Thomson from Exeter University, Professor Viv Gardner, and Professor David Mayer from Manchester University were among the first to read and comment on my book proposal. Their encouragement and support was important for the project, and I thank them for these. I'd also like to thank Professor David Punter from the University of Bristol, whose paper entitled 'The Hatred of Europe: Postcoloniality, Psychoanalysis, Culture', delivered at the ESSE conference 2000, helped me to shape my own thinking. The two anonymous readers of my original proposal to Cambridge University Press offered useful comments which influenced the scope of this project – my sincere thanks to them.

Staff at the Theatre Collection of the Drama Department of the University of Bristol, in particular Frances Carlyon, were most helpful whilst I stayed there. I also received support from staff at the Theatre Museum in London, including Susan Croft with whom I emailed briefly, from staff in the manuscript collection of the British Library, and from staff in the Special Collections of Leeds University Library, which holds archival material from West Yorkshire Playhouse. At West Yorkshire Playhouse Stacey Arnold graciously and swiftly provided some source material.

In the hunt for production photos the following photographers were particularly helpful: Sheila Burnett, Suki Dhanda, Shangara Singh, Simon Annand, Tim Smith. Their work in all bar one cases appears in this volume.

Among my PhD students Anjona Roy, Sarah Yetunde Tuakli, and Honorine Ranivoharisoa have been particularly important;

discussions about their work have impacted on my own writing. Elaine Aston, Professor of Theatre Studies at the University of Lancaster, has been a friend for many years, and our collaboration during the late 1980s and first half of the 1990s, when we interviewed women's theatre groups together and co-edited four volumes of plays by women, provided some of the impetus for this work. My thanks to her.

Finally, I'd like to say thanks to Simon Gunn for his unstinting support, advice, suppers, and . . .

1 Introduction

Since the 1980s there has been a steady increase in the number of Black and Asian women playwrights working in Britain.[1] In the main these are either women whose parents migrated to the UK, or women who arrived in the UK as young children, or women who were born and educated in Britain.[2] Frequently college- or university-educated,[3] they tend to work across a range of media including radio, television, film, the newspapers, and literary forms such as poetry and fiction since it is impossible for most playwrights to make a living from their theatre work. Black and Asian women playwrights often create their plays in response to calls for submissions or commissions to write for a particular company or on a specific topic. Maria Oshodi, for instance, was asked to write a play on sickle-cell anaemia by a member of staff from the Sickle Cell Centre in Lambeth (Brewster 1989: 94). Tanika Gupta responded to a call from Talawa inviting 'new, black women to send in stage scripts' (Stephenson and Langridge 1997: 116). Gurpreet Kaur Bhatti's *Besharam (Shameless)*[4] was written as part of Birmingham Rep's Attachment Scheme, designed to promote new playwriting and nurture young writers for theatre. The emergence and publication of work by Black and Asian women playwrights in Britain (e.g. Wandor, ed. 1985; Remnant, ed. 1986; Brewster, ed. 1987, 1989, 1995; Davis, ed. 1987; Harwood, ed. 1989; Remnant, ed. 1990; George, ed. 1993; Gupta 1997; Mason-John 1999; Rapi and Chowdhry 1998) has coincided, in Theatre Studies, with the establishment of postcolonial theatre/theory, intercultural theatre, world theatre, and performance studies. These developments reflect the hold of the globalization process on the cultural imaginary. They also bespeak the histories from which these theatres have emerged, histories of colonization, of cultural appropriation and commodification, of cultural exchange, curiosity, transformation, and international engagement, mostly on a highly politicized, uneven playing field on which the drama of the politics of the day found – and continues to find – cultural expression in contemporary theatre, performance, and theory.

Postcolonial, intercultural, and world theatres

Neither postcolonial nor intercultural nor world theatre has paid any sustained attention to the Black and Asian women playwrights now active on the British stage. As Sandra Ponzanesi in relation to writing more generally has put it: 'migration literature and post-colonial literature in general hardly focus on the internal differences present within Europe' (2002: 211). There are many reasons for this. In the case of postcolonial theatre/theory, the focus – as the term itself suggests – has been on the relation between the colonial and what came/comes after, often very much with the head turned back towards the colonial and with an emphasis on the current cultural productions in the former colonies.[5] 'Postcolonial theatre' indexes a political paradigm and reality shift (from colonial to postcolonial), a historico-temporal period (signifying what comes after the end of the colonial empires), and a reaction to all that coloniality entailed. Helen Gilbert and Joanne Tompkins' *Post-Colonial Drama* (1996), for instance, centres on the drama produced in former colonies, predominantly in Africa. Gilbert's later edited volume *(Post)Colonial Stages* (1999) includes discussions of theatre from across the world, still very much roaming the former colonial territories. In its focus on the theatre of the former colonies, this work offers important insights into the transformations which the impact of colonial forces and changes in political regime have wrought upon that theatre, even if and as it critiques past colonial conditions and their impacts. It gives voice and reception to the work of those formerly colonized. But it does not engage with the work of those who migrated to Britain or who are the children of such migrants, now living in Britain. Indeed, Ponzanesi claims that 'The post-colonial debate tends to be dominated by the English language as it rotates around the axis Britain/India, re-proposing the old dichotomy of empire while claiming to voice subaltern histories and marginal positions' (2002: 211).[6]

'World theatre' references theatre from around the world in an apparently politically and historically neutral manner that is, in fact, belied by the specificities of the 'theatres' discussed under that heading. J. Ellen Gainor's *Imperialism and Theatre: Essays on World Theatre, Drama and Performance* (1995) in every contribution challenges the assumption of a politically and ideologically unimplicated theatre. But it also frequently leaves intact the notion that theatre is sited in unitary, homogeneous geopolitical sites, referencing nations and ethnicities in ways that suggest that they have been unaffected by the flux of people, pressures of differences, and diasporic movements that go hand in hand with current forms of globalization.

'Intercultural theatre' comes in many guises but its chief characteristic is the conjunction of theatrical elements from different cultures, hence the 'inter' (see Pavis 1996). That theatre has been the object of much recent critique (see Bharucha 2000). Julie Holledge and Joanne Tompkins begin their *Women's Intercultural Performance* (2000) with the following telling words: 'Intercultural projects that originate in the west tend to focus on aesthetics first and politics second . . . Interculturalism all too frequently is perceived to become "political" only when a critic complains about (mis)representations of otherness or appropriations of culture' (1). Much of the focus of intercultural theatre has been on the conflagration of east and west, the use of Japanese, Chinese, Indian performance elements or narratives in theatre by western directors. Again, this work leaves intact a geopolitical imaginary that distinguishes, in a seemingly unproblematized way, between 'them' and 'us', between an 'other' and a 'self'.

Insofar as Black women's production for performance has been analysed, this has occurred at the intersection of postmodern, postcolonial, and subaltern theories, with drama or theatre work understood – with reference to the anthropologically based work of Victor Turner (1982) and Richard Schechner (1985; 1994) – as an extension or enactment of ritual and/or as what is now termed 'live art' or performance art (e.g. Ugwu 1995; Gilbert and Tompkins 1996).[7]

Turner's work especially, but also Schechner's, is invested in understanding performance as an evolutionary process, with continuities across time, cultures, and histories, ranging from everyday practice through ritual to 'high art'. This evolutionary model, referencing a certain cultural and historical past, is rather well encapsulated in Schechner's diagram of 'the evolution of cultural genres of performance from "liminal" to "liminoid"' that forms part of his foreword to Turner's *The Anthropology of Performance* (1987). Turner's work, more heavily anthropologically inflected than Schechner's, harks back unabashedly to 'primitive societies', 'tribal cultures', and other such vocabularies which inform what he describes in *From Ritual to Theatre* (1982) as his 'personal voyage of discovery from traditional anthropological studies of ritual performance to a lively interest in modern theatre, particularly experimental theatre' (7). Indeed, Turner's last writings before his death in 1983 were moving towards a sociobiology of performance,[8] now of course a hotly contested terrain. Some Black and Asian British female performers' work has thus found itself the object of a certain (albeit limited) amount of attention because placing that performance work into lines of continuity which connect it with 'tribal cultures' and 'primitive societies' continues to embed that work in a postcolonial tradition which maintains those visibly different in a by now imaginary space of colonial otherness, part of the empire we'd still love to have. Avtar Brah (1996) has rightly talked of the problematic of the 'indigene' subject position and its precarious relationship to 'nativist' discourses. In some of the theoretico-critical work on performance we find ourselves back on that terrain. Indeed, Robert Young (1995) has shown how certain vocabularies, encapsulated in his work in and as the term 'hybridity', and commonly used in postcolonial theory, unselfconsciously and uncritically repeat ideas that informed the very coloniality which the new theories seek to critique.

In a thought-provoking essay Julie Stone Peters (1995) discusses critiques of postcolonial and intercultural theatre; she points to 'studies of the superimposition of European high culture on local cultures (and hence the suppression of the local); studies of the "orientalist" (inevitably falsifying) representation of the "non-Western"; studies of

4

the ethnographic voyeurist spectatorship that serves such representation' (200) as evidence for the west's cultural imperialism. Her argument is that many of these studies reproduce 'the history of theatre in the empires [a]s the history of two sides' (201) which 'often unconsciously perpetuate . . . the unnuanced bifurcation of West and East, First and Third Worlds, developed and undeveloped, primitive and civilized' (202). Stone Peters' attempt to rescue postcolonial and intercultural theatre from such accusations translates into an assertion of 'theatre's position as an explorer in cultural forms' (208) and a celebration of the notion of translation, of the mutability of all cultural forms, and of identity as a way forward in the debate, a plea for viewing postcolonial and intercultural theatre as expressive of (ex)change where 'what is lost in translation may be gained in communication' (206). Stone Peters' argument is in many ways persuasive although she has to lose sight of her early point that cultural exchange does not happen on a level playing field in order to make it stick. In looking for a theatre which might exhibit the transformative potential she seeks to celebrate, Stone Peters references Una Chaudhuri who discusses '"the drama of immigrants" (196), in which an oversimplification or essentializing of cultural identity becomes untenable – in which it becomes impossible radically to subdivide the world into the "foreign" and the "familiar," the "exotic" and the "standard," "them" and "us"' (209).

The notion of the 'drama of immigrants' is contested by Mary Karen Dahl contributing to the same collection of essays as Stone Peters. Dahl refers to a discussion between her and a colleague in which she wanted to describe 'black theatre' as 'postcolonial' whilst the colleague thought it was 'immigrant drama' (1995: 40). Dahl ultimately refuses the term 'immigrant drama' after outlining the ways in which Britain's immigration policy is racist (see also Solomos 1993). Her argument is that the term 'postcolonial' gestures towards a history, that of colonization, which is conveniently obliterated by 'immigrant', a word that does not reference the prior histories that motivated that migration.

Three issues arise from these debates: one is the clear politicization of all the terms that are used; the second one is the question of who does the naming; and the third one is the question of what real-ities and/or histories we wish to address through such naming. Given Britain's colonial pasts and histories of migration that involved both shipping out and shipping in, the politicized specificity of terms refer-ring to theatre by Black and Asian playwrights is inevitable. Indeed, it is noticeable – bearing in mind how little writing on this work there is, notwithstanding the size of the actual corpus – that most of the texts dealing with Black and Asian (women) playwrights' work are explic-itly political in their scope, with titles such as 'Postcolonial British Theatre: Black Voices at the Center'; 'Bodies Outside the State: Black British Women Playwrights and the Limits of Citizenship'; or 'Small Island People: Black British Women Playwrights'. All these titles also reference space, articulate explicitly or implicitly a tension between margin and centre, between inside and outside, which points to the imbrication of the *polis* as space and as political entity in the fashion-ing of Black and Asian identities. They tend to do so from a position permeated by a sense of colonial history, the present as expressive of the past.

The socio-cultural geographies they address are dealt with rather differently in Avtar Brah's discussion of 'the politics of loca-tion'. Understanding the importance of articulating the relationship between space, history, and present, Brah focuses on 'diaspora' as en-capsulating that relationship. Arguing that 'if the circumstances of leaving are important, so, too, are those of arrival and settlement' (1996: 182), Brah explores 'how different groups come to be relation-ally positioned in a given context' (182–3), and proposes the concept of *'diaspora space'* (208) to designate the terrain in which, as she puts it, 'multiple subject positions are juxtaposed, contested, proclaimed or disavowed; where the permitted and the prohibited perpetually in-terrogate; and where the accepted and the transgressive imperceptibly mingle even while these syncretic forms may be disclaimed in the name of purity and tradition' (208). Brah's concept of diaspora space importantly entails the recognition that that space is inhabited 'not only by those who have migrated and their descendants, but equally by those who are constructed and represented as indigenous' (209). Brah argues that both migrants and those who remain in one place are affected and effected by migration, that diaspora is the contemporary condition of being in multi-cultural spaces and that people from diverse ethnic and racial backgrounds are equally shaped by diaspora, equally but not necessarily in the same way. Brah's conceptualization privileges the here and now, and it is this which makes her theoretical framework relevant here.

Empire and migration

The imaginary which nostalgically retains coloniality at its core is unsettled by the work of contemporary Black and Asian women playwrights in Britain because, as will become clear, these 'black [and Asian] voices at the center', to borrow the subtitle of an essay by Mary Karen Dahl, are not merely 'at the center' but, indeed, *of* the centre. Contrary to Paul Gilroy's assertion that *There Ain't No Black in the Union Jack*, this work reveals that 'black' is a constitutive part of the 'Union Jack' as a metaphor for Britain, and it is the need to engage with this constitutivity that has prompted this volume. That need arises in part as a function of the increasing, and increasingly public, debates about race relations in the UK,[9] necessitated by continued racist attacks against Black and Asian people, racial harassment, and racialized violence in institutional and extra-institutional settings.[10] These debates and the race-related tensions and violence of the period since the 1980s are themselves expressive of the socio-political changes that Britain has undergone since the Second World War. Key to those changes has been the decline of the British Empire, a much more recent occurrence than its commodification through phenomena such as the Merchant-Ivory films about India would have us believe. Hong Kong, it is worth remembering, was only relinquished in 1997. And Britain continues to exercise sovereignty over bits of land and over people geographically significantly removed from the British Isles, such as the Falklands and, closer to home, Gibraltar.

The decline of empire has been matched by successive waves of migration into Britain of people from the former colonies, of Black people from the Caribbean and various African countries and of Asian people from India, from Pakistan, and from East Africa in the wake of political turmoil there (see Wilson 1978; Owen 1992, 1993; Solomos

1993; Luthra 1997; Visram 2002). These migrants were initially encouraged to come to Britain as part of the post-war reconstruction and economic expansion.[11] Their arrival into Britain shattered the presumed dichotomy between Britain and its colonial 'others', creating the beginning of a transformation of what 'being British' means, a shift encoded, *inter alia*, in the various successive immigration and race relations acts designed to regulate the collapse between 'margins' and 'centre' as a consequence of migration (see chapter three in Solomos).

The migrations of Black and Asian people to Britain have their socio-economic, political, and historical, as well as geographical specificities (Wilson 1978; Solomos 1992; www.movinghere.org.uk). Whereas migrants in the mid-twentieth century, both from the Caribbean and from India and Pakistan, often but not invariably came from very impoverished rural areas, the Asians who arrived from the East African countries as political refugees during the 1970s, for instance, were frequently middle class with histories of considerable economic success. 'Black' and 'Asian' migrants to Britain thus did not constitute a homogeneous group of people, even if they were treated as such. Their diversity of backgrounds, languages, customs, religions, and everyday practices remained unrecognized as Britain, itself not a unitary entity, sought to come to terms with – as Avtar Brah has described it – its 'diaspora space'.

Brah's *Cartographies of Diaspora: Contesting Identities* (1996) is conceptually significant for this volume because Brah seeks to shift the discourse from coloniality and postcoloniality, from migration and immigration, to *diaspora* which for her signals *'multi-locationality across geographical, cultural and psychic boundaries'* (194). For Brah 'the concept of diaspora offers a critique of discourses of fixed origins' (180), a critique all the more necessary as British identities increasingly include people of mixed-race origin (Alibhai-Brown and Montague 1992; Alibhai-Brown 2001); migrants who have settled in the UK, sometimes after successive migrations that render any notion of a fixed origin untenable; and children of migrants who were born and brought up in Britain. Moreover, and equally important, Brah argues strongly that migration impacts not only on those who migrate but also on the communities into which they migrate. In this diaspora space multiple subject positions occur (208); fixity of origin becomes indeterminate and identity equivocal. This 'liquid condition of modernity', as Zygmunt Bauman has termed it, is the condition in which plays by contemporary Black and Asian women playwrights in Britain have been forged, and they bear the marks of that condition.

As the preceding pages indicate, *Contemporary Black and Asian Women Playwrights in Britain* seeks to engage with a body of theatre work that has, on the whole, escaped critical attention. It has escaped this attention in my view because it does not readily fall into the remit of postcolonial, intercultural, or world theatre. The latter frequently perpetuate historical divisions by exploring 'the other' as *other*. Instead, I want to argue that although the plays under consideration bear the mark of those divisions, the work itself is produced by writers who do not necessarily view themselves as 'other' within Britain and who are now claiming their place at the table of British high culture. Their points of reference – in theatrical terms – are thus not the rituals, performances, or theatre works that are prevalent in the West Indies, parts of Africa, India, or Pakistan, but those of contemporary British theatre. These playwrights' work does not, in other words, readily fit the categories of postcolonial, intercultural, or world theatre as these are currently understood, but should be viewed as part of British theatre now. As subsequent chapters illustrate, as such this work comments on the lived conditions of diasporic peoples in contemporary Britain, giving voice to their preoccupations and experiences. My concern, expressed through the thematic approach taken in this volume, is thus with the issues raised in this work and their relation to contemporary Britain.

Naming identities

To talk of the work of Black and Asian women playwrights instantly begs the question of what 'Black' and 'Asian' mean. Both terms have political and cultural histories in the UK that are very different from their histories elsewhere. These histories have been variously charted (e.g. Wilson 1978; Mama 1984; Gilroy 1992, 1993; Mason-John 1995, 1999). As Mary Karen Dahl, looking in from the outside, observes

9

of Britain: 'Hegemonic political and popular discourses combine diverse groups representing diverse cultures into a single category, the "not white"' (1995: 52). Playwright and performer Valerie Mason-John, commenting from within, graphically endorses this view: 'We were all wogs, all niggers, all coons. As a young child . . . I was called coloured along with children of Indian, Pakistani, Chinese, and Japanese descent, and anyone else who didn't resemble white' (1999: 11). During the late 1970s and early 1980s in the UK this homogenization in part led to a politics of coalition-building and strategic political alliances among people of West Indian, African, Indian, Pakistani, and other diverse origins, fuelled by a desire to achieve greater visibility and political impact through such coalitions. The history of the Organization of Women of Africa and African Descent (OWAAD), renamed the Organization of Women of African and Asian Descent, is instructive here and illustrative of that phase of identity politics and coalition-building that, *inter alia*, shaped the race politics of the UK in the 1980s (see Mason-John 1999: 12–14; see also *Feminist Review* special issue on *Black Feminist Perspectives*, 17, Autumn 1984). The 'blackification' of women from diverse communities in Britain facilitated the adoption of the term 'black' as the signifier of a political allegiance of people who suffer/ed racialized oppression in Britain.[12] It also related to the (re-)appropriation and revaluation of the term 'black' as one associated with pride and power. Mason-John argues that 'during the 1970s it seemed quite clear that women of African, Caribbean and Asian descent were black' (1999: 12). However, it also became clear that the strategic utility of the term had its limits in the very different needs and issues diverse communities faced as is expressed in the plays written by women from these very different communities. In the same way that the question of arranged marriages, for instance, does not affect Caribbean communities, so the issue of single motherhood tends not to be foregrounded within Asian communities.[13] The recognition of these differences led to the demise of OWAAD and, more generally, to the foregrounding of diversity as key to contemporary Britain.

The homogenizing term 'Black' can no longer easily be used in 2003. There is a recognition now, for instance, that contemporary

British culture has been differentially shaped by Black and Asian influences. Whilst the popular music and dance scene of the 1980s and early 1990s, for instance, was strongly influenced by Black cultures of various kinds, meaning cultures that bear the signature of African, Caribbean, and Black American backgrounds, the 1990s and early years of the twenty-first century have seen the rise and increasing visibility of Asian cultures in Britain. West Indian carnivals have been matched by Asian melas in towns such as Leeds, Bradford, Manchester, Leicester, and London. In 2002 in Britain much publicity was given to the arrival of *Bombay Dreams*, a Bollywood musical brought to the British stage with a script by Meera Syal, by now a household name in the UK through the television series which she co-scripts and in which she stars such as *Goodness Gracious Me* and *The Kumars from No. 42*, as much as her acclaimed novels *Anita and Me* and *Life Isn't All Ha-Ha, Hee-Hee*. Zadie Smith's novel *White Teeth*, an epic about multi-cultural twentieth-century Britain, has been televised. Bollywood is widely discussed and can be viewed in all major British cities as well as on late-night British television. There are numerous theatre companies such as Kali Theatre Company, Clean Break, Red Ladder, Pilot Theatre Company, and others, which promote new work by British Asian – as well as Black – women playwrights. Bands such as Asian Dub Foundation have generated new fusion sounds that collapse cultural boundaries. The cultural identity that diverse Asian communities have carved out for themselves in Britain during the 1990s is both prominent and distinct from Black British cultural identities and operates across somewhat different cultural terrains. In the Britain of the twenty-first century both 'Black' and 'Asian' presences thus mould British culture in different but highly articulated ways.

Recognizing diversity

To understand the work of Black and Asian women playwrights in Britain, one needs to understand something of the patterns of migration underlying the emergence of that work. The patterns of migration which have informed the arrival of Black people in Britain are distinct from those of Asian people though much of the migration by Black and Asian people into Britain took place after the Second

World War and in many ways mirrors Britain's colonial history. The arrival of the SS *Empire Windrush* in 1948 saw the entry of some 400 British subjects from the Caribbean into Britain (see Solomos 1993; Wambu 1998). Mass migration from the West Indies thus in some respects preceded migration from African countries, and also that from the Indian subcontinent. These migrations, a function of both labour market opportunities in the UK and changing economic and political climates in the countries from which people migrated, are the histories which inform the plays by Black and Asian women in Britain, frequently providing the central dynamic of the plays as their characters seek to live the diasporic lives which those migrations have meant for them.

As this volume demonstrates, diversity among Black and Asian populations, as much as between Black, Asian, and white populations, is central to the diasporic identities they – we – inhabit. Many plays by Black women playwrights, for instance, *inter alia* thematize the issue of the differences between Black people coming from African countries and Black people coming from the Caribbean. In Maria Oshodi's *The 'S' Bend* (n.d.), for example, her mother forbids Fola, one of the protagonists, to go to a party with the words: 'You mix with all these West Indian people who never pick up a book and read; do you want to end up like them? Go to your room and study, don't talk to me about West Indian parties!' (1, 3: 6). When Fola tells her West Indian friend Claudette that she is not allowed to attend the party, Claudette responds: 'You're under that African woman's power a bit too much' (1, 4: 19). And when a white girl, Mya, asks Fola about the differences between West Indians and Africans, Fola asserts that they have 'a different sort of general outlook, values, I suppose' (1, 6: 28), which she characterizes as 'A high educational value in the African, and I guess a high material value in the other, coupled with a lack of cultural identity' (1, 6: 29). Fola's view is that whilst Africans and West Indians can mix – her best friend, after all, is West Indian – 'one of the two has to make a sacrifice – SELL OUT, and too often, in most cases, it's the African half' (1, 6: 29). In her attempt to resist the materiality and loss of cultural identity she ascribes to West Indians, Fola in the end decides to return to Nigeria, inspired by a talk with her uncle:

he showed me the possibility of avoiding a sell out. He seemed to understand my feelings precisely. He had been brought up in England himself and found that the only way to escape the pressure of conflicting cultures was to completely avoid them and live in a less conflicting environment. This can only be done in your own native land, so he suggested I try life in Nigeria for a while.

I thought about this for weeks. To accept a total change to a new life-style; would it work in my case? I tried to visualize my future in England and just saw a life torn by my submission to superficial cultural groups. This would mean a continuation of the confusion . . . I may stay in Nigeria just long enough to gain some sort of identity, strong enough to keep me afloat for when and if I return to England. But, whatever the outcome, Mya, the feeling of NOT completely selling out is a feeling that has totally re-shaped my views and my life. I've managed to carry out my own small rebellion.

(1, 7: 45)

Fola's response is of course only one version of how one might deal with diversity; her repatriation at the end of the play, both into the 'custody' of her uncle and into the country her parents came from, as well as her insistence on the possibility of the preservation of a singular specific identity under diasporic conditions, raise as many questions about female identity as they seemingly resolve for Fola. The point here, however, is the articulation of differences among Black people, the assertion of (a not invariably celebrated) diversity in a context – Britain – where homogenization is the norm. Indeed, as the discussion of Ahmad's 'Song for a Sanctuary' in chapter five shows, such differences, emblematized in Ahmad's play in the clash between two Asian women with radically different diasporic histories and trajectories, are themselves often a source of conflict and are presented as such in many of the plays, providing both dramatic tension and narrative movement.

Brah's argument concerning diaspora space constitutes a significant rupture with those postcolonial positions that continue to operate in homogenizing and binarist terms. It also opens an avenue for considering new identities as they emerge and are articulated in the twenty-first century (see, for example, Ang 2001). The monolithic 'Black' or 'Asian' – which often figures as an ascription – is thus invited to contemplate identities that refuse such homogenization (see Ang-Lygate 1997). Geraldine Connor's self-description in her afterword to the programme for *Carnival Messiah* (2002), for instance, states:

> In this third millennium, I see myself as a living exponent
> of the meeting of Europe, Africa and Asia four centuries
> ago, the living product of African enslavement, of European
> colonisation and domination and of the ensuing crosscurrent
> of latter-day mass migration from the Caribbean to Britain. I
> carry all that cultural baggage with, I am what is defined as a
> 'New European'.
>
> (n.p.)

When I contacted writer Rani Drew[14] about her work she emailed me with the following comment:

> I do not seem to fit the bill of either Black or Asian Women. I
> resist the category and the concept. I wouldn't have come to
> England, if I wasn't married to an Englishman. So, I didn't
> come as an immigrant and can't be defined as the first or
> second or third Asian (not so young) immigrant generation.
> Again, I resist the definition.
>
> (personal communication, 29 June 2002)

Interestingly, Drew's play *Myself Alone/Asia Calling* (1996) focuses on a man, the child of a Hungarian father and an English mother, seeking to establish a sense of identity by travelling the world in pursuit of the occult and a spirit world that eludes him. Forever confined to an imaginary and a real liminal space, the man recounts his father's theory of the origins of the Magyar people: 'When you see a peasant in the countryside leaning on his spade and gazing eastwards, be sure he is listening to the call from Asia' (2–3). Here Asia figures as a non-specific eastern source of origin quite different from the ways in which Asia is presented in other plays by 'Asian' women playwrights. The play offers testimony to the potency of the imaginary in shaping people's lives.

Signatures of diaspora

Black and Asian women playwrights' work bears the signatures of the multi-locationality that informs their lives. Many of these scripts are written specifically for Black and Asian actresses and actors, something which rarely if ever occurs in plays by white (women) playwrights who are entirely unused to contemplating either themselves as in any way 'coloured' or the fact that they inhabit diasporic communities.[15] Plays by Black and Asian women playwrights thus provide performing/acting opportunities for women from diverse ethnic groups who are still rarely seen on the British stage. As Maria Oshodi in her preface to 'Blood Sweat and Fears', for instance, put it: 'I felt the need to provide good, strong main characters for young black actors' (94). Black and Asian women playwrights thus also place such actresses at the centre of the action, asking the audience to focus on people from social groups that are not often present in high-cultural forms.

Secondly, playscripts by Black and Asian women playwrights tend to thematize issues of race, colour, and ethnicity. They may do so in the form of an afterword that disavows these issues (see, for example, Rudet, as discussed in chapter seven of this volume) but whereas white playwrights do not usually feel compelled to comment on issues of race, colour, and ethnicity at all, thus reinforcing the frequently discussed fact that dominant cultures register no awareness of their specificities,[16] Black and Asian women playwrights virtually invariably do. Indeed, many of their plays, as this volume shows, focus on issues of race, colour, and ethnicity as key determinants of their characters' experiences. This is almost inevitable given the political climate in Britain in which questions of difference, migration, ethnicity, and regulation are perennially high on the agenda. Despite this, it has to be recognized that not all women playwrights of diverse ethnic origin centre their work on these issues. Ayshe Raif, for instance, the daughter of Turkish-Cypriot immigrants, is much more preoccupied with relations between women than with thematizing issues of race and ethnicity. Her play *I'm No Angel* (1993) centres on Mae West and her relations with various people as she asserts – and this is one of the central concerns of the play – that 'There ain't nothing closer in life than a mother and daughter. A mother and her child' (2, 2: 52). Another play, *Café Society* (n.d.), features three elderly women who meet regularly in a caf' (the title functions ironically here, providing an antidote to the actual corner caf' that is the women's regular meeting-place) in Hackney in London. Their interdependence and regular meetings are temporarily threatened when one of them starts to think about moving to another part of London and another one is courted by a man who wants her to move in with him. They all have Cockney accents; their colour, race, or ethnic background are never mentioned so that they could be played by white or black actresses, for example, but this is not specified. In fact, one might argue that the play constitutes a version of Anton Chekhov's *Three Sisters*[17] since it features three women who are peers and have a close long-term relationship dreaming of a change that ultimately never takes place. Raif's plays 'Caving In' (1990) and 'Fail/Safe' (1991) similarly do not foreground race or ethnicity issues – their focus is much more on other key concerns and relationships that affect women's lives. So, although the thematization of race, colour, and ethnicity may function as one of the signatures of Black and Asian women playwrights' work, this is not inevitably the case.

Apart from writing for Black and Asian actresses, and thematizing race, ethnicity, and colour, Black and Asian women playwrights prominently engage with historical and contemporary social and political issues that impact on their communities in particular ways, not only in Britain but also in the places from which they migrated to Britain. Migration thus features both as a historic and as a contemporary phenomenon. In the plays it takes several distinct forms:

- the contemplation of migration within a certain home setting;
- migration within the country one was born in – usually from country to city;
- migration to another country, usually the UK, and its impacts;
- the contemplation of migrating back home for those who came to the UK in the middle decades of the twentieth century;

- travel to countries from which parent generations migrated, a kind of impermanent reverse migration;
- making a life in a Britain in which Black and Asian people are categorized as migrant figures by virtue of their appearance, no matter what their individual histories are;
- breaking with one's community as an effect of changing values and attitudes across generations and between women and men, a migration effect;
- living in peer groups outside specific ethnically and/or racially defined communities as a function of one's particular history, development, and identity, another migration effect.

Pinnock's 'A Hero's Welcome' (1989), for instance, addresses the issue of the return of a Jamaican man who has fought for the British in the Second World War to his village in 1947. His presence stirs the imagination of other island inhabitants, who consider whether or not to leave to make their fortune elsewhere. Lisselle Kayla's 'When Last I Did See You', too, centres on the question of whether or not to migrate from Jamaica to the UK, Cuba, or America. In Prabjot Dolly Dhingra's *One Night* (1996) and Maya Chowdhry's *Kaahini* (1997) the issue of migration from India to Britain becomes fatefully entangled with sexual and emotional choices. Both Tanika Gupta's *Skeleton* (1997) and Rukhsana Ahmad's *Black Shalwar* (1998) explore migration within India from rural communities to the city and the impact this has on the protagonists' lives. They map geographies of unbelonging and liminal states as their characters seek to come to terms with the alienation that migration, even within one country, entails, signalled by the impossibility of a return to the place left behind. The nostalgia that the desire for return – to the place from where one has migrated, to the state one was previously in – engenders is manifested in plate 1, in which the characters from *Black Shalwar* are posed gazing longingly and wistfully down and off-centre to the left, a backward-looking gesture rather than a forward-looking one. Their conventionally romantically encoded body positioning, the male 'protectively' embracing the female from a position of relatively greater height (she leans into him), references the posters of romantic Bollywood movies, the stuff

Plate 1 Adele Selim as Sultana and Ashvin Kumar as Khuda Buksh in Kali Theatre Company's 1999 production of *Black Shalwar*.

that dreams are made of with all its lack of groundedness, a key feature of that play.

Migrating 'back home' is a key issue in plays such as Jacqueline Rudet's 'Money to Live'. In this play, the father of the central character wants to return home to live a life free from racism, economic exploitation, and insecurity. Moving down a generation, travel to countries from which parent generations migrated, a kind of temporary reverse migration, is at the heart of Maya Chowdhry's 'Monsoon', Ahmad's *River on Fire* (2000), Pinnock's 'Talking in Tongues', and her play *Mules*. The impact of these reverse migrations is discussed in chapter three of this volume. Making a life in a Britain in which Black and Asian people are categorized as migrant figures – with all that that entails in terms of social exclusion – by virtue of their appearance, no matter what their individual histories, is perhaps the most common form that the theatricalization of what one might term a 'migration effect' takes. Jacqueline Rudet's *God's Second in Command* (1985), Mary Cooper's 'Heartgame' (1988), Meera Syal's 'My Sister-Wife' (1993), Paulette Randall's 24% (n.d.), Yazmine Yudd's *Identity* (2000), Zindika's 'Leonora's Dance' (1993), and Winsome Pinnock's *Water* (2000) all speak to that experience.

Breaking with one's community as an effect of changing values and attitudes across generations and between women and men, itself a migration effect, underlies the dynamics of plays such as Grace Dayley's 'Rose's Story' (1985), Rukhsana Ahmad's 'Song for a Sanctuary' (1993), and Kaur Bhatti's *Besharam* (2001). These breaks are almost always involuntary on the part of the female characters who decide to move out of their communities, involving violence both psychical and physical to effect ruptures that mark the characters' exodus in a frequently tragic manner. Living in peer groups outside specific ethnically and/or racially defined communities as a function of one's particular history, development, and identity, another migration effect, occurs in Zindika's 'Leonora's Dance', in Kaur Bhatti's *Besharam*, in Jackie Kay's 'Chiaroscuro', and in Valerie Mason-John's 'Sin Dykes' (1999). Here the characters form part of peer communities, determined in the latter two cases by issues around sexual identities rather than racial/ethnic ones. In consequence, the plays have protagonists from a number of – rather than just two as is more commonly the case – different cultures and ethnic/racial backgrounds, offering a more consistently multi-cultural, as opposed to bi-cultural, view of contemporary Britain.

If migration in its various effects constitutes one major topic in Black and Asian women playwrights' work, so does spirituality. A common feature of plays by Black writers is the construction of the religiously over-invested mother or parents who drive their children away through a failure to understand that religion has a different place

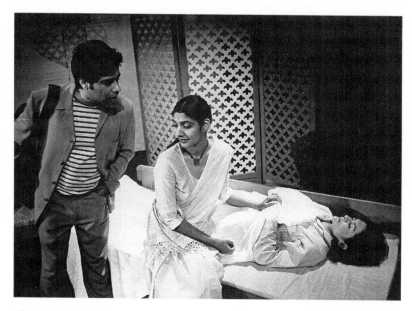

Plate 2 Shiv Grewal as Bobby Siddiqui, Parminder Sekhon as Zara Metha, and Shelley King as Seema Siddiqui in Kali Theatre Company's 2001 production of *River on Fire*.

in contemporary Britain than it has in the parents' lives. Typical examples include Zindika's 'Paper and Stone' (1989) and 'Leonora's Dance', Oshodi's *The 'S' Bend*, Dayley's 'Rose's Story', and Kara Miller's *Hyacinth Blue* (1999). Part of this differential investment in spirituality manifests itself in scripts by Asian women in the construction of ghostly presences. For example, in Ahmad's *River on Fire* one of the central characters, Seema Siddiqui, comes back to life after her death and watches the impact of her death on her three children (see plate 2). Similarly, in 'Song for a Sanctuary' Pradeep, the abusive husband of Rajinder, hovers as a ghostly and threatening presence over his family (see plate 10 on p. 155). In Gupta's 'Skeleton', the skeleton in question comes alive at night as a beautiful woman. In her play *Sanctuary*, the shadow of a woman appears as one of the characters tells her story (1, 3: 45–6). Yudd's *Unfinished Business* (1999), a play that defies the naturalistic boundaries with which it opens, raises questions as to the materiality of one of its characters as its narrative unfolds. Pinnock's 'Talking in Tongues', Gupta's *The Waiting Room* (2000), and her *Inside Out* (2002), too, invoke presences that defy material definition. The presence and invocation of ghosts is of course not unfamiliar within western theatre traditions. Ghosts appear or are invoked in many of Shakespeare's plays, but their haunting contemporary presence is much less familiar to us. In the plays discussed above, spirituality and manifestations of the spirit world, of ghostly presences, are treated much more matter-of-factly than the secularity of western culture normally allows.

There are a number of other thematic concerns that one might discuss as typical of Black and Asian women playwrights' work such as the specific but differential treatments of family and community, the representation of young single mothers, of forced and arranged marriages, of inter-generational conflicts that involve multi-cultural dimensions. Since these are dealt with in subsequent chapters, I want briefly to turn to the issue of embodiment and visual notation to discuss some of the gestural and visual specificities of plays by Black and Asian women playwrights. One of the striking aspects of theatre in general, including contemporary theatre, is that although it relies on embodiment and staging for its final articulation, relatively little notation in the form of stage directions is given over to specifying the gestural and bodily frames within which plays are (to be) enacted. This is left to the practitioners – actors, producers, directors – rather than being (pre)specified by the playwright. Playwright Ketaki Kushari Dyson, for instance, told me in an interview: 'In the Bengali production [of *Night's Sunlight*] . . . they were very keen to do a lot of English things, just as here in the English production they were very keen to do very Indian things. So always the cross-cultural thing' (2001). Black and Asian women playwrights occasionally identify bodily gestures in their scripts that are culturally specific. These are in particular teeth sucking or teeth kissing, simultaneously a bodily gesture and an utterance, which tend to occur in scripts by writers with a Caribbean or African background. That embodied utterance has a variety of meanings dependent on context but it frequently serves to express annoyance, fed-upness, or disgust. In *Shoot 2 Win* (2002) by Tracey Daley, Jo Martin, and Josephine Melville, for instance, teeth kissing appears fairly frequently in the stage directions, marking attitudes and offering commentary on the action. In Gupta's *Sanctuary* (2002) the stage directions indicate palm-slapping as a form of greeting (e.g. 1, 1: 17). But such gestural referencing of culturally specific embodied practices is comparatively rare in the plays in question, bespeaking both the absence of that kind of bodily encoding in play texts more generally, and, possibly, the erosion and/or transformation of such embodied practices as part of the diaspora effect.

Helen Gilbert and Joanne Tompkins have articulated the attraction of difference in performance and the ways in which cross-cultural differences are sometimes accentuated in productions along stereotypical lines in order to preserve notions of authenticity and purity (1996, esp. chapter two). This is evident in the production of plays with an Asian dimension on the British stage where 'Asianness' is frequently illustrated through the use of fretwork screens, characters wearing traditional dress such as the shalwar kamiz and dhupatta, or, less frequently, saris, and through, in particular, hand gestures that are associated with greetings or worship (see plate 3). These cultural signatures assert cultural particularity and simultaneously respond to certain images of Asianness common in British and other cultures.

Playwrights themselves articulate cultural specificity in several different ways including the introduction of languages other than English (as Cooper does in 'Heartgame') or through the use of particular accents or dialects such as patois. Many Black playwrights detailing West Indian experiences use forms of patois to locate their characters culturally. This can be experienced as personally liberating for the playwright. Pinnock, for instance, has said: '[*A Hero's Welcome*] was . . . the first time I'd used patois and I found that so liberating. It was another voice and it freed me in some way to be myself as a writer. It was a breakthrough for me personally . . . It was like discovering my voice' (1997: 50). Kushari Dyson has commented in an interview on how liberating she finds writing in Bengali, in which language she is not 'under Western eyes' (2001). And in her notes on the language of 'When Last I Did See You', Kayla states: 'In England today parents, young adults and children whose history is Caribbean, see very little of their oral tradition in written form. For too long the Afro-European

Plate 3 Parminder K. Nagra as Kiran Siddiqui in Kali Theatre Company's 2001 production of *River on Fire*.

based languages of the Caribbean have been regarded as almost without value. Because of this, there still isn't a standardized dictionary widely accepted, but these languages definately [sic] do have a rich and colourful tradition, uniting and sustaining the self confidence of the peoples of these islands' (1987: 97). Languages are clearly a way of uniting communities and fostering social cohesion. The articulation of languages such as creole, patois, Hindi, or Gujerat on British stages simultaneously speaks to those audiences familiar with these languages, ascribing value to these languages through their presence in a high-cultural space conventionally reserved for standardized forms of English, and installs those languages within British culture as part of that culture, not as a cultural space apart.

In this context the 'Dramatis Personae' or 'List of Characters' serve to indicate the racial politics of any given play. In some scripts, such as Mason-John's 'Sin Dykes' as discussed in chapter six of this volume, Gupta's *Sanctuary*, or Kaur Bhatti's *Besharam* the characters' racial or ethnic identity is stated in the list of characters, indicating that that identity is at issue in the play. This usually occurs in terms of either inter-racial or inter-ethnic differences, as in Dolly Dhingra's *Unsuitable Girls* (1999) in which differences in attitude towards arranged marriages between Asians and whites are explored. Alternatively, the articulation of the characters' racial/ethnic background in the list of characters signals the thematization of intra-racial or intra-ethnic cross-generational differences. Such is the case both in Patricia Hilaire's *Just Another Day* (n.d.), which deals with the issue of teenage pregnancy, and in Yemi Ajibabe's *A Long Way from Home* (1990), in which different moments and generations of migration and their associated socio-ideological implications are explored. What all these plays have in common is that they re-articulate, for a variety of reasons and in diverse ways, the boundaries between different racial and ethnic groups that have been central to the colonial enterprise. They thus affirm that 'there ain't no black in the union jack' – to quote Paul Gilroy – through the maintenance of those boundaries.

That position is in some respects exploded in those plays where the characters' racial and ethnic identity is not detailed in the list of characters. The absence of such articulation, as is the case in *Shoot 2*

Win and in Trish Cooke's 'Back Street Mammy' (1990), does not mean that the plays contain no markers of racial or ethnic identity. Frequently names such as 'Dynette' or 'Shenequa' serve as one such marker of difference, as do the use of particular accents, dialects, or languages, the articulation of culturally specific bodily gestures and costumes in the stage directions, and the reference to culturally specific phenomena such as certain food-stuffs etc. However, by not foregrounding difference through naming a racial or ethnic identity, the playwright can unmoor that identity from its racial/ethnic boundaries, so that the subject, rather than being set into a racialized frame that denies her subject status within a Britain that has 'no black in the union jack', is re-figured as a subject who is constitutive of the Britain depicted in the play. In this sense, Black women writers, and not only they, 'living now within the administrative center of what was/is left of the British Empire . . . are now able to launch an internal/external critique that challenges simultaneously the history and meanings of imperialism, the projects of postcoloniality, the implications of various nationalistic identifications of home, and the ways in which masculinity interacts with these various systems of domination', as Carole Boyce Davies puts it (1997: 100).

This highlights the historicity of the work done by Black and Asian women playwrights in Britain. As a consequence of all the plays written, produced, and published since the early 1980s, it has become possible to create a map of sorts of the concerns that have informed that writing and production, concerns which mirror the changing situation of Black and Asian women playwrights in Britain. Whereas during the 1980s plays were dominated by inter-generational conflicts as expressive of the difference between the adult subject who migrated and the child who, so to speak, *was migrated,* and their different accommodations to that situation, by the 1990s plays tended to focus much more on how to live in Britain now, beyond the experience of the moment of migration, as part of a generation that had grown up in the UK. As Jatinder Verma puts it: 'The rise of a second-generation [*sic*] of "foreigners" – children born of immigrant parents – . . . provided a powerful motive to *achieve presence*' (1994: 55). How difficult this is to do is clear when one considers the difficulties Black and Asian women playwrights have had, and continue to have, in achieving cultural visibility in this country, even as they inhabit key stages on the new playwriting scene.[18]

Since the 1980s in particular, certain theatre venues have become critical for the production of new work by Black and Asian women playwrights as well as their male counterparts. These include, in London, the former Soho Poly Theatre, now the Soho Theatre; the Royal Court Theatre which has significantly supported the work of Winsome Pinnock, for example; the National Theatre where Tanika Gupta was writer-in-residence in 2001–2; the Tricycle Theatre in Kilburn; the Theatre Royal, Stratford East;[19] the Lyric Theatre, Hammersmith; the Oval House Theatre; and the Ritzy in Brixton where I saw Ntozake Shange perform. Increasingly, venues outside London – usually in cities and towns with large Black and Asian populations – promote work by Black and Asian playwrights. Among them are the Birmingham Rep, the Leicester Haymarket and the Phoenix Arts Centre in Leicester, the West Yorkshire Playhouse in Leeds, the Liverpool Playhouse, and the Priestley Centre and the Mill Theatre in Bradford. These sites offer one opportunity for Black and Asian women playwrights to achieve presence.

Another such site is the critical reception of their work. Black British Studies, which has emerged as a lively arena of debate during the same period that the work of these playwrights has become more prominent on British stages, has not taken up that writing. Black British Cultural Studies has been mainly sociological in focus,[20] and the cultural sites that have been its most sustained objects of interrogation have tended to be those designated as popular culture such as film, music, and dance, with the consequence that Black and Asian women's presence in British theatre has been marginalized in its critical and theoretical debates. Some feminist theatre scholars, however, have begun to engage with these playwrights' work. Mary Brewer's *Race, Sex, and Gender in Contemporary Women's Theatre* (1999), the only volume of this kind to emerge in Britain to date, still centres predominantly on plays by Black American playwrights. In *An Introduction to Feminism and Theatre* (1995) Elaine Aston devotes a chapter to 'Black Women: Shaping Feminist Theatre' which focuses on Black women on the British stage. Liz Goodman (1993) includes a chapter on Black British theatre companies; Mary Karen Dahl writes on 'Post-colonial British Theatre' (1995), and May Joseph on 'Bodies Outside the State: Black British Women Playwrights and the Limits of Citizenship' (1998). Jatinder Verma, a male founding member of Tara Arts, a British Asian theatre company, has contributed to volumes such as Richard Boon and Jane Plastow's (1998) *Theatre Matters* and Theodore Shank's (1994) *Contemporary British Theatre*. Meenakshi Ponnuswami like-wise has contributed chapters to Elaine Aston and Janelle Reinelt's (2000) *The Cambridge Companion to Modern British Women Play-wrights* and to *Women and Performance* (1995). The dates of these texts, and there are some but not many others, indicate a very grad-ual increase in critical interest in the work of Black and Asian women playwrights in Britain during the 1990s. William W. Demastes' *British Playwrights, 1956–1995* – covering a period when Black and Asian women playwrights were coming to the fore in the UK – for instance, asserts in his preface that 'Women have found a voice in the theatre; ethnic minorities have likewise increasingly found a place' (ix). How-ever, this is not the case in his work: of thirty-six entries, only seven are devoted to female playwrights, and none to Black or Asian women playwrights at all. Susan Croft has done much sterling work to remedy this situation; following on from her chapter on 'Black Women Play-wrights in Britain' (1993), she has compiled bibliographies of works by Black and Asian (women) playwrights (2000; 2001[21]) which indi-cate quite how much material by such playwrights has been produced. But overall the extensive research and scholarship on Black American women playwrights, for instance, even taking into account the very different migration and socio-cultural patterns which inform the US history of Black women playwrights' work, has not been matched by similar developments in the UK.[22]

Ponzanesi (2002) has pointed out the difficulties of achieving presence in a location dominated by an absence of focus on the first, second, and third generation of 'migrants' as constitutive subjects of contemporary Britain. Indeed, one might argue that appellations such as 'migrant', 'immigrant', and 'foreigner' – as well as all the more abusive terms commonly employed in racist contexts – are misnomers since many of the people to whom they are applied were born and grew up in the UK and identify culturally with that space, even if in a problematizing way (see, for instance, Carole Boyce Davies (1997) on this issue).[23] This is exemplified in an excerpt from an interview conducted by Anjona Roy[24] which mirrors the experience of Kamla, one of the characters in Ahmad's play 'Song for a Sanctuary':

> INTERVIEWEE: In fact, I'm seen as an outsider more or less. Not as . . . not as an Asian at all. Asian in colour, but not as an Asian because for one I don't speak an Asian language, and for two, I have come from the West Indies. So by Asians I'm not seen as an Asian and by statutory organisations I'm not seen as an Asian . . .
>
> AR: So what do you think that they see you as?
>
> INTERVIEWEE: I think they see me as a Brown British or a Westernized British . . . Well, I dress western. I would say, my body language is western and that in itself is a barrier.
>
> AR: Right, it's a barrier, but it is something you choose to do. Is that because it's important to you?
>
> INTERVIEWEE: I didn't choose to do it. I didn't have a second language. I've never had a second language.
>
> AR: OK, but you are saying that you dress western . . .
>
> INTERVIEWEE: I come from a western country.
>
> AR: OK. Right.
>
> INTERVIEWEE: I think it would be a bit of a hypocrisy if I were to dress Asian, because what messages will I be giving then . . . and then somebody comes up to me dressed in Asian dress and starts to speak to me in an Asian language and I'm saying, 'I don't understand what you're saying.' Can you see the complications of that?
>
> AR: Is it important to you that you present yourself in the way you do?
>
> INTERVIEWEE: Well, there is no other way to present myself, to be honest.

Underlying this exchange is the notion of a coherent identity, be it 'Asian' or otherwise, which the interviewee cannot produce because her physical appearance – according to prevailing stereotypes – is at odds with her demeanour or bodily practices and her self-encoding through dress. Exactly that contradiction is at the centre of the clashes between two Asian women in all the plays discussed in chapter five of this volume. The difficulties of adequately or appropriately labelling the multi-locationality of many contemporary subjectivities accounts for the dilemma faced by the interviewee and, indeed, faced by the characters in Syal's 'My Sister-Wife', Cooper's 'Heartgame', and Ahmad's 'Song for a Sanctuary'.

Some of the characters in these plays struggle with what might be termed bi-culturality, that is the question of how to negotiate effectively between two cultures with frequently very different norms, values, and demands. However, for many within the plays and outside the question is not just one of that negotiation but also one of what identity/ties to inhabit as values, and norms shift. Where ascriptions of identity tend to assume a congruity between appearance and a set of values, norms, and behaviours – itself of course a fossilizing move – such ascriptions come unstuck when appearance, values, and norms do not cohere in the expected way. Indeed, it is that expectation of coherence that needs interrogation, for it is not coherence *per se* that is at issue but what is presumed to cohere. That recognition involves the re-writing of a script that has held both self and other in place to explode the boundaries of our identities. It means assuming the diasporic as axiomatic and also assuming change. What this means – in the context of this volume – is that we need to recognize that the plays discussed within it bespeak a particular historical period. Nowhere does this become more obvious than when we consider one of the effects of 11 September 2001 when the World Trade Center in New York was bombed. As that terrorist attack was associated with Muslims, so in the aftermath of that attack did people of Asian appearance find themselves vilified if suspected of being Muslim, and a new differentiation among Asians – between Hindus and Muslims – arose in western cultures. The impact of that process is already visible in Rani Drew's *Bradford's Burning* (2001).

A word on the research process: in an article entitled 'White Out' (2000), Michael Billington asked, 'Is there a crisis in black theatre in Britain?' and answered it with, 'You bet. And it seems to be getting worse.' He cited Nicolas Kent of the Tricycle Theatre in north London who said:

> In the past two years alone a number of companies and events have disappeared: Carib, Temba, Couble Edge, the Black Theatre Season, the Roundhouse Project. Along with the companies, the regular African–Caribbean audience is also dissolving. But I could go on and on listing the problems. The fact that there is no black children's company and that theatre staff and boards are overwhelmingly white. If you read the Arts Council-commissioned Boyden Report into English Producing Theatres, you discover that only 16 out of 463 board members nationwide are black. Given that we at the Tricycle Theatre have eight of them, Stratford East five and Hampstead two, that must leave one black board member for the rest of the country.
>
> (1)

Billington goes on to point to the fact that 'Once there were 18 revenue-funded black and Asian theatre companies, now there are two. All but 80 of the 2,009 staff permanently employed in English theatres are white. And with odd exceptions . . . contemporary black and Asian experience goes largely unrecorded' (2). In fact, Black and Asian women playwrights have increasingly contributed to the recording of that experience. However, they – especially the Asian women playwrights – can feel that it is difficult to get their work produced. Tanika Gupta, for instance, argues that 'Asian theatre companies like Tara Arts and Tamasha really only develop new writers on a small scale, although Tamasha's production of Ayub Khan-Din's *East is East* was a huge success; but it was a bit of an exception. Their work is usually based around reinterpreting the classics. And although black theatre companies like Talawa develop new writers: Biyi Bandele Thomas and Zindika, for example, they don't seem to produce any Asian plays. So there isn't really anywhere for a new writer to go'[25] (1997: 117). It can thus be or become difficult to access these playwrights' work. Most theatres and theatre companies are insufficiently funded to archive their materials – and that includes playscripts and production photos – properly, or indeed at all. For touring companies on a shoestring budget and theatre companies operating on project funding such archiving understandably cannot be a priority. Although copies of performed plays are meant to be deposited in the British Library this is, as I found, both insufficiently well known and inconsistently followed. Where material is donated to special collections, it often lacks basic information which can become hard to track. Thus a collection may hold production photos but not details of the photographers who took them, making it difficult to reproduce these photos as part of the documentation process of the work. Much more needs to be done publicly to preserve all of this material, including financial support and education of companies and playwrights regarding the process of publicly preserving their work and accessing funding to do so.

This is continuous with the consistent marginalization of Black and Asian women's work for theatre (Ponnuswami 1995; 2000). To admit the existence of that work is to recognize that we inhabit a diasporic space, that high-cultural forms partake of and enable the formation of such space, and that we need to re-think our relations, and ourselves in relation, to those still viewed as colonized and colonial 'others'. It also means attending to the voices of those others, to try to understand their experience of diasporic space and to re-frame our own experiences in that light. The problematic of multi-locationality is graphically illustrated in all the plays discussed in this volume which, one might argue, have multi-locationality at the heart of their concerns.

Diaspora as theatre

Contemporary Black and Asian Women Playwrights in Britain is organized thematically. Each chapter offers extended readings of two or three plays (as well as referencing a number of additional plays) within a specific thematic and theoretical frame. Following on from the introduction, chapter two, on 'Diasporic subjects', utilizes Avtar Brah's notion of diaspora space to examine the representation of migration as a movement which places the individual into an estranged

relation both to her country of origin and to the place to which she mi-
grates, resulting in a longing for the homeland on the one hand and a
recognition of the impossibility of return on the other. Caught in this
'entre-deux' (Cixous 1997), the characters in Trish Cooke's 'Running
Dream' (1993), for example, negotiate complex and ambivalent longings across generations as they interrogate their own and their children's life choices. Winsome Pinnock's 'Leave Taking' (1989) frames
this problematic in terms of itinerary and a social isolation which
places the memory of childhood into the same space as the memory
of the homeland, an irretrievable space which is both the point of departure and the place of the impossible return. The chapter analyses
the theatricalization of the spatialized problematic of inhabiting diasporic spaces, suggesting, in alignment with Brah's argument, that
the diaspora effect impacts not only on those who migrate but also on
those who stay in one location.

Chapter three on 'Geographies of un/belonging' investigates the
articulation of re/turns to countries of origin by second-generation
migrants. For these children of the diaspora their parents' country of
origin does not necessarily figure as the 'homeland' but may generate a
new sense of unbelonging where difference is articulated not through
skin colour but through the attitudes and behaviours which second-
generation migrants have acquired as a consequence of living in a
racialized and racist western context. This issue is treated very differently in Winsome Pinnock's 'Talking in Tongues' (1991) and in Maya
Chowdhry's 'Monsoon' (1993). Where Pinnock, within a naturalistic
frame, portrays the problematic of an alienated second generation,
whose relation to Jamaica is that of exploitative tourism, augmented
by the replication of the sexual exploitation of black people which
structured the experience of slavery as much as the practice of sex
tourism in the late twentieth century, Chowdhry, working more ex-
perimentally, projects the possibility of a turn to the homeland acting
as a liberator for the displaced individual. The result is not a reintegration of those who have migrated or are the children of migrants
but a recognition that the space and culture with which the central
character is associated can speak to the identity of the individual in
enabling ways.

32

The impact of inhabiting diasporic spaces on individual identities is explored in chapter four. Following Ang-Lygate's (1997) discussion of the inadequacy of the homogenizing and monolithic 'black' to encompass the diversity of identities representing 'ethnic minorities' in Britain, the chapter focuses on inter- and intra-racial differences as they are articulated in Winsome Pinnock's 'A Rock in Water' (1989), Zindika's 'Leonora's Dance' (1993), and Maya Chowdhry's *Kaahini* (1997). At the centre of this articulation is the isolation of the individual whose sociality has been undermined by the impossibility of mapping categories of identity onto individual realities and, indeed, collective experience. The chapter argues that the destabilizing effects of the diasporic experience, reinforced through the racist attitudes prevalent in British culture and the epistemic violence achieved through labelling, are constructed in these plays as resulting in degrees of alienation within individuals living in Britain that lead to social isolation and breakdown, and fracture both individual and community identities.

Chapter five, entitled 'Culture clashes', centres on the representation of a particular issue, arranged marriages and polygamous households within a western context, in three plays: Mary Cooper's 'Heartgame' (1988), Rukhsana Ahmad's 'Song for a Sanctuary' (1991), and Meera Syal's 'My Sister-Wife' (1993). Each of the plays articulates the culture clash between 'Asian' and western attitudes towards marriage in radically different ways, indicating that conventional western attitudes towards arranged marriages, 'Asian' families, and intra-familial relations are incapable of accessing the cultural and social codes which regulate these arrangements and relations. The characters' difficulties in reconciling divergent socio-cultural positions on marriage, domestic violence, and cross-cultural differences in gender role expectations are constructed as the key to the dilemmas which the plays present. Significantly, these dilemmas, although portrayed in realist mode, are not resolved within the plays in terms of conventional happy endings. Instead, the plays, inspired by 'real-life' events such as the killing of Balwant Kaur in the Brent Asian Women's Refuge in 1985 (Southall Black Sisters 1992), raise questions about the violence done to women in their negotiation of culture clashes.

The debates about hierarchies of oppression and the relative positions occupied by sexuality and race, the impact of racism and homophobia, and their shared imbrication within structures of inequality, have generated plays by Black women which seek to interrogate the complex intersections of racialized marginalization and homophobic rejection which Black lesbians experience in this culture. These are discussed in chapter six which investigates the racing of sexualities in Jackie Kay's 'Chiaroscuro' (1984) and Valerie Mason-John's 'Sin Dykes' (1998). Importantly, the plays emerged at two very different moments of lesbian and of Black politics. Kay's play, rooted in pre-Clause 28 and pre-queer/performance theory days, projects the difficulty of lesbian closetedness and invisibility in an interrogation of racialized visibilities and the politics of female friendship. Mason-John's play, on the other hand, is fully invested in the politics of sexuality as performative within racialized power structures that extend across race boundaries and re-enact the dominance-submission dynamics which echo historical forms of slavery and enslavement. The chapter argues that shifts in lesbian and in identity politics replay racial oppression as sexual oppression while querying the meaning of identity.

Jacqueline Rudet's 'Money to Live' (1984), Grace Dayley's 'Rose's Story' (1984), and Winsome Pinnock's *Mules* (1996) are all issue-based plays focusing on the Black female body as a site through which Black women interrogate their sense of identity and socio-economic positioning. These plays are analysed in chapter seven in order to establish the impact of racialized positionings on attitudes to issues which are not in themselves in any way race-specific. 'Money to Live' centres on a Black woman who decides to become a go-go dancer in order to make a living both for herself and for her family. In contrast to plays by white women playwrights on the topic of sex work in the 1980s which portrayed 'objections to sex and violence' (to quote Caryl Churchill), this play emphasizes the economic possibilities offered to women through their sexploitation and constructs them as making considered choices in which economic independence and security emerge as more important than the sexual politics of sexploitation. 'Rose's Story' focuses on a Black teenager's pregnancy (in some respects rather like Shelagh Delaney's *A Taste of Honey*, 1958)

34

and the single teenage mum syndrome that has, in fact, a long history of post-war theatrical representation as well as a history of racialization, stigmatizing Black women as sexually promiscuous and likely to engage in unprotected, teenage sex. *Mules* presents the issue of the use of Black women as carriers of drugs across borders which made the news in the early and mid-1990s. This play's structure, as much as the others', reflects the notion of entrapment which Black women suffer through sexploitation. All three plays also engage with the problematic of gender relations in Black communities.

In the final chapter, 'Living diaspora now', the emergence of a new figure in recent plays by Black and Asian women playwrights such as Amrit Wilson's *Survivors* (1999) and Tanika Gupta's *Sanctuary* (2002) is discussed, that of the refugee and asylum seeker. This final chapter asserts that plays by Black and Asian women playwrights in Britain continue to reflect the socio-cultural, political, and economic realities which women from diverse racial and ethnic backgrounds encounter in the UK. Many of the plays which have been published to date present the issue-based, socialist-realist frame that informed much of women's theatre work in Britain from the late 1970s onwards. The necessity of articulating Black women's experiences of diasporic existence, fractured identities, racist and homophobic attitudes as well as the difficulties of negotiating inter- and intra-cultural differences, as portrayed in Pinnock's *Water*, also discussed in this chapter, has generated a body of work by Black and Asian women playwrights which interrogates the colour regimes, social codes, and cultural imperatives that govern British culture. The invisibilization of that body of work in (feminist) theatre history replicates and reinforces the marginalization of Black and Asian women's work in British culture. This volume attempts to intervene in that process, arguing implicitly for the need to establish a critical and theoretical apparatus to accompany the publication of works by Black and Asian women playwrights in Britain.

2   Diasporic subjects

The diasporic subject is one who experiences displacement and estrangement. The two, displacement and estrangement, are not synonymous. For whereas displacement is an effect of location associated with the forced as opposed to the voluntary removal of a person from 'her place', and place does not have to refer to a literal space here although that is frequently the case, estrangement is an effect of that displacement and relates to the violation of one's sense of belonging which may be experienced by those who are displaced. Both displacement and estrangement are central to Winsome Pinnock's 'Leave Taking' (1987) and Trish Cooke's 'Running Dream' (1993). In these plays, as in others by contemporary Black and Asian women playwrights,[1] diaspora exhibits specific traits which are articulated through the plays' structures, their characters' social relations, and the semiotics of performance. They correspond to Hélène Cixous' notion of the *entre-deux* as described in her *Rootprints: Memory and Life Writing* (1997), 'a true in-between – between a life which is ending and a life which is beginning' (9).

The notion of the in-between conjures up the idea of polarity, of opposites, of binarisms. And, indeed, both plays in different ways operate within binarist parameters, reflected in their symmetrical structures. In 'Leave Taking', this is underscored by the symmetrical positioning of the characters (see diagram).

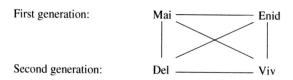

36

'Leave Taking' consists of two acts of four scenes each; 'Running Dream' is divided into two parts. This structural device underlines the fact that the structure of diaspora is not random, chaotic, or unpredictable but rather, that diaspora occurs along identifiable lines, in chartable and specific directions, and with particular and definable effects. Diaspora is thus not about some kind of scattergram dispersal but about explainable and purposeful movements, with causes and effects. In this context the common distinction[2] in the UK between economic migrants, at the beginning of the twenty-first century virtually a term of abuse, and so-called 'legitimate' immigrants, meaning asylum seekers whose human rights have been violated, is revealed as deeply problematic, since the desire to improve one's economic position which may lead to diasporas is tied to the human right to have adequate food and shelter and to preserve one's bodily integrity, an integrity threatened by poverty. This is particularly the case for women who in many cultures, including the British one, are severely economically disadvantaged, not least because their biological ability to bear children makes them exploitable as reproducers of the labour force. Diaspora, then, has historically specific dimensions;[3] waves of migration from the UK to America, Australia, and the so-called former colonies have in the twentieth century been supplanted by waves of migration to the UK from the former colonies, as well as from other countries where groups of people, such as the Jews during the Nazi regime in Germany, found themselves in distress and persecuted.

Living diaspora

'Leave Taking' features a group of first-generation migrants from the West Indies who came to Britain as young adults in the 1950s and 1960s in search of a better life. In making that move, the three characters who represent that generation in Pinnock's play, Enid, Mai, and Broderick, incurred a psychological cost which, especially in the case of Enid, haunts them in their later years. Economically, they have survived, although their story of being able to manage economically is juxtaposed in the play with the narrative about Gullyman, another migrant from the West Indies, who 'let England fly a him head' (1, 2: 151),[4] and who went from rags to riches, and back to rags, seemingly living on the streets now, begging. Gullyman, his name already emblematic of a quasi-mythological figure not dissimilar to the 'everyman' of morality plays, figures as an example and a warning of what can happen to those who 'forget everybody, all him friends, him people back home, just cut everybody off' (1, 2: 151). Gullyman is described as a figure who wanted to fit into English society and in the process became estranged from his roots.

The different positions Enid and Broderick take vis-à-vis Gullyman's fate are expressive of their divergent views about how to deal with the position of being a diasporic subject. Broderick insists on the importance of retaining ties to one's culture and community of origin and takes the view that Gullyman 'get what him deserve' (1, 2: 152). Enid, on the other hand, thinks: 'He was right. You come here, you try to fit in. Stick to the rules' (1, 2: 152). Her position is informed by her view that 'England been good to me. To all of us. I love England an' I bring up the girls to love England because they English' (1, 2: 152). Broderick's less enthusiastic attitude is occasioned by recent experiences of being classified as 'a alien' whose previous love of England was dislodged through receiving a 'letter say if I don't get my papers in order they going to kick me outa' the country' (1, 2: 152). Broderick's experience that despite having spent 'the whole a' my life standing to attention whenever I hear the national anthem' (1, 2: 152) he remains, in the eyes of the authorities, an alien, has led him to re-assess his relationship with England. Gullyman's and Broderick's attempts at enacting Englishness – emblematized in Gullyman's case through trying to speak standard English,[5] in Broderick's case through standing up when the national anthem is played – come to nothing as they remain 'aliens' in the eyes of the authorities and the English who do not reward the enactment of Englishness through a welcoming, integrating attitude.

Diaspora, then, is a permanent condition for first-generation migrants who have to negotiate between their culture and community of origin and the society into which they have migrated. Gullyman's story of a rise and fall, in the narrative directly related to his attempt to integrate into English society, presents the key dilemma faced by all the characters in 'Leave Taking' and played out in its narrative: how to negotiate, and not merely negotiate but negotiate successfully, the *entre-deux* of diasporic existence. That negotiation is made evident in the opening scene of 'Leave Taking' when Enid takes her daughters[6] to see Mai, another first-generation migrant from the West Indies and an obeah woman, in order to get readings for herself and her daughters.

Ritual interventions

In Enid and Mai's culture of origin, obeah is an important cultural tool for regulating people's lives. Its efficacy in part depends on the belief structures which support it, and along with these, on the appropriate enactment of a variety of rituals and behaviours. Simultaneously, it is understood to be a transaction with an economic base; obeah is how Mai makes her living, and there is an actual price to be paid for the invocation of her powers. This would be the case in the West Indies as much as it is in England.[7] But the conditions under which obeah has to be practised in England are less propitious to the effective enactment of ritual than they are in the West Indies because of the differing living conditions and belief structures in the two countries.[8] In discussing the enactment of traditional ritual in postcolonial theatre, Gilbert and Tompkins (1996) assert that 'traditional enactments have special functions in post-colonial societies and are often key sites of resistance to imposed values and practices' (54).[9] They suggest that 'ritual remains the event/practice which attracts the most attention in the west because of its "difference"' (55). In 'Leave Taking' ritual related to obeah, associated with the culture of the West Indies and beyond that with Africa, becomes a way both of asserting difference and of offering resistance to white British culture. For one thing, to put obeah on stage in the UK is to suggest that belief systems other than those commonly practised among white English people have validity and value; that such different systems occur within the culture that disavows them; and that they are part of a counter-balance to the attempt to efface difference through assimilation. As Gilbert and Tompkins argue: 'The combining of ritual with other cultural forms can . . . provide new performative events and practices that acknowledge the changes wrought by colonialism' (58). These changes encompass effects such as displacement which are a function of diasporic movement. Enid seeks Mai's advice as an obeah woman because English culture is unable to accommodate, and cater for, her needs. When Mai asks Enid if she 'bin to a doctor?' (2, 2: 174), Enid's response points to the gap between obeah and western healing practices: 'What doctor know about our illness? Just give you few pills to sick you stomach and a doctor certificate. What they know about a black woman soul' (2, 2: 174). Enid articulates the inadequacy of what is regarded by many in western culture as the most effective – and most advanced – way of dealing with feeling unwell, that is conventional medicine, to effect the healing she desires. The interventions offered by conventional medicine, pills and a certificate, do not respond to her needs which, as the play makes clear, are psychosomatic rather than purely somatic. They are a diaspora effect, a function of the *entre-deux* existence Enid has lived since coming to Britain.

That *entre-deux* existence is articulated through the opening scene of 'Leave Taking' when Enid seeks help through obeah in a London bedsit, a seeming incongruity which the play gradually deflates as it reveals the effectiveness of the obeah woman's interventions in the lives of Enid and her daughters, particularly Del. Ritual changes as it travels. Mai, the obeah woman, is not able to enact obeah in the UK as she would in Jamaica. Ritual itself thus becomes diasporic, being enacted in mediated form, as well as mediating between two cultures.[10] Thus when Enid seeks help to deal with her troubled relations with both her mother and her daughters, Mai says: 'If this was back home I woulda' say bring me two a' you best fowl as a sorta' sacrifice. Over here I don't think the blood a' two meagre chickens going to make you better' (2, 2: 175). Mai understands the need to adapt ritual to circumstance; hers is not a fossilized relation to her practices but a knowingly pragmatic and adaptive one. In talking of 'old time obeah' (1, 1: 145) and stating that 'the old ways are dying' (2, 4: 185), Mai demonstrates her understanding of ritual as subject to change, to diasporic inflection.[11] She wishes to help Enid but knows that such help has to take account of the context in which it is asked for. Here Jamaica and England are presented as two different cultures, requiring different practices and solutions. Therefore Mai resorts to an integrative practice of pills and symbolic gestures: '(*Moves to cupboard and takes out a small bottle, which she gives to* ENID.) Take these. Make a sign a' the cross on you' forehead with this one in the morning and this one at night. The pressure soon ease. Soon you notice life picking up again' (2, 2: 175). The mixture of medicine and religious act Mai prescribes presents a hybridized form of intervention expressive of the protagonists' *entre-deux* condition, the conflation of two types of curing systems whose combined forces cater to the different aspects of Enid's needs, her 'black woman *soul*' (emphasis added) and her somatic responses to her condition.

One might argue that Mai's capabilities as a healing woman lie in her ability to understand the psychological disposition of her clients and their needs. An ethnocentric white view would be to suggest that it is the symbolic actions required of the client, their embeddedness in certain belief structures, which enable Mai's remedies and interventions to be effective. Towards the end of the play, when Mai teaches Del how to be an obeah woman, she says to her: 'You see everything you need to know in their eyes' (2, 4: 186). This suggests that Mai's interventions are based on her reading of her clients' eyes, the 'windows to their souls'. Yet Mai has a series of props and paraphernalia such as palm reading, card reading, candles, and the salt that she utilizes in enacting her various rituals. The question thus raised – both for the audience, and, intradiegetically, for the other characters – is what is the significance of these props and what is the relative efficacy of Mai's devices as opposed to her psychological insights into people?

Signifying diaspora

One of the most interesting semiotic devices Mai uses in the context of obeah, a prop significantly never spoken of but referred to only in the didascales (or stage directions), is 'a large Afro wig' (1, 1: 141). In the opening scene this wig sits on the middle of the table in Mai's bedsit. Mai puts it on before she opens the door to Enid, who has come for a reading. The wig thus acts as a liminal marker, a threshold symbol between Mai's position as a private individual and her role as an obeah woman. The placing of the wig on Mai's head signifies Mai's *entre-deux* status, her position between 'ordinary' and 'obeah' woman. When wearing the wig Mai enters another state. That state, significantly, is one that needs to be signalled to her clients, because it is when her clients appear that Mai wears the wig. It forms part of the socio-cultural contract between Mai and her clients whereby she signals the status they ascribe to her by the mere fact that they come to seek her help, that of an obeah woman, through a ritual marker of that status, the wig. Such use of a wig is not unusual or culturally specific. One need only think of the wigs worn to this day in British courts of law, where they similarly serve a transformative function, divesting their wearers of their individual and private identities in favour of a specific role within a particular kind of socio-cultural exchange. Exactly as in those instances, here too the shape and size of the wig is heavily semantically invested.

In his pioneering essay 'Black Hair/Style Politics', Kobena Mercer (1994) discusses the function of the Afro as a hair style in black aesthetics, history, and politics.[12] He points out that the Afro emerged 'as a symbol of Black Pride and Black Power in the 1960s . . . marking a liberating rupture, or "epistemological break", with the dominance of white-bias' (104). When Mai puts on her Afro wig she becomes a different woman, taking on symbolically an identity materialized through the wig, that of a woman embodying her relation to a certain idea of black identity and black culture. The epistemological break from the dominant white culture effected through that transformation articulates a validation of that practice. In addition this particular Afro wig, given its size, demands a space which feeds directly into the notion of pride and a sense of the rightful claiming of the space the associated practice deserves. Mercer (1994) argues:

> [The Afro's] morphology suggest[s] a certain dignified body
> posture, for to wear an Afro you have to hold your head up in
> pride . . . As Flugel pointed out with regard to ceremonial
> headdress and regal crowns, by virtue of their emphatic
> dimensions such items bestow a sense of presence, dignity
> and majesty on the wearer by magnifying apparent body size
> and by shaping bodily movement accordingly so as to project
> stature and grace. In a similar way, with the Afro we wore the

crown, to the point that it could be assumed that the larger
the Afro, the greater the degree of 'black' content to one's
consciousness.

(106)

Mai's wig signals both her function as obeah woman and the relation
of that function to an older history, for, as the term 'Afro' indicates,
the style, and thus Mai's wig, gestures towards an African heritage enacted in her role as obeah woman. The wig thus signals a continuity
between Africa, Jamaica, and London as the practice it materializes
travels as part of the diasporic dispersal of peoples of African origins.
As a quotation of that history, however, it makes no claims for its
authentication. For not only does the Afro, as Mercer (1994) shows,
have no 'given reference point in existing African cultures' (111); indeed, 'there is nothing particularly African about the Afro at all' (111).
As a 'reconstitutive link with Africa', however, the Afro is 'part of a
counter-hegemonic process helping to redefine diaspora people' (107).
It is, in fact, 'specifically diasporean' (112).

Mai's validation of her status of obeah woman through the
wearing of the Afro wig when she is being consulted thus functions
as a form of validation not only of her own role but of her clients'
choices in seeking out her help. Her wig says to the clients that she is
what they think she is. Her authentificatory move in wearing the wig
pertains to the practice she engages in, not to the history towards
which the wig gestures. Indeed, all such notions are undercut by the
very fact that it is a wig, rather than her own hair. Mercer analyses
the complex relationship between ideas of African-ness, naturalness,
and the Afro, and argues that hair as an ethnic signifier is virtually
never in a natural state but almost always manipulated to articulate
particular meanings. As such the wig, as the epitome of artificiality,
highlights its own symbolic function, its un-naturalness, through the
naked display of its constructedness. One might be tempted to argue that the mobility of the wig, the fact that it can be put on and
removed at will, underscores the performativity of Mai's function of
obeah woman, that it is something she can put on and off. But, more
than that, in the course of the play the wig comes to signal the fluidity

of Mai's identity, the ways in which private individual, obeah woman, friend, member of the displaced West Indian community, and guide at your side merge and mingle, at times crystallizing more firmly into one shape, at times dissolving, but never sharply separated.

The fluid contours of Mai's identity emerge clearly in her inter-actions with Enid whom she sometimes treats with the authority of the obeah woman, sometimes as a friend in need. During the consul-tation that takes place in the first act, for instance, Mai at one point 'scratch[es] her wig so that it rides up a bit' (1, 1: 147). Later on in the same scene, when she switches to talking to Enid woman to woman, mother to mother, displaced person to displaced person, she 'takes off her wig and scratches her head thoughtfully' (1, 1: 148). The very mobility of the wig semantically encodes the range of Mai's identi-ties that manifests itself as she engages with Enid. One might argue that that motility signals artificiality and therefore possibly insincer-ity and lack of trustworthiness (and Mai's financial demands on Enid, her money-grabbing behaviour certainly would reinforce that), under-scored, by the multiplicity of Mai's personae. However, it seems to me that it is utilized in the play to suggest the very opposite, namely, first and foremost the sincerity of Mai who understands her business as well as people and treats the latter in accordance with their needs, which are sometimes for the obeah woman and sometimes for a friend. Second, the fluidity of identity embodied through the wig bespeaks the reality of diasporic life in which obeah may be carried out in a Lon-don bedsit as part of the global movement of cultural capital, as an expression of that movement rather than as a threat to some fantasy of unity, exclusion, and cultural closure.

The movement of the wig may also be read in a different way. Like all the other characters in the play Mai faces a crisis – hence her presence in the play. Like Enid she has not had an easy life, marred as it was by her estrangement from her son on the one hand and by the burden of her gift as an obeah woman on the other. Mai's mother wanted her to have a life that would be different from her own, not marked by living in rural poverty and perpetual pregnancy. As Mai says, 'When I was a little girl mother got down on her hands and knees each night and prayed to God to save me' (2, 2: 178). However, the price for being saved from one fate was having to endure another, that of obeah woman.

> MAI (*angry*). Come here, expecting me to give you the
> answers – palm reading, herbal bath, tricks with cards, read
> the bumps on your head – expect me to look into your lives
> and alter the future for you. You have sucked me dry. I've
> come to an end. My battery dead. Finished. I have had enough.
>
> (2, 2: 177)

Mai's crisis is a crisis of succession, of moving from one life into another without damaging the role she had in her community and whilst ensuring that her knowledge survives and is passed on. In this context the shifting of the wig on Mai's head symbolizes the shifting of her role, her desire to divest herself of her obeah function, to pass on the 'crown'. In effecting this change she helps shape the identity of another character in the play who, likewise, is undergoing a crisis.

All the characters who seek Mai's advice question her powers. That interrogative stance has several functions within the play and in relation to the play's audience. It is, in the first instance, part of the intra-ritualistic exchange between the characters, acting to protect both the client, who may not get what she expects, and Mai, who not only may not be able to deliver what the client wants but who can also point to the client's lack of belief as an explanation for any inefficacy of her interventions. Obeah itself is thus tied into the *entre-deux* of belief and un-belief, which, in turn, is an expression of the diasporic experience, although even that, within the context of ritual, has its antecedents in Jamaica. Enid's revelation that 'my mother always say to me, never you trust a obeah woman or a priest' (1, 2: 149) is indicative of a scepticism towards older belief systems that goes back to the simultaneity of multiple beliefs within a culture, placing its peoples *entre-deux* and demanding choices between seemingly mutually exclusive ways of believing and acting. It bespeaks the impact of colonization on cultures that were forced to endure Christianity as part of their subjugation to colonial forces. However, the prevalence of such multiplicities in western cultures too creates a parallel between Enid and her sceptical daughters, and a contemporary London audience of the play, who might adhere to religious belief structures at the same time as reading horoscopes, attempting all kinds of alternative medicine, and seeking relief in therapies and interventions imported into Britain from a variety of cultures and traditions. Ambivalence or scepticism as a disposition is thus not specific to Enid but part of contemporary existence where diaspora and globalization enable cross-cultural choices for healing interventions prised loose from their context of origin, and functioning as moving signifiers of possibilities whose efficacy is under scrutiny as a reverse effect of an increasing sense of the inefficacy of 'the tried and the tested', whether this be conventional medicine or traditional ritual.

However, the very fact that Enid repeatedly goes to an obeah woman in London underlines her need for help and desire for ritual interventions which, on some level, she presumably believes might be effected through obeah rather than through other types of resource. Her scepticism mirrors a scepticism that might be felt by the audience of this play who both know that ritual here is 'only play' in the sense of being theatre but simultaneously understand that 'alternative' forms of healing or intervention may prove efficacious. The play thus projects an interesting recognition of parallels that exist between the migrant communities' own attitudes of scepticism towards the efficacy of their traditional ritual interventions and the white west's increasing doubt in the efficacy of conventional medicine. Within the play obeah becomes the pivot in a triangle that maps healing systems from diverse cultures, attaching scepticism to them all (see diagram).

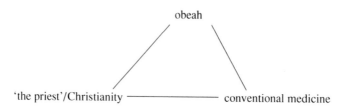

The relativism which underlies this position of scepticism reinforces the ambivalence that diaspora generates within the characters both in terms of what one has left behind and in terms of what one has inserted oneself into.

For Enid as a first-generation migrant, obeah is part of the past and the culture she has left behind in Jamaica – it constitutes a continuity with something once familiar but now displaced. The need for that continuity is at the centre of all the characters' longings in 'Leave Taking', and the play powerfully suggests that a complete break with one's past leads to breakdown and terrible estrangement. This is the fate that befell Gullyman. Enid, too, is constructed as in danger of experiencing a history not dissimilar from that of Gullyman. Like Gullyman she has embraced Englishness and is, in fact, variously (sometimes even bitterly) by herself described as 'Miss Holy Drawers' and 'Miss English'. Enid was ambitious which – for women of her generation in the West Indies – meant trying to avoid being perpetually pregnant from an early age and economically dependent.[13] That ambition translated into the desire to go abroad, either to America or to England. A certainty of being able to realize one's ambition through diasporic dispersal went hand in hand, in Enid's case, with the notion that assimilation was the best strategy to achieve one's ends. Indeed, both Enid (in 1, 2: 152; 156) and Mai take the line, 'you want to stay here in *my* house you abide by my rules, y'hear. You got to learn respect' (2, 1: 168). Enid and Mai have themselves been brought up with the importance of respect, expressed through abiding by the prevailing rules, as the appropriate way to act in a given territory. That stance makes for an assimilationist position in that it requires submission to the rules of the territory you are in. Enid and Mai, as first-generation migrants, have reached a certain accommodation in relation to the rules that govern English society. In that respect they are representative of first-generation migrants, many of whom adopted an assimilationist stance on first arriving in Britain. Both Enid and Mai to differing degrees attempt to fit in, *and* to retain a sense of self connected to their culture of origin. Thus Mai keeps chickens in her backyard, a thing not commonly done in contemporary London, to remind her of the outdoor and backyard life which typifies Jamaica for her. At the same time she has had to give up one of her rituals, the 'healing bath', because 'Damn' fool landlady keep complaining how I was bringing complete stranger in she house use bath. Think she going catch something. An' I know say all my clients does hundred times cleaner than she' (1, 1: 146).

Remembering Jamaica

Enid's relation to Jamaica is not nostalgic. Her and Mai's memories of home are permeated by an overwhelming sense of poverty and lack of opportunity for women. But the play raises questions about the relative importance of material and social impoverishment. Enid's view of Jamaica is that material deprivation was mediated through sharing and through community. When Del accuses her of failing to support her folks in Jamaica materially, Enid responds: 'You think one little gift going to make their life all right? You poorer than they are. Least them all in it together. When I was a girl you kill a cow, you share it up, everybody in the distric' get a piece. Here, you poor an' you by you'self. Nobody cares' (2, 2: 176). Enid here manifests a nostalgia for community which is reinforced through the fact that all the characters in the play are on their own throughout the play, the only demonstrated relation the blood bond between mother and daughter. Having come to England, Enid has lost that community. Her hopelessness becomes manifest when she says: 'I want . . . I want to go home' (1, 4: 166). The play constructs a symmetry between that final moment of Act One when Enid articulates her longing for a return and for belonging, and the final moment of Act Two when Enid and Del are poised to embrace in an act of reconciliation. Home is where the maternal relation is.

Del in particular accuses Enid of always giving money, implying that whilst Enid meets her daughters' material needs she does not provide for their emotional and social needs. The impression is given that Enid has bought into a soulless capitalist system of monetary exchange in which her only way of articulating a relation is through money. However, to take that line is to ignore Enid's history of extreme poverty as a child, a history which made her value money since it was something she did not have. But, again, the meaning of money is very different for her than it is for Del. Del has never known abject poverty. For her money is part of everyday life. She therefore wants something

48

else, ultimately a way of attaining a sense of self. Where Enid had to negotiate between her past, Jamaica, and her present, England, Del has to manage as a Black woman in a racist white culture. That is her history, the dilemma she faces.

Enid and Mai, the first-generation migrant women, are caught in the *entre-deux* of

past	present
Jamaican heritage	English life style
desire for change	repetition of behavioural patterns
movement	stasis
their generation	their children's generation
aspiration	denial
ideal	reality
memories of childhood	demands of adult life
idea of community	social isolation
rural past	urban present

Their Jamaican heritage is juxtaposed with their English present articulated through

ways of speaking	manners
ritual/obeah	social climbing
idea of community	being single
poverty	capitalism/money
sexploitation of women	self-sufficiency of women

Gendered asymmetries

With the exception of Broderick, all the males referred to in the play are absent. Indeed, the relative absence of men compared to the presence of women on stage constitutes one of the major and most telling asymmetries of the play, reinforced by the fact that the main call on Mai's powers of obeah seems to be in relation to 'man trouble'. As she tells Enid: 'Look, lady, if is man man you come 'bout you might as well go straight home. So many black women over here does come see me 'bout man: how to catch him, how to get him back, how to get rid of him. Mostly them does want to get him back. So many a' those women lef' lonely on them own. Some a' them gone mad over man' (1, 1: 145). The play offers an extensively documented and repeated explanation for this situation centring in part on the men's unwillingness or inability to take responsibility, in particular for the women they impregnate or whom they (promise to) bring over to England once they themselves have migrated, and, as articulated by Broderick, the difficulties black men face in making relationships with black women: 'Black women so hard to love. They do every damn' thing by themselves. Them so blinking self-sufficient they don't need a man for anything' (2, 3: 183). Broderick takes a line often encountered in writings by Black women in which Black men figure as incapable of dealing with what Michele Wallace (1990)[14] has famously described as *Black Macho and the Myth of the Superwoman* in her book of the same title.[15] As he reviews his life Broderick is able to make a link between his own sense of self-worth, or rather, his lack of such a sense, and his inability to treat black women well, especially in his youth. Now, older, he is able to recognize that 'Lov[ing] you'self' (2, 3: 183) is the key to being able to love others, but he has also found himself prevented from loving his wife because she had and embodied things that he did not feel he had himself: 'I hated her intelligence, her beauty because I felt none a' these things in me. I wanted to destroy them' (2, 3: 183). Although Broderick does not wish to make excuses for his younger self, his simultaneous disavowal of how he acted ('I was never as bad as some a' these men' (2, 3: 183)) and assertion of a similarity between him and Enid's former husband points to the importance of the diasporic experience as a key factor in shaping their behaviours: 'I never see a man eyes look so empty. Him never use to behave them ways in Jamaica. What do that to us? Englan'?' (2, 3: 183).

Broderick's sense that England is at the heart of the destruction of men like himself and like Enid's husband connects with the ways in which he is treated as an 'alien' in England. Made to feel worthless through the continual racism that haunts their lives, men such as Broderick turn against those who are like themselves to externalize the feelings foisted upon them. In this move he replicates a stance frequently described in writings on the impact of racism and colonialism on Black men. As Bryan *et al.* (1985) put it:

Black men in this society [the UK] are as much the victims of race and class oppression as we [Black women] are. The resulting projection of worthlessness cannot help but have a negative and damaging effect on how social and personal relations are perceived by both parties . . . Thus their attempts to subjugate Black women who are in a position of even less power must be seen as the evidence of their alienation. This is not to make apologies for their oppression of Black women, for it is clear, from where we stand, that their abuse of us only serves to increase *our* alienation as women both from Black men and society at large. But it *is* to recognize that Black men's oppression of us is merely a façade of power.

(214)

'Leave Taking' very clearly constructs its single present male character as much as its female characters as victims of both the colonial legacy which subjected them in the first place and the diasporic experience which succeeded that subjection.

The marginalization and limited presence of Black men in this play replicates their structural position in British society as much as their tangential role in the Black female characters' lives, on which they have an enormous impact but in which, especially in their younger years, they do not figure as permanent presences. Broderick as an older man seeks to reconnect to Enid as a man ready to engage in an intimate committed sexual relationship. He repeatedly states that his bad behaviour towards women, and not just his but also Enid's husband's, for example, happened when he 'was a young man' (1, 3: 161). The implication of his representation of their early days in England is that those days constituted a rupture that could only be endured through various forms of 'wildness' that not merely he and men but Enid, too, for instance, engaged in. As he says at one point: 'Drink. It was then I learn how to drink. We needed a lot a drinks to get through. Rough times, I tell you' (1, 2: 151). One of the diaspora effects articulated here by Broderick is the way in which the erosion of black people's sense of self-worth following migration dissolves the social fabric of black communities through the circulation of the devaluation of self and, consequently, of others. All the women in this play, both first- and second-generation, are left by the men in their lives, or throw them out for being unfaithful. Importantly, this seems true for both first- and second-generation migrants, as Del breaks up with her boyfriend, who always seems only tangential, just as Enid's husband did.

The difficulty of a permanent commitment by Black men to that which is denigrated by the dominant white culture, Black women, results in all of them experiencing the loneliness that can be the hallmark of the individualism fostered in western cultures at the expense of community. Significantly, every character in this play is single at the beginning of the play as much as at the end. Colonialism and diaspora thus become destructive of the social ties between those displaced. This is as true of their sexual as of their emotional ties, and is marked both within and across generations of diasporized peoples. None of the women is in a sexual relationship that might be described as 'committed' or permanent, whether it be heterosexual or lesbian. Similarly, both Enid and Mai have either (as in Enid's case) strained or (as in Mai's case) broken relationships with their children. Mai has not seen her son in years and does not know where he is; much of the play is about Enid's attempt to re-work her relationship with her daughters. The problematic, as diagnosed by Broderick, at the heart of these inter-generational problems, which are to some extent the same for both female and male offspring, is that 'The tragedy a' parenthood is that you bring up you children as if you preparing them to live the perfect life that you never had. Only thing is, you got to send them out into an imperfect world. You mother can't change the world' (2, 3: 183–4). Broderick's diagnosis produces a narrative of the conflict between aspiration and reality which Enid in particular experiences, both in relation to her own history and in terms of that of her two daughters.

Mothers and daughters

Enid's ambition to leave behind the perpetual pregnancies and poverty which are the fate of many of her peers in Jamaica had a significant influence on her decision to adopt an assimilationist stance towards

England, the country expected to move her beyond that fate. To acknowledge that England cannot or has not delivered all that Enid had hoped for would involve a re-reading of England that Enid cannot afford, because it would raise questions about the appropriateness of her vision of England and, by implication, raise questions about the judgments and decisions she made. Those decisions have cost her dearly. In two extremely moving exchanges, one with Broderick and one with her daughter Del, Enid describes key scenes in her life involving her own mother. The first scene relates to the time when Enid left Jamaica. In this narrative it becomes clear that Enid's mother herself migrated but then returned to Jamaica, a sign perhaps that the hoped-for improvements her exodus was meant to provide did not happen. Enid says: 'You know, the day I leave home, she never say goodbye to me. She must be never want me to go. I did think she woulda' understand: in the twenties she leave home go Cuba fe cut cane' (1, 3: 160). Enid never indicates why her mother returned from Cuba rather than stay there. Her mother's silence as Enid leaves, a silence that generated 'this . . . big, dark hole inside' (1, 3: 160), is thus ambivalent; it might indeed suggest that her mother did not want Enid to leave, not necessarily, however, because she did not understand, but rather because she knew full well the cost of such a departure. Enid does not ask herself why her mother might not have wanted her to leave. But as she reviews her life she returns to the cost of the loss of the mother in the scene where she finally reveals to Del why she did not send money back home for her mother's medical expenses when her mother lay dying: 'I knew she was dying. When I went out there you could just see it. She wanted me to put a' end to it . . . She made me promise that I wouldn't send anything out for her, said that I was Miss English, that I should forget them and get on with my life here . . . How can a person forget? To do that you would have to tear your heart out' (2, 4: 188). Enid, faithful to her mother, suffers from the guilt incurred in enabling her mother to die, an involuntary guilt which is part of the price she has been asked to pay for becoming a diasporic subject. Her mother's notion that 'Come from big big England mus' have something that would put a' end to the waiting [for her death]' (2, 4: 188) displaces the responsibility for helping the mother to die from those immediately around her to Enid, far away in England. The spatial remove of the diasporic subject from her country of origin is, however, not matched by a symmetrical emotional remove. As a first-generation migrant, Enid remains deeply attached to that country, and her mother's request to help her die by refraining from providing financial support is the greatest sacrifice Enid is forced to make as part of her diasporic life. Significantly therefore, and in contrast to the first act, by the second act the didascales describe Enid with the words *'There's something frail about her now, in contrast to the strong woman in earlier scenes'* (2, 2: 175). The news of her mother's death propels her to review her life choices.

'Leave Taking' is prefixed by quotations from Alice Walker's *In Search of Our Mothers' Gardens* (1983) and Simone de Beauvoir's *The Second Sex* (1949) which construct the significance of the play within a western feminist framework that – at the time of the writing of the play and in the preceding few years – was powerfully invested in the interrogation of relationships between mothers and daughters, as the many texts from that period, both non-fiction and plays,[16] testify. At the centre of this play, as of Cooke's 'Running Dream', are thus the relationships between women, between sisters and women of one age group on the one hand, and inter-generational relations between women on the other. These relationships are structured in specific ways that map the diasporic experience. A division emerges between those who leave their country of origin and those who stay put as both plays present the experiences of first-generation migrants and their children in the UK.

The history of migration to Britain is frequently constructed as one of male migration in the first instance, followed by women. 'Leave Taking' re-reads that history in terms of female migration and shows very clearly that migration is a gendered process, motivated by different agendas for women and men. Enid wanted to escape poverty and, almost more importantly, being condemned to a life of child-bearing from an early age. Her move is thus also an articulation of a refusal to be the object of male subjugation. In *Cartographies of Diaspora* Avtar Brah writes of 'a flight from the restrictions of patriarchal relations as they obtained in Uganda at the time' (1996: 5) as part of the motivating

54

force that encouraged her to seek a scholarship to study in the States. A similar motivation obtains in Enid's case. However, this refusal to be subjugated by men comes at a cost. As a heterosexually invested woman Enid suffers, as indeed do all the women in this play, from the isolation that comes with the (involuntary) severance of relations with men. The move from Jamaica to England of the first-generation migrants depicted in 'Leave Taking' embodies for Enid the process of dissociation she had already experienced in Jamaica where life choices are constructed as limited, particularly for a girl. The play constructs diaspora as a gendered process, generative of its own particular social structures both among those left behind and among those who move.

In the play Broderick acts as a mediating figure, mediating between the past and the present, as well as between Enid and her daughters. Marked by the experience of diaspora, his recognition of the racism which pervades Britain helps him to build bridges between Enid who on the surface seeks to deny that racism and her daughters who live with it. Enid understands that she lives in a racist society – talking of her daughters she says: 'Them think the world at them feet. They not going to end up like the old woman: no getting down on them knee an' scrubbing hospital floor for them. But this is white man country, a black woman less than nuttin' (1, 1: 148). Enid is not naïve about black women's situation in Britain but she simultaneously needs to think that her sacrifices have had a meaning, a meaning to be realized through her daughters. As she sees Del gliding towards the life she herself had desperately wanted to escape from, she becomes very anguished. Del, however, is not the exception. Viv tells her at one point: 'They're dropping like flies in the sixth form: one by one all the black girls are falling pregnant. It's like ten little Indians, everyone's placing bets about who's going to be next' (2, 1: 171). What this reveals is that migration does not necessarily result in improved living conditions; Del's partying is her response to the racism she faces on a daily basis, an impoverishing condition which fails to move her beyond the situation poor Black girls from rural areas in Jamaica might find themselves in. This negates the notion of some form of transgenerational teleological progress which Enid hoped for.

Broderick understands Enid's position but his own disillusion-ment with England also enables him to understand Enid's daughters. Unlike Enid, whose crisis of faith leads her seemingly to give up, Brod-erick has come through his own despair and puts his faith in the pos-sibility of a relationship with Enid. The audience's final glimpse of Broderick is when he leaves to 'serenade you Mooma [sic] under she window' (2, 3: 184), still hoping that Enid will relent under his persis-tent courtship. For Enid, however, a reconciliation with her daughters is much more critical than a relationship with Broderick.

Spatializing diaspora

'Leave Taking' has two locations, Mai's bedsit and Enid's living room. All but one scene of the first act take place in Enid's space; the sec-ond act occurs entirely on Mai's territory. Mai and Enid are in many ways constructed as opposites: Mai is untidy, floating between her Jamaican identity and the English context in which she now lives, calculating but kind, able to live her life despite the privations she has suffered; Enid is presented as tidy, aspiring, anxious to make the best of her life and of that of her daughters, wanting to be integrated but not quite managing it. Mai and Enid represent different responses to the diasporic situation. Within this framework, their on-stage loca-tion is important. The space that occupies them is not the space they occupy. But the space they occupy functions as a symbolic affirma-tion of their state of mind and of the diasporic experience as a state of mind. Enid is trapped between her past and her daughters' future. Her own life has ceased to matter to her. The life she has left behind con-tinues its hold on her, not merely through the requests for financial support from those who have stayed behind, but also through the loss of the sense of belonging Enid has to endure. Driven by the promise of opportunity and release from poverty with which Britain is synony-mous, Enid left Jamaica to improve her life. The cost of that move is enormous.

The play does not show diaspora as movement but focuses in-stead on diaspora as effect. Its location in two interior spaces points to the interiority of the diasporic effect, its poignancy beyond the movement which constitutes diaspora itself. The diasporic subject is not permanently on the move. Even though Mai states that 'home is a figment of the imagination. You know, sometime I think our people are condemn' to wander the earth' (2, 2: 178), she is also very clear about the fact that diaspora is not about perpetual physical motion, or a nomadic existence, but about a state of mind. Thus she says of her son: 'he English as they come – a Cockney – though he don't think so. All the time he roaming in him mind, round and round like he want to escape, but where the hell he going to escape to? If he could find some peace in himself – journey inside himself – everything would be all right. You at peace with yourself, you at home anywhere' (2, 2: 179).

Mai's diagnosis of the diasporic condition as an internalized and interior restlessness does not address the reasons for this inner roaming, the reasons for the need to escape. Her son's inability to settle, his alienation from her, is played out and given embodiment through the mirror of the tensions between Enid and her two daughters. These daughters represent two aspects of Enid's self. Del, the older daughter, is a bit wild as Enid is said to have been in her younger days. Del likes to go out dancing because in that bodily activity she experiences herself as her self: 'I spent all last night dancing. The music just picks you up and throws you around the room. You can't stop. *I always feel like me when I'm dancing.* You can't pretend. Why don't you want me to feel like that?' (1, 2: 156; emphasis added). Del's use of dance acts as a form of catharsis through which, as Kobena Mercer (1994) puts it, 'a momentary release might be obtained from all the pressures on mind and body accumulated under the ritual discrimination of racism' (118). Del's sense of alienation, her 'running wild', is – as she clearly articulates when accusing her mother of not 'giv[ing] us anything we can use out there' – fostered by her experience of racist behaviour: 'Every day', she says, 'we go out and they can do what the hell they like with us' (1, 2: 157). The experience of racism is acknowledged by Del in ways that Enid can never accept. As Brah puts it: 'we believed in the narratives of progress' (1996: 4). Enid came to England expressedly to better her situation, to live the progress alluded to by Brah.

For a long time Enid tries to hold on to this dream of progress and improvement. But 'Leave Taking' ultimately refutes these teleological narratives of progress which propel diasporic movement, through Del's and Viv's perspectives on the life their mother has enabled them to live. Neither is happy with her situation. Del attempts to deal with her sense of alienation by 'being wild', going out and enjoying herself, with the consequence that she falls pregnant, and becomes one of the many young single black mothers. Of – and to – her mother she says: 'You're always telling us to be grateful. For what? You move around with your back bent, dancing attendance on some illusion that was exposed years ago' (1, 2: 157).

The *entre-deux* which is the experience of the second-generation migrants is very different from that of their first-generation elders. The second generation live the reality that the first generation dreamt about. They have to come to terms with the space between that dream and the reality which is England. Without a prior experience of extreme rural poverty and perpetual pregnancy, Del and Viv, as much as Mai's estranged son, have to find the rationale that enables them to live in a society which judges them by their skin colour. The older generation's rationale is guaranteed through their prior lives; for the second generation a different situation pertains. Enid judges her current situation by her past in Jamaica; her daughters have no such past to compare their present with. This is a key difficulty faced by Enid whose own vision of her daughters' life is determined by her history in Jamaica, not by their history in England. Whereas that history and Enid's sacrifice of her relation with her mother is the price which justifies Enid's endurance and repression of any experience of racism, Del and Viv have to forge their identities against other grains. As they struggle to become themselves, they are initially constructed in Enid's image, seemingly representing, symmetrically, a 'good' and a 'bad' version of how one might live as a Black woman in Britain. Del is 'wild' and has become pregnant (although pregnancy in her early twenties, the age she is in the play, is nothing like as problematic as pregnancy at fourteen), manifesting a rebellious attitude towards her mother whose assimilationist position she despises. Viv, on the other hand, seems to have internalized the notion of bettering oneself through education, an idea much more important in the West Indies than in the UK. Her academic achievements are Enid's pride and joy since they seem to embody all that she strove for. However, having been born and brought up in England does not make Del and Viv belong in the way Enid dreams of. Both girls feel displaced and without an identity they can inhabit. In articulating her sense of estrangement Viv says: 'I sometimes feel like I need another language to express myself. (*Slight pause.*) Swahili perhaps' (2, 1: 172).

From the beginning Viv takes an interest in her ancestry and her family's history. At Mai's place she '*picks up an African figure*' (1, 1: 144), for instance and says that she wants 'to go to the West Indies, do a grand tour' (2, 1: 145). This desire is repeated later when she asserts again that she wants 'to go to Jamaica' (1, 3: 162), stating, 'I want to see for myself. What it's like and everything. It must be part of me' (1, 3: 162). However, this desire is never realized within the play. By the end of Act Two Scene Two, Viv has faded from view, her 'one act of rebellion' (2, 1: 172) as she describes it – walking out of an exam – and giving away the money Enid gave her as a reward for being so good at school, resulting in Enid throwing her out. Viv's future life is left hanging at the end. Her mother dismissed her sense that Jamaica might be part of her as 'nonsense' (1, 3: 162), precisely for the reasons that make Enid's being in England a different form of diasporic experience from that of her daughters, namely that Viv would not know how to survive there because she has no experience of extreme poverty. Enid thus cuts off one of the routes Viv might have towards her own sense of self independent of her mother. Indeed, the play offers no solution for Viv in her quest for a sense of self. The play thus registers the uncertainty that haunts the diasporized imaginary as to its belonging. Thrown out of her home by her mother, her possibility of her roots in Jamaica denied her, and with an uncertain future in the education and employment market, Viv is left to fend for herself with no obvious solution as to the way forward. While Viv's path, seemingly certain at the outset of the play, is overturned in the course of the play into one of uncertainty, her sister Del's situation undergoes the reverse scenario, moving from uncertainty to certainty (see diagram).

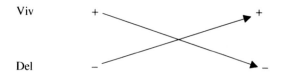

Here is another symmetry in the play's structuration of diasporic experience, suggesting, rather like the narrative about Gullyman, the possibility of the changeability of fate, the unpredictability of the future, but within a context where change does not necessarily imply change of location. Broderick describes Viv and Del's situation astutely when he admonishes Enid to teach them where they come from: 'These girls ain't English like them newsreader, them people got English stamp on them like the letters on a stick a' rock, right through English. These girls got Caribbean souls' (1, 2: 153). Broderick pleads for Enid's girls to be allowed to inhabit their diasporized selves, to participate in Jamaica, even if only at the level of learning about it. Enid, having felt compelled to leave Jamaica behind, does not want to be reinscribed into it, or to have her daughters return to it in any way since that motion would disturb her teleological perspective of her life. Del and Viv thus have limited knowledge of Jamaica and of West Indian history, with Del especially manifesting both scorn and disbelief in the early scenes of the play regarding that heritage. This manifests itself in particular in her mocking attitude towards obeah, her seeming refusal to believe in it. But when she leaves her mother's house, pregnant and with nowhere to go, it is to Mai, the obeah woman, that she turns for help and support. Mai takes her in and trains her to be an obeah woman, thus simultaneously solving her own problem of succession and Del's problem about how to support herself from home with a small child. For most of the play Del retains her attitude of incredulity towards the efficacy of obeah, mocking Mai's rituals and accusing her of being 'a phoney' (2, 1: 169). Eventually she is forced to admit, 'Maybe I am lost' (2, 2: 177), a moment that offers Mai the opportunity to spell out to Del why she tolerates her insufferable behaviour in her house and supports Del who shows little appreciation of that fact: 'I want you to have my thoughts. I don't have a daughter

to pass them on to' (2, 2: 177). Del's taking on of clients of her own
at the end of the play, her cleaning of Mai's bedsit, and her reconciliation with her mother signal the sense of self she has acquired in the
course of the play. In this context Broderick's earlier assertion that Viv
and Del need to connect to their 'roots' through knowing about West
Indian history is endorsed, since Del's emerging sense of self depends
significantly on her changing relationship to obeah, also part of her
Jamaican heritage.

Significantly that sense of self is forced upon her by her unwanted pregnancy: 'now, for once in my life I can't run away. For the
sake a' my kid I got to stand and face up to who I am. For once in my
life I feel like I got a future' (2, 4: 189). Ironically, in saying this Del
is investing in her as yet unborn child in exactly the ways in which
Enid invested in her children – the children represent the future that
determines the women's present course of action. In referencing that
future Del replicates her mother's history of emotional investment.
At the same time, she hankers after the certainties and securities of
childhood, saying to her mother, 'Every night I go to bed and curl
up tight and pretend I'm a kid again: when you used to hold me and
whisper secrets in my ear, remember?' (2, 4: 189). Caught *entre-deux*,
between a childhood that has irrevocably passed and a future that has
not yet occurred, Del reveals the emotional fabric which joins those
two states stretching across the present, covering its needs. This provides her mother with the opportunity to assert her similarity to Del,
to show how she, too, is caught in that *entre-deux*:

> ENID. And don't I need to curl up in somebody lap and to be
> told stories to make the sun shine? Don't I need somebody to
> touch my cheek as though I was a prize not a curse and to
> stroke my hair like Mooma never did? What about me?
>
> (2, 4: 189)

Both mother and child: in their final gesture of reconciliation, Del and
Enid are simultaneously mother and child, not only in themselves but
to each other, expressing their need to be child and to be mothered,
as well as the need to respond to the demand for mothering, in themselves and in others. A parallel of recurring needs is thus established

within a structure of cyclicity whereby the daughter undergoes the same emotional experiences and socio-economic processes that structured her own mother's decisions. In finding a way for herself, Del becomes like her mother and is also enabled to understand her mother's needs and decisions.

The play thus offers a particular take on diaspora as a recurrent cyclical effect which mirrors women's journey from childhood to adulthood, mapping the evacuation from the security of childhood to the insecurity of adulthood. In the process childhood and adulthood emerge as sites of fantasy, of an unrealized because unrealizable desire for security and comfort. Diasporic movement is here reinterpreted as an adult version of the exodus from childhood already previously enacted, the point at which unbelonging is installed at the heart of the diasporized person. Within this context assimilation, conceived of as one answer to the longing for belonging, is constructed as a provisional remedy the efficacy of which is scrutinized through the return of the repressed which is the price paid for a temporary assimilation. The repressed is the heritage Enid seeks to divest herself and her children of. It returns, however, through the continuous connection Enid retains to her family back in Jamaica, through her memories of Jamaica and of her mother, and through Viv and Del's unsettled senses of self. Where Enid's exodus from childhood was compounded by her leaving of Jamaica for England, her daughters' exodus from childhood is compounded by their second-generation migrant status in England, of which they simultaneously feel and do not feel a part. Del recovers her sense of self through taking on her mother's history of being a single parent and through forging a connection to her Jamaican heritage and community by serving the latter by taking on the role of obeah woman. For Viv the future is less certain. The play thus dispels the notion that there is a single solution for dealing with the trauma of diasporic existence. It makes, however, the point that diasporic experience, the actual movement from one location to another, from one culture to another, has affinities with the exodus from childhood into adulthood, installing in the diasporized the same longing for belonging, for a forever imaginary place of safety to return to, that is always already lost as part of one's experience of growing up and growing older. That affinity secures recognition for an audience that may regard diaspora as the problem of the other.

Diaspora in 'Running Dream'

Where 'Leave Taking' focuses on life in the diaspora, on life as a diasporic, post-migration state, 'Running Dream' weaves together past and present in a complex semiotically articulated movement between two locations, simultaneously temporal and spatial: the past and the present, childhood and adulthood, life in Dominica and life in England. Like Pinnock, Cooke explores West Indian diasporic experience, and like Pinnock, Cooke does so through the exploration of inter-generational relationships between women. But whereas Enid's daughters are born in England and their dilemma is the *entre-deux* of living in a predominantly white society as young Black women, Cooke's play moves into another direction as she explores one of the key experiences of many West Indians who came to the UK between the 1950s and the 1970s: the fragmentation of families as a consequence of that move, and the price of that fragmentation.[17] Importantly, in this context, diaspora is constructed as affecting not only those who leave, and the societies into which they migrate, but those who are left behind, for whatever reason. The play thus moves from the binary to the triangular as it interrogates the relationships between three generations of women, those who moved or 'travelled' as Cooke describes it and those who stayed behind.

Like Pinnock, Cooke is very clear about the fact that diasporic movement comes at a cost, a cost which is not just associated with loss of culture, home, and community but also with loss of family, the most intimate of ties. Speaking of her own family, Cooke writes: 'within my own generation (my brothers and sisters) there were two parts – a generation who travelled to England from Dominica and those who were born here . . . Those who travelled remembered a world we English-born knew nothing about and as I got older I envied their memories. They spoke of a grandmother who brought them up. My grandmother died before I met her' (187). 'Running Dream' replays those experiences but sets them into a context which mythologizes and, as a consequence, de-personalizes those experiences, through its theatrical devices which, *inter alia*, link the play to Greek tragedy, where family drama translates into an interrogation of the relation between the private and the individual and larger systems and institutions such as the pantheon of the gods and the state. The opening scene brings together all those elements as Effeline, the old woman and grandmother in the play, speaks in an incantatory manner, repeating in Dominican patois (here given in the play's own parallel translation):

> My dearest
> My dearest
> Everything you say
> Everything you do
> It stays with you
> We will not forget
> It stays with you
> Like a spirit
> Like a spirit
> Like a spirit
>
> (1: 188)

This incantatory speech is marked by repetition and underscored by the sound of music, the sea, and 'a slow unoiled regular croak' (1: 188). Within the significatory economy of cultural representation all of these elements associate Effeline's speech with what Julia Kristeva (1984) has described as the semiotic, the rhythmic, repetitive, associative, present-oriented articulation of the time of the primary relation with the mother, predating the intervention of the (law of the) father. The world of 'Running Dream' as much as that of 'Leave Taking' is a maternal, female-centred world in which – in contrast to most western plays – older women play a key role as markers of transition, as bearers of a past and a culture that now seems threatened, as the liminal figures between what is lost and what cannot be found. These older women, symbolic[18] as much as actual mothers, are, as Kristeva describes it in 'Stabat Mater' (1986), 'the *fantasy* that is nurtured by the adult, man or woman, of a lost territory; what is more, it involves less an idealized archaic mother than the idealization of

64

the *relationship* that binds us to her, one that cannot be localized – an idealization of primary narcissism' (161). To underscore this fantasy, described by Cooke in her preface to the play as the coming to life of her grandmother, the one who mothered her siblings but not her, in her dreams, hence the 'running dream' as the continuous – running like running water – dream, always a dream, or fantasy, rather than reality, the thing desired but unreachable except through fantasy, through dreaming. It is for this reason that Effeline's invocation at the opening of the play is poetic, rhythmic, repetitive, employing the present tense. Its incantatory quality evokes the maternal as fantasy, eternally present, outside of time. To quote Kristeva's 'Women's Time': 'Female subjectivity would seem to provide a specific measure that essentially retains *repetition* and *eternity* from among the multiple modalities of time known through the history of civilizations' (191). Both repetition and eternity are articulated in 'Running Dream' through various structural and theatrical devices, and through the invocation of the spirit world.

'Running Dream' echoes the narrative of 'Leave Taking'. Here too we have an older generation, embodied by Ma Effeline, left behind in the West Indies, as the next generation, the first-generation migrants to the UK, represented by Florentine and William, leave because they 'want to do something with [their] li[ves]' (1: 203). William, like Broderick, is another tangential male who fails to support his wife and children in his younger years, having taken up with a white woman on his arrival in Britain. He explains that he 'jus' change track . . . because I cannot look after you the way I want' (1: 206), a change of track he regrets in his later life. But the effect of his change of track is that both he and Florentine end up by themselves, isolated and without community. Like 'Leave Taking' this is a narrative of female abandonment by males, and again, not just in the third generation. Like Del, Bianca, Flo's last child, born in the UK, is without direction and seeks her salvation through men. Like Del, she is abandoned, eventually finding her self through travelling to Dominica to reconnect to her family.

At the heart of 'Running Dream', a dream that runs through the protagonists' lives, a dream about running and searching, a continuous dream, is the trauma of female abandonment which structures the

diasporic existence of all the characters in the play. That abandonment, in many respects the experience of the first separation from
the mother and, in Kristevan terms, the shift from the semiotic to the
symbolic, operates symmetrically, reciprocally, and cyclically: in the
three-generation context of the play every abandonment is simultaneously an abandonment of the mother and of the daughter. The opening
refrain, repeated several times throughout the first act, thus does not
articulate the consolation of memory but commemorates the trauma
of loss. The play demonstrates that diaspora is loss and its reference
to Greek tragedy through the use of a chorus reinforces this. Diaspora
generates a traumatic rupture, comparable only with – and in this play
always associated with – the loss of the mother, which remains un-
compensatible. Significantly, the chair on which Ma Effeline takes her
seat in the opening scene is described as *'a rocking-chair (a throne, an
altar)'* (1: 188). That description signals that contrary to Freud's notion of 'his majesty the baby', at the centre of the play is her majesty
the mother, as idealized and idolized form. Indeed, within this play
the baby is semiotically encoded as simultaneously the desired and the
debased other: a reverse discourse to match the reversal of the conventional focus from the baby to the mother. For the first materialization
of the baby occurs when the female characters playing in the yard
uncover the coffin that is sitting there: *'(The women take the lid off
the coffin inside is a white, blonde, blue-eyed doll. The rocking-chair
moves. A baby cries)'* (1: 189). The conflation of the uncovering of the
doll with the crying of the baby prefigures a later scene when Clem and
Grace, left behind by their mother Flo who has gone to England, are
sent white blue-eyed dolls by her, and Clem, the daughter who is never
sent for to come to England, ends up with the broken doll. The white,
blue-eyed doll figures repeatedly in this play,[19] always as that which
you cannot have or cannot be but which embodies a dream, a broken,
soiled dream which itself mirrors the broken lives of those left behind. For the baby, supposedly what every woman desires, is not what
is desired in this play: it is the mother who is yearned for: 'Plane bring
my Mammy back to me. Plane bring my Mammy back to me' (1: 190)
shout Clem and Grace as a plane flies overhead. Clem's emotional
life is destroyed by the fact that Flo never had the money to send

for her to join her and Grace in England. And although that rationale explains what happened, it cannot compensate for Clem's feelings of abandonment. Simultaneously Grace, the daughter who was sent for to come to England, has had to live with the loss of Ma Effeline and, as it turns out, with the loss of her mother Flo, too. When Grace returns to Dominica as an adult to visit Ma Effeline, who is ill and likely to die, she tells Clem:

> I can't even remember Mammy at home, and if you honest
> you can't either. Ma Effeline brought us up. I only got to know
> Mammy when I went to meet her in England, and we didn't
> mis [sic] her when she went away because we had everything.
> We had each other, we had everybody all around. You still had
> that when I left, you still had everybody around. I had nobody
> Clem. Can't you understand what you're jealous of is nothing?
> I had nobody. I lived for your letters too.
>
> (2: 225)

But Clem's response remains: 'Mammy left me' (2: 225).

The invocation of community in Dominica which Clem sets against the social isolation she experienced in England – a comparison already familiar from 'Leave Taking' and itself in some respects a manifestation of a nostalgic yearning – cannot alleviate Clem's sense of abandonment. Neither can Grace's assertion of the idea of the mother as fantasy, as idealized and desired object that does not match the reality she and Clem lived. For, as Kristeva rightly diagnosed in 'Stabat Mater', it is the *relation* to the mother that is mourned, the ideal of that relation, tied to the moment of childhood, which was both generated and sustained by separation from the mother. This is evident in Clem's and Grace's treatment of their mothers, actual and symbolic, in adulthood. Grace, who has been with her birth mother from her teenage years until adulthood, yearns for her grandmother Effeline who brought her up during her childhood. Clem, who has lived her life around Effeline, yearns for her birth mother. The one woman in the play, Bianca, who has spent her life continuously with one mother, her birth mother, finds it difficult to maintain a relationship with her as an adult and is constructed as always searching for something that

she can 'hold on to, something you can say is yours' (2: 223). Like
Del in 'Leave Taking', Bianca, who has been the object of racist taunts
and behaviours, does not feel that England is *her* country despite the
fact that she was born there. Her search for an identity, for a sense
of belonging, like Del's translates into motion, but whereas Del goes
dancing, Bianca goes running: 'Running', she says, 'eases the tension.
Makes me feel at home with myself. Makes me relax with what I know
to be me' (1: 209). That finding of the self, temporarily, through motion
points the diasporic person back to self as the source of identity and
belonging. Significantly, when Bianca says, 'I ran for the school/ran for
the country/Wanted to run for the country' (1: 209), the chorus replies:
'Which country?' (1: 209), revealing the gap between an assumption
that identity is forged around place and nation, and identity as psychical response to circumstances. Bianca ends up admitting that 'I ran for
myself – I don't know . . . ran for my life. Ran away – from my mother'
(1: 210). She feels her mother loved her too much, invested in Bianca
what she could not invest in herself: 'Loved me because you couldn't
love yourself any more' (1: 210).

Bianca's narrative of loss of self and re-finding of that self –
initially through a relationship with a man – echoes the narratives
in Ntozake Shange's *for colored girls*, which Shange wrote 'for colored girls' in order to enable them to 'become all that is forbidden
by our environment, all that is forfeited by our gender, all that we
have forgotten' (Shange 1992: xvii). In the same way that *for colored
girls* moves towards its triumphalist, transformative ending where the
put-upon colored 'everywoman' says: 'I found god in myself/ & i loved
her/ i loved her fiercely' (Shange 1992: 63), Bianca's, and indeed the
other women's narratives in 'Running Dream', are constructed as ones
in which they need to find themselves rather than their mothers in
order to move on from their sense of inadequacy and abandonment.
'Running Dream' references *for colored girls* in a number of ways,
including in its focus on women, poetic form, use of patois and a chorus, representation of heterosexuality as exploitative of women, and
in its exploration of the need for the colored girl or black woman for
self-affirmation. The major difference between the two plays is that
for colored girls focuses on one generation of women, constructing a

series of parallel experiences among a group of female peers, whereas 'Running Dream' takes a longitudinal view, reflecting upon women's experiences across generations and anchoring them directly in colonialism and diaspora. Clem's and Grace's loss of their birth mother occurs as a consequence of her migration, a migration propelled by the desire, exactly as was the case with Enid, to escape a life of gendered drudgery and, like Enid, Flo ended up in a three-women household as a single mother. She tells Bianca:

> FLORENTINE: I was the only twenty-one year old
> woman . . . that didn't have children yet. I *was* a fighter, a real
> how you call it? Tom boy? I had no use for a man. I was
> strong. I could do most things a man could do by Mammy,
> Mammy did want me to be like other woman. Make children,
> be a wife ha . . . Well I make children, did all the things I had
> to do, played the part . . . but all I wanted to do was –
> BIANCA: Run?
> FLORENTINE: You know me because you is me.
>
> (2: 219)

Flo submitted to what Adrienne Rich (1980) famously termed 'compulsory heterosexuality', forgetting her self. And just as *for colored girls* ultimately exhorts the black girl to find god in herself and to love herself, so this play exhorts its female characters not to forget themselves, not to be overtaken by the imperatives of compulsory heterosexuality or indeed by desire and fantasy, for both propel the women to forget themselves, to do that which engenders loss because it entails the abandonment of the primary narcissistic relation, the relation of self to self.

The focus of 'Running Dream' on the maternal is theatrically encoded in its non-naturalistic form. Its vaguely linear narrative, itself archetypal rather than particular, and centring on the story of loss and separation, is disturbed by scenes which shift back and forth between past and present, childhood and adulthood, Flo's youth and Flo's middle age, England and Dominica. Similarly the dialogues, both between the characters and between the characters and the chorus, shift between past and present, between appearance and inner psychical reality, between the reality the characters inhabit and the dreams, repressions, traumas they suffer. In this they mirror the lines of the opening refrain that everything you do and say stays with you and, as the play demonstrates, haunts you in the form of memories and unassuaged desires. That basic assumption of the text, the simultaneity and perpetual presence of all that one experiences, determines the structure of the play and its non-naturalistic mode. It co-articulates this with the notion of the primacy of the maternal for which the play uses, *inter alia*, the emblem of the sea, a kind of cosmic amniotic fluid the atavistic memory of which haunts the imaginary of the expelled.

The play begins and ends with the sounds of the sea. But whereas in the opening scene the sea symbolizes an eternal enveloping presence reinforced through the opening chant, by the end of the play the sea has taken on the contradictory identity of the mother both as the figure who is most immediately and intensely desired and as that which has to be let go of, that which is irrevocably bound into loss. In the opening scene, which sees Clem and Grace with Ma Effeline, Flo having left for England, the children are playing as if they are washing clothes (1: 190), an activity involving water, and whilst playing Clem sings:

> Wash away my sorrow/Wash away my grief
> Wash away that love/that once belonged to me
> Wash away my sorrow/Wash away my grief
> Wash away that love/that once belonged to me

(1: 190)

At the end of the play she sings that song again, not only indexing the perpetuity of the effect of that loss and grief, but also referencing a gesture Grace has forced her to make in an effort to enable Clem to move on from her grief at having been abandoned. Where in the opening scene the washing away of the love that once belonged to Clem refers to the actual removal of the mother from Dominica to England, articulating the raw grief felt by the girls recently left behind by their mother, by the end of the play the refrain refers to the doll that is being washed away by the sea, having been laid 'to rest in the sea' by Clem. The doll constituted a tangible connection between Clem and her mother Flo, representing that which drove Flo to leave in the first instance, namely the seductiveness of material opportunities in the white world, as well as the colonial legacy which impoverished the countries from which people migrate in the past and in the present – in the past through straightforward exploitation of these lands' resources and in the present through draining these lands of a particular resource, their people. Clem's sense of abandonment has led her to over-invest in the doll, using her fetishistically to externalize her feelings of loss and resentment regarding her situation. The continued presence of the doll has become a way for Clem to keep hold, quite literally, of the feelings she developed as a child as a consequence of her abandonment. Now a woman, Clem – abandoned again by her husband and sons who went to America, and about to lose to death in old age the woman who brought her up – has remained emotionally rooted to the spot where she was as a child, the girl left behind. Clem thus emblematizes the emotional costs of diaspora for those left behind whose separation from their families, here very specifically from the mother, creates a trauma which is very difficult to come to terms with.[20]

In the final scene, then, Clem and Grace pick up the fight over the doll they had as children, fighting again over the doll but this time as adults with histories that invest this scene with a new semantic significance. Grace asks to see Clem's doll, snatching it from her because 'it cause you too much pain already. Is jus' a doll and you put so much meaning, so much anger, so much hatred in this' (2: 226). Grace rightly identifies the doll as the fetishistic object of Clem's emotional landscape, and her intention to divest Clem of her feelings of anger and resentment through divesting her of the doll is a logical conclusion of this understanding. In order for Clem to move on, however, she herself has to consent to letting go of the object which has become the repository of her emotional needs. Clem's attachment to the doll – '*My piece* of what you had. *My piece* of what all you had. Yes, it break up and ugly but it mine' (2: 226) – cannot be undone by Grace without Clem's consent since such an action would only do further violence to

Clem. Only *she* is able to effect the reconciliation with her experiences that she needs to undertake in order to restore her sense of self-worth. Having been the object of others' decisions, having had to submit to a forced separation from her mother, she needs to have agency restored to her, becoming the subject of her own situation rather than the object of others' decisions. Encouraged by both Ma Effeline and Grace to 'Let it rest Clemoi' (2: 226), Clem becomes still, accepting her sister's help. In a cleansing and purification ritual Grace begins to wash the doll in the sea, symbolically reuniting the child with the mother and simultaneously cleansing the doll of the meanings Clem had attached to it. Grace *'lowers the doll to the sea and begins to wash it'* (2: 226), whilst Clem accompanies this ritual with the refrain 'Wash away my sorrow . . .', thus literally invoking the sea to heal her anguish. The jointly executed ritual of divesting the doll of its emotional hold over Clem reunites the sisters who stand with their arms around each other as the moon, another symbol of the maternal, *'glows on the doll in the water'* (2: 227).

The play ends with the chorus singing

> If I sail on a sailing boat and I don't come back,
> stay home and mind baby . . .
> Brown skin girl stay home and mind baby
> Brown skin girl stay home and mind baby
> If I sail on a sailing boat and I don't come back
> Stay home and mind baby . . .
>
> (2: 227)

The 'I' of the song remains unspecified, its gender ambiguous and enforced as such through the use of a chorus as the singers rather than a single gendered voice. It is thus unclear whether the persona of the song refers to a man or a woman. The addressee is without question the 'brown skin girl' exhorted to stay at home and mind the baby, though whose baby – her own, someone else's – is also not specified. In the play itself both women and men, identified as daughters and as husbands or sexual partners respectively, sail away. For the 'brown skin girl' both staying behind and going away entail loss and separation – she is in the no-win situation. Clem, who has stayed behind and minded baby in the form of the doll, has nurtured her sense of abandonment which she needs to move beyond. But the doll is also the fetish object rather than a 'real' baby, and the play suggests that Flo's failure to stay home and mind baby has effected Clem's disconsolate state. Yet one of Flo's desires was to escape the constraints of the kind of gendered role that – like the brown skin girl in the song – would lock her into recurrent cycles of reproductivity and perpetual poverty. The play thus registers a profound ambivalence in which the reality of diasporic experience is mapped against the emotional landscape of all those inhabiting the diasporic space, counting the cost of that experience.

Simultaneously, the play suggests that the diaspora enacted by those leaving Dominica and the West Indies for a better life in England replicates a prior diasporic movement, played out at the point of childhood when the separation of girl child from mother occurs. Not only do both experiences entail loss and a sense of abandonment but they also produce situations of no return. Just as Clem and Grace can never recover their childhood, can never be reunited with the mother who, in any event, was always a fantasy of relation, so those diasporized can never recover their original relation to their country and culture of origin. There is no going back. Thus Grace tells Clem: 'it nice to come back to but it not my home again. I remember all the good times we had but they're memories you know . . . they're just what we used to be . . . and now we're different people' (2: 225).[21] 'Running Dream' makes clear that it is impossible to move on without confronting the past. For Clem to be able to move on emotionally she has to come to terms with her sense of abandonment, emblematized in letting go of the doll. Flo articulates her dying as 'going home': 'Something not right. May be my modder calling me – Maybe is my time' (2: 224). She also tells William, her estranged husband, come to reconcile himself with her after years of absenting himself, 'I want bath. Put blue in the water!' (2: 224). Immersion in water as a symbolic return to the mother figures here as the desire which governs Flo's last moments. The urge to be reunited with the mother is constructed as the lasting impulse installed at the moment of separation and perpetuated through the estrangement experienced as a consequence of diaspora. Diaspora, too, thus becomes a permanent condition – not a temporary

73

state, reversible through returning, but an experience without remedy, obliterated only in death.

Language and diaspora

'Running Dream' opens with Ma Effeline speaking in Dominican patois, a kind of French Creole. As such it is not immediately accessible either to an audience whose primary language is English or to an audience whose only languages are particular versions of French. French Creole, here as Dominican patois, reinforces the notion of the *entre-deux*, an in-between-ness generated by the mixing of an indigenous language with that of the colonizer, signalling the simultaneity and persistence of both the indigenous history and the presence of the colonizer. Since the play was first performed in London,[22] an audience with a Dominican history would have understood some if not all of the patois whereas native English speakers would have had great difficulties understanding what was being said, at least some of the time. This linguistically particular point of entry into the play thus generates a language-based rapport between a patois-speaking audience and the figures on stage whilst creating an alienation effect in those in the audience not familiar with patois. Within the play text, the localized patois is juxtaposed with a translation into English in brackets, and although the texts appear side by side, the very fact that the translation is in brackets and is to the right makes it second, indeed secondary, thus relegating the dominant to the position of echo. On stage, the language issue can be dealt with in a number of ways, one of which is simply to retain the alienation effect for those who do not understand patois as part of the theatre experience, or through having some of the chorus, echo-like, sing the English version of the text, or through projecting the English text, or through appropriate programme notes. However it is done, English in this context is always secondary to Dominican patois. Gilbert and Tompkins (1996) discuss the incorporation of indigenous languages into plays as a way of proclaiming 'radical alterity in a context where non-indigenous viewers can neither "look up" the meaning nor quite imagine how such words might be scripted' (170). They argue that 'When a playwright chooses an indigenous language over English, s/he refuses to submit to the dominance of the imposed standard language and to subscribe to the "reality" it sustains' (169). Instead, the use of indigenous language entails a validation of that language and its attendant reality and culture. Transporting dominant-language speakers onto unknown linguistic territory thus generates in those viewers a diasporic effect in which the primacy of their culture and knowledge is displaced in favour of the indigenous address. At the same time this play signals that its focus, its terrain, is intra-Dominican, that it is dealing with intra-ethnic rather than inter-ethnic concerns, although the former are powerfully conditioned by the latter. Language as a form of cultural self-definition becomes a source of affirmation in a context where indigenous languages are frequently seen as inferior or not 'correct'. Thus 'the strategic use of languages in post-colonial plays helps to reinvest colonised peoples and their characteristic systems of communication with a sense of power and an active place on the stage' (Gilbert and Tompkins 168). In 'Running Dream' the use of Dominican patois by Ma Effeline, and by Clem and Grace as children, signals their rootedness in a culture from which the latter two become displaced as their mother moves to England in search of a better life. For those who move patois can come to signify 'only "history" . . . and a superseded past at that' (Gilbert and Tompkins 171). This is the case for Grace, for whom the return to Dominica does not lead to renewed identification with that country but to an affirmation of her diasporic self.

For Bianca, born in Britain and thus a second-generation migrant, patois has different meanings from the ones it holds for Grace. Significantly, Grace initially sees her as 'one of them tiny dolls that cried real tears' (1: 207). This association of Bianca with a doll is repeated later when Clem meets her for the first time in Dominica and says she is 'a doll. A real English doll' (2: 221). Bianca thus carries the weight of both the desired and the abjected already emblematized through the doll. Whilst Grace has to go through the process of recognizing that neither the place she came from nor the country she now inhabits can be 'home' to her in the fullest sense of that word, Bianca's diasporized subjectivity is confirmed through the way in which she is 'other' even to her own sister since she has never lived in Dominica. The surprise that another character, Dennis, registers at the fact that Bianca can speak 'patwa' measures the sense of distance assumed by those who stayed behind or live in Dominica in relation to second-generation migrants. Bianca is not completely alienated from her mother's culture, because her mother speaks patois at home. But like Clem, Bianca is at home in neither culture. Bianca has to insist repeatedly that she is not English, and that England is not 'hers'. Racism creates the gap between her and England which leaves her in the limbo of the *entre-deux*. This play, as indeed does 'Leave Taking', makes explicit the impossibility of return as much as the difficulty of (re)connecting.[23] But it also suggests the breaking down of the binarisms that themselves underpin racism. The movement between patois and English which occurs in the play, its co-mingling, points to the possibility of participation in both.

3   Geographies of un/belonging

Diasporic identity demands the management of an unsettled self, of a subject permanently *entre-deux*, in process rather than 'becoming', without a necessarily teleological structure to support that process and relieve it of some of its destabilizing impact. This is particularly evident in the context of the lives of second-generation migrants. As Nancy Foner (1977) put it in relation to migrants to the UK from the West Indies: 'Jamaican migrants in England are caught between two worlds: they are no longer just like Jamaicans back home but they are also not exactly like, or fully accepted by, most English people' (121). But whereas economic despair and aspiration may have prompted the first generation of migrants to undertake the journey to the UK, and that very history mediated between the past in Jamaica and the present in the UK, second-generation migrants face a present without that particular past. Thus whilst first-generation migrants may think of their country of origin as 'home', especially when faced with discrimination and racist experiences in the country they migrated to, for second-generation migrants the question of where you belong is not easily resolvable,[1] either in terms of a spatialization of belonging that points to a geographical place as the site of their belonging, or within the imaginary. As the children of migrants seek to develop their identities and negotiate their sense of belonging in a society, Britain, which is often hostile towards them, one of the reactions, presented in the plays discussed in this chapter, is the turn or return to the countries or places of familial origin by second-generation migrants. As I shall discuss, the two plays dealt with in this chapter, Winsome Pinnock's 'Talking in Tongues' (1991) and Maya Chowdhry's 'Monsoon' (1993), articulate very different interpretations of the meanings of those re/turns. They share, however, the position that the space and culture of familial origin towards which the central characters re/turn can speak to the identity of the individual in enabling ways.

Problematizing peer culture

Winsome Pinnock's 'Talking in Tongues' is divided into two acts, with the first act taking place in London and the second in Jamaica. Between them lies a journey, a re/turn to the country of familial origin for some of the central protagonists, simultaneously invisibilized and highlighted through the locations of the two acts. The play thus lays less emphasis on the journey itself than on its start- and endpoints, and the positions that these locations imply. The play focuses on 'being there' rather than on 'getting there', juxtaposing the central characters' positions and experiences in London with those they have in Jamaica. In and through the sequencing of the acts London becomes the place which necessitates the journey to Jamaica, laying the ground for the re/turn to Jamaica.

In 'Talking in Tongues' Pinnock articulates the problematic of the unsettled self through the politics of personal relationships. At the heart of her play is the question of how that unsettled self manages her or his inter- and intra-racial relationships.[2] Unlike many plays by Black and Asian contemporary women playwrights in Britain, which focus on inter-generational relationships as a way of exploring diasporic existence,[3] Pinnock's play centres on peer relationships,[4] and specifically on a group of young, heterosexually active black and white women and men. Jeff and Bentley are friends from college days where, apparently, they were known as the 'two-tone twins', going around saying that they were 'unidentical twins, one of us a throwback baby' (1, 2: 181)[5] in order to attract women. The play inverts the usual stereotype of the successful white male versus the unsuccessful black male through the figure of Bentley, a young black man, who is professionally successful, even if not as upwardly mobile as his former mate Jeff suggests. Jeff, in contrast, has not made it, and is drifting from job to job, seeking refuge in memories of his college days. Jeff and Bentley represent different positions vis-à-vis the potential of male alienation in a racist and capitalist economy. Bentley wants to get on, to overcome any potential alienation through moving forward and assimilating to the idea of socio-economic success. Jeff is incapable of taking the same stance. He is presented as the one who experiences a powerful sense of alienation: 'I can't breathe here. I don't feel at home. Of course, it's home, I was born here, but it doesn't feel like home, more like a place you rest at overnight on your way to somewhere else' (1, 2: 180). Jeff's statement articulates the importance of the imaginary in inhabiting location. His sense of belonging is determined by his emotional relation to place, and in his case that emotional relation is disturbed by his inability to achieve a sustainable socio-economic position through either employment or personal relationships.

It is the latter which proves problematic for both Jeff and Bentley. Jeff's relationship with his white wife Fran is on the rocks and destroyed in Act One while Bentley's relationship with his black wife Leela is under stress and also disintegrates in the course of the first half of the play, which sees Bentley and Fran leaving together. London is constructed as a site of stress, not only because of the racism black people may encounter but also because of the pressures of upward socio-economic mobility.[6] The suggestion of the first half of the play which sees the disintegration of intra-racial heterosexual relationships seems to be that differences are not merely a matter of race, but perhaps more importantly of personality and of how one can establish belonging.

At the same time the first half of the play counts the costs of racism in Britain. There is a clear sense in which certain constructions of black subjectivity are invoked to explain behavioural patterns of intersecting racialized and gendered inflections. In her postscript to the play Pinnock explains: 'I was interested in exploring whether relationships can, in fact, be politicized. Claudette is a fanatic when it comes to expounding her particular brand of racial politics, which are based on a form of separatism, the belief that interracial relationships are a betrayal of the community and, more seriously, a betrayal of the black woman which is connected to her historical degradation' (226). Pinnock explains Claudette's political position in terms of her personal experience as presented in the play: 'Claudette's fanaticism is an attempt to avoid her own pain and longing caused by the traditional double oppression (both within and outside their communities) that some black women experience' (226). When Claudette, a single black woman, asks her friend Curly: 'Did you see the look in Bentley's eye when he caught sight of the living Barbie doll?' (1, 1: 177),[7] she articulates both her personal dismay at Bentley's behaviour and her dislike of white women who from the beginning of the play are constructed as preying on black men. The key issues in exploring peer-group relations in Pinnock's play are thus the gendered, indeed sexualized relations among black and white women and men within two sets of geopolitical space – the UK and Jamaica. Claudette, in many ways the central female character who is present both in the opening and in the closing scene of the play, as well as the other black women in the play, is angry about the ways in which black men desire white women, and make black women like Leela, Bentley's wife, feel inferior.[8] As Leela says at one point: 'I never forget my body. That's the trouble' (1, 2: 183).

Embodying un/belonging

Leela is in a sense in no position to forget her body since it is the cultural reading of her body as 'other' that generates her insecurity. Her husband Bentley rightly diagnoses that she 'is trying to make something of herself' (1, 3: 189). But he denies his white lover Fran's assertion – when he insists that she would not understand – that 'It's a black thing' (1, 3: 189). Instead he interprets Leela's behaviour as a function of an individualized meritocratic ideology of achievement to which she subjects herself: 'I know how hard it is even though I do believe that it's up to the individual to rise above all the shit' (1, 3: 189). The play makes clear that, compared to Jeff for instance, Bentley has 'made it' and has done so, in a sense, in spite of his race. Bentley is aware of this but, precisely because of this awareness, he does not want to allow for the race factor even as he seeks to explain his disaffection from his black wife to his white lover. But implicit in his critique of his wife and his choice of Fran as lover is the racialized reality he seeks to deny: Fran as a white woman in a predominantly white society does not have to make the efforts Leela has to make to be what she wants to be, and that relative ease translates both into a more relaxed attitude towards life and her situation, and into a drive to achieve. Where Bentley is disaffected with a wife struggling to make something of herself, Fran is disaffected with a husband who confides in his friend Bentley that the fight has gone out of him, that he cannot cope with the demands of his situation. Significantly, his boss is a woman – Pinnock depicts a contemporary Britain in which women have considerable power and the possibility of financial independence. They are also the ones to force issues: Fran egging Bentley on to tell Leela about his relationship with her and to leave Leela; Curly, another black woman, making love with Jeff and telling him about Fran and Bentley's affair; Claudette and Curly comforting Leela.

These realities are, in the first act which is predominantly naturalist, accompanied by two scenes dominated by narratives that break realist conventions, but importantly conventions governing ideas of the body rather than of theatricality. Both narratives are told to Leela, the woman who most immediately has to come to terms with her body, the woman struggling to make something of herself, who by the end of the play has learnt that 'You've got to be in touch with your body' (2, 7: 225). Leela's story of coming to her body mirrors the narrative arc of Ntozake Shange's *for colored girls* which is also concerned with enabling black women to be in touch with their bodies, to love themselves. It is the narrative of the racialized other whose embodied otherness leads to a dissociation from and struggle with the body, resulting in the inability to inhabit that inalienable but simultaneously culturally alienated space, the black female body.

The first of the narratives, which breaks with conventions of a certain kind of naturalized body, occurs in the prologue where Sugar, a black woman, tells Leela the story of how she secretly observed a group of women, who had gone down to a waterfall to wash clothes, 'talk in tongues' and be seized by a spirit. The narrative foregrounds the bodily changes which occur in the women, from dragging their feet to go washing to being seized by and transformed by the experience of the spirit. As the narrative focuses on the female body as object of transformation and alleviation of burden, so the scene itself reinforces that body focus through Sugar massaging Leela while she is telling her the story. The simultaneous relieving of Leela's body stress through massage and of the life stress the women in the narrative experience

Plate 4 Ella Wilder as Irma in the Royal Court Theatre Upstairs 1991 production of 'Talking in Tongues'.

through their bodily experience of the spirit becomes the key to the play, in which the meaning of the body as a possessed and dispossessed territory is at stake.

This is also highlighted in the second narrative of the first act, told by Irma (plate 4), a black hermaphrodite,[9] whom Leela meets at the party when Bentley has just left her for Fran. Whilst Leela is sobbing, Irma laughs. She represents the affirmative principle, a mixture between the bald primadonna and Irma La Douce, a person at home in her indeterminate body that defies gendered specificities and an unambiguous bodily identity. Irma's narrative demonstrates that it is possible to inhabit ambiguity with confidence. Her mother's initial decision to allow surgical intervention so that Irma might be a 'girl' rests on the mother's belief that 'black men were too often in the limelight, and that a woman might quietly get things done while those who undermined her were looking the other way' (1, 5: 193).

However, she changes her mind, finding Irma perfect the way she is. At the point when Leela encounters Irma, Leela is struggling but not yet 'getting things done' – by the end of the play, whilst Claudette has spent her time engaged in exploitative sex tourism, Leela has quietly got things done, come to her body, through walking the length and breadth of Jamaica. Irma advises Leela: 'Distance. That's what I'd do. I'd go away' (1, 5: 194), and Leela takes that advice. Irma thus functions as a kind of *deus-ex-machina*, appearing only in this scene in the play to suggest to Leela the affirmative position that may move her beyond her entrapped sense of self.

Irma's narrative is one of 'thinking back through our mothers', as Virginia Woolf put it in a different context.[10] Referencing the opening narrative of the play of the possessed women on the beach, Irma reminds Leela of the function religion had in their mothers' lives and the exercise of spiritual possession with all its physical manifestations which they engaged in. But whereas Leela interprets that possession as a form of 'total surrendering up of the will' (1, 5: 194), Irma understands it as 'a way of releasing pain', of not allowing oneself to become a victim (1, 5: 194). Irma thus views spiritual possession as a form of empowerment, a way of (re)inhabiting the body in a context of multiple oppressions, racialized and genderized. Herself a spectacle – according to the didascales '*She is wearing a multicoloured jump suit and trainers, large gold earrings and has a bald head*' (1, 5: 193) – Irma regards spectacle, specifically the spectacle of spiritual possession, as a way of reclaiming space, both bodily and geographical.

Leela, made overly conscious of her own body, and unable at this stage to overcome the inhibitions this bodily self-consciousness has caused, projects herself as the very opposite of Irma, not a spectacle but invisible. Alienated from her body, her movements gagged by the bodily awareness which a combination of racism and sexism has forced upon her, she experiences her bodily alienation most urgently in her self-consciousness 'about the way I speak' (1, 5: 195). In high-Freudian fashion the text explicitly references hysteria through Leela's assessment of spiritual possession as a form of 'mass hysteria'. Simultaneously, Leela's language and speech difficulties are presented as a form of 'hysteria', words sticking in her mouth as she describes it, difficulties with pronunciation, and other problems which Leela explains as being a function of her alienation from the language she is forced to inhabit: 'If you don't feel you belong to a language then you're only half alive aren't you, because you haven't the words to bring yourself into existence. You might as well be invisible' (1, 5: 195).

English as it is spoken in Britain is not Leela's first language: 'Not that I do have any real first language, but sometimes I imagine that there must have been, at some time' (1, 5: 195). Leela's diasporic history has led to an estrangement which encompasses actual spatial territory, the body as territory, and language, indeed all the coordinates that mark identity. That is why she is struggling to come to her self, in every aspect of that self. Her estrangement's somatic consequences – 'Sometimes it feels as though there's something stuck down here (*Holds her tummy.*) and I want to stick my fingers down my throat and spew it all up' (1, 5: 195) – literally embody the repressive effects of a racist and sexist context that allows Leela no space to be the self she is or might be. Distance becomes the means through which to enact how she feels and – through enacting that coincidence of imaginary and actual existence – to bring Leela back to her self.

(Sex) tourism as an enactment of alienation

The coming to the body is a way of marking the belonging to a territory which Leela, in the second half of the play when she and Claudette are in Jamaica to ease Leela's pain at having been left by Bentley, enacts through the endless walks she takes around Jamaica, trying to get to know the country to which she has an ancestral relation but in which she also figures as 'other'. Where the first act of the play highlights the dilemmas of inter- and intra-racial heterosexual relationships in a racist Britain, the second act articulates the diasporic effect Claudette and Leela as well as others experience in Jamaica, where they also do not belong. In Jamaica they are viewed as tourists whose whims must be indulged for the sake of the money they bring in. Here Claudette can turn the tables on the black men who prefer white women because her money and tourist status temporarily endow her with a certain power. Her treatment of Mikie, a local who – despite already being in a relationship with Sugar – becomes Claudette's sex toy during her stay in Jamaica, is no different from how any white sex tourist might treat the local inhabitants of a region in which sex tourism occurs. The fact that Claudette causes pain to Sugar, Mikie's woman, is irrelevant to her. Her disgust at Bentley for making off with Fran is thus revealed to have nothing to do with solidarity with Leela but is a function of what Pinnock in her afterword, as previously mentioned, describes as 'an attempt to avoid her own pain and longing caused by the traditional double oppression (both within and outside their communities) that some black women experience' (226). For Claudette the trip to Jamaica is not about going back to her roots but about being in a predominantly black environment where she hopes not to have to deal with the racial and sexual debasement she suffers in Britain. Further, it is a holiday and she treats it as such. She feels no particular affinity to the island or its people and, in contrast to Leela, makes little attempt to get to know the place. Her main source of enjoyment is the sense of power she derives from the superior position she finds herself in as a tourist from England. As she says to Leela: 'Everybody knows what the score is. You don't begrudge me a little holiday fling, do you? We all use each other. Everyone goes home happy. No one gets hurt' (2, 1: 206). But Claudette's reckoning, which of course ignores Sugar's plight, comes unstuck when Mikie decides to pursue white tourist Kate.

Kate has come to live on Jamaica, a move that her brother David, out to visit her, cannot understand: 'I couldn't live in that strange vacuum of belonging neither here nor there. Wanting here when you're there and there when you're here' (2, 2: 209). But Kate's response, rather like Irma's from the first act, is one of embracing that position of unbelonging, constructed as a surrender of the self: 'The great thing is feeling yourself disappearing. A little part of you dissolves every day, but you hang on to those things that distinguish you: an accent, the way you walk . . . People think I'm mad. But the best times are when I feel myself stateless, colourless as a jellyfish' (2, 2: 209). Kate desires the kind of invisibility which Claudette and Leela find so painful in their lives in Britain, but she does so, of course, from a position of visibility, indeed, in Jamaica, from a position of heightened visibility. Kate's perception of herself as colourless[11] is, of course, not shared by

those around her, and within the play her attempt at living in a territory that is not hers is compared unfavourably with Leela's attempts
to get to know the island. Both Kate and Leela are struggling towards
an idea of self, but whereas Leela's struggle is legitimated through her
activities on the island, Kate's is thrown into question by her sexual
relationship with Mikie, who finds it easy to treat her as just another
sex tourist.

When Claudette discovers that Mikie has had sex with Kate,
her wrath is unleashed: 'Travel halfway across the world and they're
still there acting like they own the place' (2, 4: 216). In an act of revenge she and Leela de-face Kate by smudging lipstick upon her and
cutting off her long hair.[12] It is a gesture designed to disempower Kate
and simultaneously constitutes an attack on that 'other' object, long
straight hair, which has been constructed as an emblem of desirable
beauty imbued with racialized significance.[13] The action triggers a
phase of release for Leela.

As Claudette feels challenged by Kate's sexual interaction with
Mikie, so Mikie feels challenged by Kate's brother David inviting him
to hand-wrestle, an act of physical competition which Mikie at first
seeks to resist. David, riled by an awareness of being perceived as a
moneyed tourist, baits Mikie with money: 'What's the matter? Isn't
that enough incentive for you? That's a surprise. Everybody else here
has been quick enough to take our money from us' (2, 5: 221). Initially,
Mikie lets David win, continuing to treat him as the tourist he is
whose trade is important and whose behaviour, even if problematic,
is therefore tolerated. But David pushes Mikie too far and in their
final wrestle, Mikie makes clear to David the extent to which he is
tolerated rather than viewed as a friend: 'You see, now, at this time a
night, I not on duty. You see, now, I don't have to smile. You see, now, I
don't have to pretend that you have something special about you. You
see, what happen out here in the daytime, it's a game, just a game,
understand?' (2, 5: 222). In the juxtaposition between night and day,
day – the 'white' time – is constructed as a time of pretence and deceit,
of make-belief, during which the local population is forced to tolerate
its own exploitation as part of the economic exchange which governs

tourism. Night time, the 'dark' time, however, is the time owned by the black people when they can assert their independence and can stop pretending. Significantly, Claudette's and Leela's de-facing of Kate happens during the night.

The consequence of Claudette and Leela's behaviour is that Sugar – accused of cutting off Kate's hair to revenge herself for Kate's affair with Mikie – loses her job. Both black and white tourists alike thus cause havoc on the island. In a pivotal scene, Leela confesses her act to Sugar, and in their exchange finally moves towards the release she has been seeking from her own sense of rage and pain. Sugar relates Mikie's analysis of their way of acting: 'He say you all sick, say unno come out here because you broken people . . . You come here looking for . . . Unno tourist think you belong here. But you come out and you don't know where to put youself: one minute you talking sisterhood, the next minute you treating us like dirt. You just the same as all the other tourists them' (2, 6: 223). Mikie's analysis of tourist behaviour articulates the diasporic experience of perpetual alienation, the inability to (re)turn to a country of origin as a way of experiencing belonging in a context in which where you live does not equate with belonging. Claudette and Leela respond to that sense of alienation differently. Both feel rage and anger, but whereas Claudette vents that anger through aggression and the sex tourism that affords her a temporary sense of desirability, Leela uses her body in a different way to come to that body and thus to herself. In a scene which mirrors the 'talking in tongues' referred to in the opening prologue, Leela talks in tongues on the beach, following her confession to Sugar (plate 5):

> **Leela**'s speech becomes a garble as she struggles to get the words out, her body trembling out of her control. She's breathing very quickly. She starts to mutter under her breath. **Sugar** stands and watches, not quite sure what to do. **Leela**'s muttering becomes louder and she starts to talk in tongues. **Sugar** is bewildered at first, then frightened as **Leela** releases all the rage and anger that she has repressed for so long.
>
> (2, 6: 223)

Plate 5 Joanne Campbell as Leela and Cecilia Noble as Sugar in the Royal Court Theatre Upstairs 1991 production of 'Talking in Tongues'.

Coming to self

Leela's 'talking in tongues' aligns her with the hysteric and with the madwoman as presented in Hélène Cixous and Catherine Clément's *The Newly Born Woman* (1987) where the spectacle of femininity serves both as a form of abreaction and as a way of 'self-constituting a subjectivity' (90). Cixous' description of the woman coming to voice maps directly onto Leela's experience on the beach:

> she doesn't 'speak,' she throws her trembling body into the
> air, she lets herself go, she flies, she goes completely into her
> voice, she vitally defends the 'logic' of her discourse with her
> body; her flesh speaks true. She exposes herself. Really, she
> makes what she thinks materialize carnally, she conveys
> meaning with her body. She *inscribes* what she is saying
> because she does not deny unconscious drives the
> unmanageable part they play in speech.
>
> (Cixous and Clément 92)

It is in this sense that the play's title 'Talking in Tongues' acquires a new and different meaning, for the title not only references a bodily part which metonymically takes on the meaning of speech; it also conjoins the notion of body and speech to point to the plurality of identities produced through the projection of speech – it is the plural 'tongues' rather than the singular 'tongue' that is referred to after all.

The cultural history of spiritual possession and talking in tongues, upon which this expression of and coming to self is based, is alluded to in the opening narrative of the play in which Sugar's story of the women going to the waterfall prefigures Leela's experience by the side of the sea. As in Maya Chowdhry's play 'Monsoon', to be discussed below, and as in 'Leave Taking' (analysed in the previous chapter), the proximity to water becomes a vital ingredient in enabling Leela, who significantly has not used her time to swim in the sea but has wandered the island's interior, to release her pain. Cixous and Clément argue that 'there is a bond between women's libidinal economy . . . and her way of self-constituting a subjectivity that splits without regret.' They state: 'Unleashed and raging, she belongs to the race of waves. She arises, she approaches, she lifts up, she reaches, covers over, washes ashore, arising again, throwing the fringed vastness of her body up high, follows herself . . . as if she recalled herself in order to come again as never before' (90–1). The unleashing of Leela's penned up feelings is preceded by her explanation to Sugar of her brokenness:

> Broken, yes. Invisible people. We look all right on the outside, but take our clothes off and you'll find nothing underneath, just thin air. That's what happens to people who have no language – they disappear. Only your feelings tell you that you exist, so you cling on to them even if they're not nice . . . I hate the world that tries to stifle me . . . I want revenge. I want to lash out.
>
> (2, 6: 223)

Leela has her epiphanic moment and, by the end of the play, she is 'not so frightened of the pitfalls'. As she tells Kate: 'It's the way you displace the weight of your body, isn't it? You've got to be in touch with your body. It soon gets used to sudden challenges' (2, 7: 225). Leela learns both literally and metaphorically to displace the weight of her body, not to place such overwhelming importance on it that it strangles her ability to be herself, no longer to be weighed down by it to the point of immobility. In contrast, Claudette at the end of the play is still trapped in an attitude that makes her as sexploitative towards black men as she feels they are towards black women. She views 'all relationships [as] some sort of business transaction' (2, 3: 212) and thus remains both perpetually disappointed and angry.

Pinnock's symmetrical play structure of two acts with seven scenes each mirrors the unmaking and remaking of Leela's world in a reference to Genesis. Where the unmaking ends in Act One with the exodus from paradise, the break-up of Leela and Bentley's marriage, and the decision to go to Jamaica, the remaking of Leela's self takes place away from the city, in the countryside of Jamaica, and by the sea.

But it does not constitute a return to paradise. As Pinnock, referencing the story of the tower of Babel, describes it:

> I have always loved the biblical story of talking in tongues. The idea that the whole world once shared the same language appeals to a certain sentimental idealism. In that story the separation of peoples is caused by a fall from grace, the ultimate punishment an inability to understand one another. Like the myth of the separation of men and women who were once one animal, this story suggests that we are potentially more alike than we know and that, while we will never again speak the same language, one of our quests is to find our way back to each other.
>
> (226)

However, and even if this is the case, male-female relationships and inter-racial peer relationships remain problematized in Pinnock's play which advocates the need for a coming to self that is less relationally focused than centred on the self. Leela's self-sufficiency – neither getting caught up in the sex tourism that Claudette engages in, nor being pushed into a new alliance with Kate – is the guarantor of her healing while her environment remains unchanged. Self in relation to self becomes the key structure through which difference can come about. The legacies of the colonial experience, both in Britain and in Jamaica, do not enable a transformation of circumstance. In both locations black people are exploited and their feelings disregarded. In Jamaica the neocolonialism of tourism has succeeded prior colonial histories; in Britain the legacies of colonial attitudes persist. Going to Jamaica allows Leela to explore her self and Claudette to express her sexual self, but it is not a 'return' to a site of origination which is signalled through this move. Rather, it enables a view of Jamaica as a place of continuing exploitation where hard work and drive might lead to recognition (Bentley in Act One is mirrored by Diamond in Act Two in this respect) but where many live in a state of exploitation and vulnerability. This does not mean, however, that the places are the same. The play makes very clear that Diamond, the relatively successful bar owner, and Sugar, Mikie's girlfriend, have a much less

threatened sense of self than the 'English' tourists do. Leela, for example, says: 'The people . . . they seem so at ease with themselves. They
have that confidence that comes from belonging' (2, 1: 206). Diamond,
a returner with some years' experience of living in Britain, confirms
that through her assertion: 'Back there I was nothing. Here I'm a lady.
You can live like a lady here' (2, 3: 209). Even Sugar, who has to cope
with her boyfriend's pandering to the sexpectations of tourists sees
Leela – in contrast to herself – as broken. Both Diamond and Sugar
are in a stable relation to themselves, if not to others. That is the
advantage they have over Claudette and Leela who experience self-
alienation through living – both literally and metaphorically – in a
state of unbelonging.

Beside herself

In Claudette's case that state is one which – for her – is inescapable;
there is no place exempt from being tainted by the racialized relations
that haunt her life. Claudette's initial 'dream' of her vacation – 'I in-
tend to rest, eat, drink, soak up as much sun as I can and fuck everything that moves. Yesterday I had three men dancing attendance on
me. All the rich American women on the beach and they're swarming
around me. You should have seen Mikie's face' (2, 1: 204), a dream
of reversing the power structures that usually dominate her life – is
shattered by Mikie's flirt with Kate. It reveals that Claudette's self-
protective assertion that 'All relationships are some sort of business
transaction' (2, 3: 212) is exactly that, a self-protective line with which
she counters her longings for romance and monogamy. Her actual attitude is much closer to Sugar's ('Sugar believe in one man, one woman'
(2, 1: 205)) but in a world in which, as Pinnock suggests, men and
women will never speak the same language, that belief is a dream
readily destroyed by the social realities the women face. Significantly,
in Pinnock's play it is women, rather than men, who aim to self-
constitute their subjectivity. This is as true for Leela and Claudette
as it is for Kate. As heterosexually active young women, that drive
towards establishing a certain subjectivity – independent, respected,
self-reliant, and confident – raises questions about their relation to

the other sex, and the relative impact of race and sexual identity on subjectivity. Both for the white and for the black women the quest for subjectivity involves a geographical shift, a being in a place other than the one you usually inhabit. Enacting a sense of estrangement through moving to a strange place becomes both a marker of the unbelonging the female characters feel and the ground upon which a confrontation with the self as a means of transcending that unbelonging can be undertaken. Unsettling the self through a geographical shift thus constitutes the process by which the unsettled self expresses her condition and thus engages with it.

Although Leela and Kate represent their relation to self in different ways – Leela wants to find and Kate, in a sense, wants to lose her self – both have a notion of a desired endpoint which focuses on self. In contrast, Claudette is concerned to experience herself differently *in relation*, veering between a sexploitative tourist position, the kind she attributes to men, and the desire for conventional hetero-romance. But the attempt to achieve the latter through the former is bound to fail – different geographies have their own structures and needs that do not readily succumb to the pressure of desire from those who come in from the outside. This becomes evident from the ways in which all the tourists – black and white – are shown to be manipulable by and gullible in relation to the local narratives they encounter. Mikie and other local inhabitants use these narratives as a way of regulating their relationships with the tourists who – despite their seeming sophistication and cynical disdain – are easily manipulated and controlled through these stories. When Kate, who has been told stories about snakes, is confronted by her cut-off plait, mistakes it for a snake, and breaks into a panic, she emblematizes her gullibility and state of disempowerment at the same time that the play semiotically raises the question, who or what is the snake in paradise. Kate is effectively confronted by herself or, rather, a part of herself. In mistaking it for a snake she constructs (part of) her self as the snake in paradise, and to the extent that she has succumbed to Mikie, she is just that – from Sugar's perspective, and indeed from Claudette's. The latter's moral right to her desire for revenge might be somewhat more in question than Sugar's, since she, too, has had sex with Mikie. At the same time, Claudette and Leela as tourists in Jamaica also inhabit the position of the snake, partly because in Claudette's case they propose or invite seduction, partly because as tourists they have the money which the local inhabitants need and which therefore places them in a position of pecuniary power. This is evident in the way in which Sugar's dismissal from her job is premised on a notion of the tourist as 'king' or 'queen'. Capital and sex coincide as forces that determine the social interactions of and with the inhabitants of a space in which economic survival is linked to tourism.

Reverse migrations

Maya Chowdhry's 'Monsoon' (1993) confronts the audience with similar issues: the return of second-generation migrants, in particular women, to a country from which their parents came; tourism, travelling, and sexual relations in that country, India, as a way of coming to self; the meaning of sexual relationships with local inhabitants; the impact of differential economic status on relationships; and the meaning of temporary sojourns. For in both 'Monsoon' and 'Talking in Tongues' it is always clear that the (re)turn to the country of the parents' origin is temporary and will be followed by a return to England. In the opening dialogue between sisters Jalaarnava and Kavitaa, Chowdhry constructs both the gap, and an approximation, between east and west as the sisters articulate their responses to the environment through which they travel. In their discussion of the Indian landscape their referents, the film *Heat and Dust* and Spain, gesture towards western excursions, both historical/colonial and contemporary/neocolonial-touristic, into foreign territories. Steeped in what have become popular cultural emblems – the successful popular film and the successful popular tourist resort – of contemporary western exploits abroad, the girls are simultaneously shown to manage the Indian context effectively. Both delight in their Indian environment, but whereas the younger sister, Kavitaa, is cautious, Jalaarnava is curious, ready to explore and embrace the differences she encounters. Kavitaa's reference points are more firmly located in the contemporary London in which she lives than Jalaarnava's who, like Leela in 'Talking in Tongues', is ready to explore unknown territory.

Being 'othered'

As in Leela's case, Jalaarnava's exploration of India is aligned with her relation to her body. Jalaarnava is unsettled by her period, and menstruation, one of the key narrative strands in this play, becomes the metaphor through which the play articulates a theory of the unsettled self which centres on the two notions of the recurrent experience and the unspoken. Insofar as menstruation is cyclical and thus recurrent, and constitutes a taboo which is not usually spoken about,[14] it mirrors the experience of racism that is both recurrent and taboo but which is inescapable, as it was in 'Talking in Tongues', even in India. When Jalaarnava, like Leela walking around Jamaica, sets off on a journey of her own to explore Kashmir, she meets Tanya, a white English tourist and an equivalent to Kate in 'Talking in Tongues', staying in the same youth hostel as herself, busily engaged in experiencing the other as 'other'. Tanya's expectations of Jalaarnava, based on her assumption of a coincidence between racial identity and specific knowledges and behaviour patterns, are introduced with the phrase 'You're Indian, aren't you?' (2, 5: 61) which serves simultaneously as a question, an attribution (to a particular race and culture), and an affirmation, designed to put Jalaarnava in her place. Tanya then tells Jalaarnava what being Indian means: 'I didn't think Indians stayed here' (2, 5: 61).

During her time at the youth hostel both her menstruation and Tanya become sources of aggravation for Jalaarnava. Tanya manifests a particular kind of racism, described by Jalaarnava as 'this English tourist who gives me the third degree all the time . . . I get indigestion listening to her going on all the time about how amazing this is, how wonderful the people are and so colourful, such interesting habits . . . you can imagine' (2, 7: 62). Tanya's way of encountering difference is both patronizing and adulatory. She tries to impose her views of India upon Jalaarnava at the same time as expecting Jalaarnava to embody India. According to the didascales she is *'surprised'* (2, 5: 61) at the possibility that Jalaarnava has never been to India before. Her expectations that Jalaarnava will know certain things such as where to eat are confounded whilst she simultaneously derogates information that Jalaarnava offers. Her contradictory behaviour bespeaks her inability to engage effectively with diasporic experience. For Tanya the other is other, and the possibility of less clear-cut structures of identity escapes her. As a repeat tourist ('Well I'm on another of my expeditions' 2, 5: 61), Tanya's investment in affirming the otherness of the other rests precisely on the maintenance of certain structures of difference that motivate and legitimate her tourism. She constitutes a latter-day version of colonial excursion, enacting, as Ryan and Hall (2001) describe it, 'a socially sanctioned and economically empowered marginality' (1) that renders 'the holiday as a source of self-identification' (1) whereby Tanya sees both her own identity and that of the other confirmed in the dualistic terms in which she conceives of herself and of the other. Her selective attention enables her to make her imaginary real, by allowing only those perceptions that reinforce her idea of difference to register in her interactions with others.

Reverse nomadism

But Tanya is, of course, not the only tourist in the play. Jalaarnava, too, is engaged in the touristic enterprise, enacting a kind of reverse nomadism through returning to her parents' country of origin. Ryan and Hall argue that 'being a tourist is to occupy a liminal role within a temporal marginality' (1). This is as true of Jalaarnava as it is of Tanya. As young women they share a social position of some marginality, both in the UK and in the country they visit, by virtue of being female and young. Since both are tourists in India, they are both temporarily levered out of their assigned social roles and usual social context, and as such have the opportunity to generate transformation or change, for themselves and potentially for others. Both women are in a position of economic power relative to those around them, and expect that status to be recognized. As Jalaarnava writes to her sister about her journey to Kashmir, for example: 'Actually I felt like a toasted sandwich, it was so crammed full, so much for the seat reservation on the Tourist Quota' (2, 1: 60).

However, the major difference between Tanya and Jalaarnava resides in their historical relation to the country: Tanya is the descendant of colonizers, Jalaarnava the daughter of formerly indigenous inhabitants. For Jalaarnava there is therefore a connection of identification between herself and those around her, whilst for Tanya the key position is that of affirming difference.

The potential for identification offered Jalaarnava through her familial relation to India is severely tested when she leaves the youth hostel where she has been staying to live with a family on a houseboat. The family rent out a room on the houseboat from financial necessity, putting Jalaarnava up as a paying guest. Jalaarnava's relation to the family is thus one governed by economic exchange. However, that relation soon becomes complicated as economic and affective orders clash. Jalaarnava inserts herself into the family, which is entirely female, with relative ease, forgetting at times that their invitation for her to join them on the houseboat is driven by an economic, not by an affective imperative. The family have a daughter, Nusrat, the same age as Jalaarnava, and it is this daughter who introduces Jalaarnava into the family. Once there, Jalaarnava's behaviour veers between enacting the role of the moneyed tourist, and expecting to be treated as a family friend. Early on, for instance, she says to Nusrat who has just come to knock on her door and say 'hello': 'Are you going into town? Would you mind getting me some stamps and posting this? Could you also get me some more writing paper too, here's the money. (*Pause, Nusrat doesn't respond, then takes money and letter*) Is that O.K.? NUSRAT: Fine' (3, 4: 64). Jalaarnava here treats Nusrat like a servant, easily slipping into the role of the economically empowered tourist. Only Nusrat's nonverbal response, articulated in the stage directions, indicates the unease generated by a situation where two women who might be peers shift into the hierarchical structure that tourism can establish between the traveller and the local population. A similar incident occurs later (4, 1: 71) when Jalaarnava offers to help Nusrat with the washing up but Nusrat's mother intervenes and forbids it. Increasingly, the play begins to ask questions about the relative status of the tourist and the local population, and how that status is altered as a consequence of the emergence of affective relations. Jalaarnava and Nusrat develop an emotional and sexual relationship and both simultaneously question and accept the fact that they inhabit different worlds which they will not be able to leave, not even for each other. As they question their relative identities, they both take issue with positions that place them into a marginalized space and 'other' them. Jalaarnava, for instance, attempts to deny her position as tourist:

> JALAARNAVA: I'm not a tourist.
> NUSRAT: Yes you are.
> JALAARNAVA: I'm not like them though.
> NUSRAT: No, except for washing your clothes.
>
> (3, 7: 67)

Similarly, Nusrat does not want to be seen as a local who serves and is exploited by tourists. In fact, they both wish to deny that status which points to the commodification of their relations with others, and elevates economic exchange to the position of prime motivator for their interactions. As their relationship deepens an affective order temporarily becomes entwined with and replaces the economic one. Changes occur.

Menstruation and monsoon

The play aligns two 'natural' specifically cyclical processes, menstruation and the advent of the monsoon, with the processes of the coming and going of tourists and with the process of falling in love. Jalaarnava's complaints about her bodily experiences of menstruation change as she realizes that menstruating women are considered to be unclean in Muslim culture and that Nusrat is debarred from certain activities such as attending the Mosque during her period. Jalaarnava, contemplating the rule that menstruating women are not allowed into the temple, says: 'Once inside [the temple] I wonder who made up this rule, that the very blood which creates life is banned from places of worship of life. Maybe they don't worship life, maybe men made up the rules, cause they're jealous that life doesn't abound deep within the warm flesh of their womb' (4, 7: 74). However, the cultural difference implied here is juxtaposed with the recognition that the taboo regarding menstruation extends to both Nusrat's and Jalaarnava's childhood experiences in what are otherwise seemingly radically different cultures. Confiding in each other both Nusrat and Jalaarnava recognize that they were brought up with the same attitude towards menstruation, namely that it was not to be mentioned.

The silencing of that experience is reversed through the play which articulates the experience of menstruation in order to revalue that experience. Initially articulated in terms of physical pain, by the end of the play menstruation is viewed as life-giving. This shift in argument moves the focus from a view of menstrual blood as abject, as something to be reviled, expelled, and taboo[15] to menstruation as nurturing and life-sustaining. Jalaarnava, falling in love with Nusrat, dreams of her menstrual blood, and of drinking it: 'My dreams are of her blood, thick ruby red, it is flowing fast and heavy into the lake. I am swimming in the lake, I lift my hands from the water, they are stained in her blood, I cup them and drink deeply' (3, 13: 69). The play generates direct associations between the beginning of a period and the release from pre-menstrual tension as the menstrual blood starts to flow, the beginning of the monsoon and the opening of the heavens, *and* the experience of a lesbian sexual relationship and the release as desire is consummated in the sexual act. In constructing these associations the play both revalidates and naturalizes those experiences in an act of celebration that moves swiftly towards closure and raises questions about the meanings of that celebration in its temporality.

Futures

As in Pinnock's 'Talking in Tongues', the focus of this play is on peer relations, with older female figures, Massi (Jalaarnava's auntie) and Nusrat's mother, hovering in the background as framing presences for some of the actions and, more importantly, for the socio-moral parameters within which the play operates. The play thus sets the younger women up as defining themselves against a context determined by the older women and the authority of the previous generation. But they are not in protest against that generation; they do not defy or want to resist the future that has been mapped out for them. The younger women's paths seem already well defined. Jalaarnava's expectation is that once she goes back to England, 'I'm going to University when I get back, to study medicine' (3, 7: 66).[16] Jalaarnava is happy to do so, and, one assumes, it is a move her parents would endorse.[17] Her journey of self-exploration is thus less about her public future and position than about her private self, associated with her bodily and sexual identity. In one of her nightmares she dreams of drowning and calls out for 'Tony' to help her, but coming out of the dream she tells Nusrat, 'He let me drown' (3, 10: 68). It is not made clear in the play who Tony is but the impression is given that he might be Jalaarnava's English boyfriend and that they have split up.[18] Jalaarnava's nightmare suggests that 'Tony' is not the answer to her dreams, but the play also leaves open what her future will be, and with whom she will spend it. In particular, the play does not make clear whether or not its narrative is one of the sexual awakening of its central characters to lesbianism or constitutes an episode in the process of coming to self. The association of the beginning of the monsoon, the beginning of the monthly menstrual cycle, and lesbian sexual experiences in the play suggests that the latter is recurrent and cyclical, not a one-off. But it is only at the level of the symbolic, rather than in narrative terms, that this is asserted. For against the cyclicity of these associations is set the symbolism of the voyage of discovery which, within this particular play, has an endpoint, prefigured by Jalaarnava telling Nusrat that she could not live in India since she 'would get really frustrated with the way women have to live, and with the levels of poverty' (3, 18: 71). Jalaarnava asserts that 'India's special to me, I love being here, but . . . I don't think it's enough' (3, 18: 71). Jalaarnava's responses here make clear that – in contrast to many adolescents' responses to romance – romance does not lead her to romanticize India, or to make promises she cannot or is not willing to keep. Significantly, place is used to assert difference – it is not Jalarnaava's relationship with Nusrat, conducted in secret, which itself suggests that it has no public forum in which to flourish,[19] that is at issue. Instead, the recognition that place demands and shapes lives, that one deals with a geosocial and geocultural rather than merely a geographical space in which location, culture, and socio-economic realities overlap and merge, is articulated here. This is reinforced in performance through the fact that theatre, in its relation to performance space and the heightened symbolic manner in which that space is en-propped,[20] foregrounds precisely this meaning of location, that is the embeddedness of the socio-cultural in the spatial. Location thus becomes meaningful through the socio-cultural which it invokes. In Jalaarnava's case, this relates both to the notion of a country of origin and to the way in which her voyage of discovery within that country transforms her as she enacts her relation to it through separating from family (her sister and aunt) and falling in love with a woman there. India is thus special to Jalaarnava in two ways, as the site of familial origin and as the site of a certain sexual and emotional awakening. That site provides Jalaarnava with a location within which to explore her identity, not as an act of rebellion or healing, but as a context for a process that remains unfinished, in process, at the end of the play when she is poised to leave India to return to England. The cyclicity of the dominant images of the play, monsoon and menstruation, gesture towards an iterative process rather than towards closure. This is reinforced by the final affirmative words of the character THE POET: 'The heavens have opened. A gift from the Goddess to be able to create life' (5, 3: 75).

Jalaarnava, come to India to explore herself, is in some respects a figure similar to Leela, gone to Jamaica to relieve the unsettled self following the breakdown of a heterosexual relationship. And in some ways Nusrat is to Jalaarnava what Sugar is to Leela, the local inhabitant whose life appears more constrained but who has an assured sense of self that is juxtaposed with the unsettled – especially bodily unsettled – identities Leela and Jalaarnava inhabit. Nusrat like Jalaarnava is still in education but her expectations are different from Jalaarnava's:

JALAARNAVA: What are you going to do when you leave college?
NUSRAT: I'm going to marry a tailor, that way I can carry on with my designing and support my Ummi.
JALAARNAVA: You don't have to get married, follow Islam, stuff like that.
NUSRAT: It's fine. At least I don't have to get involved with the man I marry, except to have children.

JALAARNAVA: Don't you like him?
NUSRAT: He's O.K., better than some, most men are bastards, they're just rude.

(3, 17: 70–1)

This exchange configures Nusrat's future as a particular, pre-determined process that embeds her in a heterosexual order in which her own wishes have to be integrated with the needs of her family. The one concession to her is to the preservation of her skills which point to a man with a particular profession as an appropriate partner. Nusrat accepts this future which will allow her to continue her 'designing' and will also enable her to support her mother. In this she both furthers her own desire to use her specific skills and expresses her commitment to her family. She thus emblematizes the interdependence and family orientation which, according to Ghuman, is valued in Asian cultures above the individualism and autonomy valued in western contexts (1999: 14–25). Nusrat is not constructed as unhappy with this future. She takes a pragmatic rather than a romantic view, and although she asks Jalaarnava about coming to live in India, she does not pressurize Jalaarnava to stay on, and she does not offer to run off with Jalaarnava to Britain. Nusrat is thus not waiting to be missionized by Jalaarnava; her life is fully embedded in her context and she is not desperate to leave that behind. Her sense of duty and of destiny are deeply intertwined, and not in opposition to the emotional structures she inhabits. The temptation presented to her by Jalaarnava, the 'tourist' with a critical perspective on Nusrat's life and future as mapped out within her community, does not lead to Nusrat abandoning that life or future. The boundaries drawn between the two women's futures thus undercut the teleological romantic narrative that usually accompanies love stories, of a life together, 'happy ever after'. That lack of romantic closure, unmediated by closure of emotional affinity (there is no sense that Nusrat and Jalaarnava's affections for and sexual attraction to each other diminish, on the contrary), functions as a critique of conventional models of hetero- and also frequently homo-romance in that – in the context of a cyclical imagery – it points to the iterativity of sexual–emotional attachments, of relationships beyond the current one, of severance beyond diminution of attachment. It thus takes an affirmative stance to romance in complete contrast to 'Talking in Tongues' where self is discovered not in relation but outside of relation, where travelling and moving become the grounds on which self can be regained but outside of social attachments. Here it is precisely through emotional attachments that self is discovered and sustained and, in fairly traditional fashion, journeying is both the actual and the metaphoric basis for that discovery of self.

'Monsoon' is thus concerned with negotiating affinities rather than difference. In Nusrat and Jalaarnava's discussions about their relative positions and experiences, an equality gradually emerges which temporarily reduces the distance between them. This distance, created out of the locations they usually inhabit and involving a power differential whereby Jalaarnava is the (relatively) moneyed tourist to whom Nusrat and her family provide a service, is – as in 'Talking in Tongues' – disrupted by the personal relationship that evolves. However, in 'Talking in Tongues' these relationships reinforce the exploitative dimensions of the differences between tourists and local inhabitants. In 'Monsoon' the relationship between Jalaarnava and Nusrat provides both women with an emotional and sexual satisfaction which equalizes their situation within the affective order without denying the locational and socio-economic differences that ultimately shape their lives. Their relationship is thus viewed as mutually supportive and rewarding, and it is celebrated within the play. The healing effect of Sugar's and Leela's exchange, in contrast, ultimately rests on a reversal of power between the local inhabitant and the tourist whereby the local inhabitant is constructed as having the settled self required to be able to give emotionally in ways in which Claudette, for instance, is unable to give.

Gynocentricity

The much more affirmative stance of 'Monsoon' towards the possibility of relationships between local inhabitants and tourists is related to its gynocentricity. The play features only women.[21] Its women-centred content is mirrored in its stylistic and theatrical specificities. Originally conceived as a poem,[22] the play has an episodic structure, consisting of five acts with varying numbers of very short scenes. The acts roughly chart Jalaarnava and her sister's arrival in India (Act One), her journey to Kashmir (Act Two), the development of her relationship with Nusrat to the point of kissing (Act Three),[23] the sexual enactment of their relationship (Act Four), and Jalaarnava's decision to leave to return to England (Act Five). Act Three as the pivotal and longest sequence of scenes (eighteen compared to the three, six, seven, and eight scenes of the other acts) charts Jalaarnava's transformation from seeking to get over her boyfriend to falling in love with Nusrat, thus presenting the central change in the play at the centre of its structure.

The play opens and closes with the figure of THE POET who – throughout the play – marks time, both the actual moments in the play and the monumental time in which the monsoon and menstruation as a cyclical release of life-giving fluid are symbolically inter-related in a mythical, goddess-centred narrative:

> The birth of Maya
> the beginning of time
> I cannot see my growing
> the new moon in my eyes.

(I, I: 57)

Chowdhry's use of poetry, but also her general use of language and varied discourses, as well as the structuring of her play and, indeed, its content place her text in the realm of the semiotic as described by Julia Kristeva, herself a migrant,[24] in *Desire in Language: A Semiotic Approach to Literature and Art*. Here Kristeva famously describes 'poetic language' as an 'unsettling process . . . of the identity of meaning and speaking subject' (1980: 124–5), aligning rhythmic, repetitive utterances and heterogeneity with the maternal, a prelinguistic semiotic order, and the subject-in-process, taking the subject back to its original union with the mother which is disrupted by the law of the father or the entry into the symbolic through the acquisition of language, the insertion into an order of homogeneity, linear time, and single meanings, of prohibitions and repressions, including that of the affective affinity to the mother and to women in general. 'Language as symbolic function', Kristeva writes, 'constitutes itself at the cost of repressing instinctual drive and continuous relation to the mother' (136). In this economy, Jalaarnava's return to the 'mother country', to India, prefigures her re/turn to women as a source of emotional sustenance. On coming to India she cuts herself off from her sister in order to come back to herself after her relationship with her English boyfriend has broken down. Once in Kashmir and installed on Nusrat's family's houseboat she writes in her diary: 'April 12. I am being fed and nurtured by women. My solitude is disallowed, frowned upon. I want to be alone. April 19. It is not a secret that I am lost. I am not keeping it from myself. The lake and the mountains enclose me, are silent, do not answer my questions' (3, 4: 65). The answer to her questions does not lie in the solitary or in location but in the social. Through her relationship with Nusrat she re/turns to women and to her self:

> Inside this room, womb, sanctuary
> I discover a taste for myself
> dipping into hot wet flesh
> into taste on tongue sucking.
>
> . . .
>
> Outside this womb, room sanctuary
> I discover a taste for women
> Dipping into hot wet flesh
> Into taste on tongue sucking.[25]
>
> (4, 7: 74)

The articulation of a relation to the maternal, evinced through the reference to the 'womb' and the 'sanctuary' but also to the taste for women which obliquely gestures towards mother's milk as well as more overtly to lesbian sexuality, the expression of that articulation in poetic language, the use of repetition with variation within that language, as well as the use of music and chanting, both choric devices in Kristeva's psychic economy and thus also associated with the maternal, stylistically reinforce the gynocentricity of the play. This is further enhanced by Chowdhry's use of diverse discourses and multiple voices within the play. For apart from realist dialogue, the play contains letters and diaries, both of which have a long history of being associated with *women* writers. In the play the letters are addressed to Jalaarnava's sister; the diary is intended to be solely for Jalaarnava herself. These texts thus convey a notion of intimacy, of the kind of enclosure, sanctuary, or protected space referred to in the poetic sequence above. That intimacy is enhanced by the extensive use of sounds in order to provide atmosphere. Many of the stage directions are devoted to sound rather than to the visualization of the play. This is probably partly a function of the fact that it was, *inter alia*, produced as a radio play where, according to Chowdhry, 'it becomes a tapestry of sound, erotic and evocative' (in George 1993: 56). That appeal to the senses, especially the aural, refers the play back to the idea of the womb where sound, including nonverbal sound, is one preeminent medium through which the foetus receives sensory stimulus. The play thus leads back to the pleasure of sound, and to the sensual more generally, through its use of the colour red – associated with the monsoon and with menstruation – as a key infrastructural element of its staging. Both sound and colour help to create a womb-like environment, augmented by the fact that Jalaarnava is staying on a houseboat on a lake, surrounded by water as in a womb. Thus both in this play and in 'Talking in Tongues' the coming to self, including the bodily self, is through the proximity to water, metaphorically associated with a re/turn to the womb, to one's origin, and to the nurturance of female support. However, Chowdhry – in contrast to Pinnock – places that experience much more firmly into the theatrically experimental through creating a more strongly episodic, associative, and expressionistic structure, through the sustained use of diverse sound structures to generate particular kinds of atmosphere, through the specificity and over-determined nature of her symbolism, through diverse textual patterns, and through the use of music. Both playwrights, however, project the same notion, namely that the re/turn to the place of familial origin is enabling for the diasporic individual. This turn to the country of familial origin is never conceived as a 'returning home for good'; it is, indeed, not viewed by the central characters as a 'return home' as such. Instead, it is a turn to a location which holds certain affinities to the central characters that may but do not necessarily allow for change to occur. That change is set, within both plays, in a maternal frame in which the presence of the mythical, proximity to water, and female support offer the nurturing structures that effect a coming to self. As Kristeva writes in 'Women's Time':

> As for time, female subjectivity would seem to provide a specific measure that essentially retains *repetition* and *eternity* from among the multiple modalities of time known through the history of civilizations. On the one hand, there are cycles, gestation, the eternal recurrence of a biological rhythm that conforms to that of nature and imposes temporality whose stereotyping may shock, but whose regularity and unison with what is experienced as extra-subjective time, cosmic time, occasion vertiginous visions and unnameable *jouissance*.
>
> (1986: 191)

In Leela's case this description approximates to her experience of speaking in tongues by the shore; in Jalaarnava's case, it is the orgasmic experience of lesbian sex which references female subjectivity as described by Kristeva. The latter juxtaposes those experiences with the monumental time of the maternal:

> On the other hand, and perhaps as a consequence, there is the massive presence of a monumental temporality, without cleavage or escape, which has very little to do with linear time . . . all-encompassing and infinite like imaginary space . . . one is reminded of the various myths of resurrection which, in all religious beliefs, perpetuate the vestige of an anterior or concomitant maternal cult.
>
> (191)

This presence is installed in 'Talking in Tongues' through the narrative of the mythic women referred to in the play's prologue (which itself moves that scene outside of the time of the play 'proper') and in 'Monsoon' through the figure of the poet invoking the goddess. Here we have the juxtaposition of 'mythic' and 'real' women alluded to in Liz Goodman's collection of performance work by women, *Mythic*

Women/Real Women, which binds the monumental into the temporal, the present into a past, and female subjectivity into the maternal. But the journeys undertaken by the central characters figure as a re-merging in order to emerge, a trip back in order to move forward, a turn to familial origins to release the unsettled self from its self-alienation. This is the meaning of the temporary sojourn envisaged in both plays, the positioning of the central protagonists as western-based tourists rather than as permanently displaced characters.

4   Unsettling identities

Theatre and performance rely on the unsettling of identities in terms of their various conceptions of the actress-character or performer-performed relationship.[1] 'De-stabiliz[ing] the boundary between the subject and its others' as theatre does in its exploration of the relation between actress and role, 'dramatize[s] the inseparability of the subject from the realms of the social and the political' (Ahmed 1997: 153), since the relation between the subject and its others necessarily always operates within the social and/as the political. As such theatre offers an appropriate terrain for the enactment of unsettling identities. Such unsettling or troubling, which takes different forms and carries different meanings within diverse diasporic experiences and representations, constitutes a key dynamic in the work of many Black and Asian women playwrights. Here I shall focus on three plays to discuss that dynamic, Zindika's 'Leonora's Dance' (1993), Winsome Pinnock's 'A Rock in Water' (1989), and Maya Chowdhry's *Kaahini* (1997). In each case unsettling identities struggle against the burden of a colonial past which has generated multiple displacements and demands constant negotiations between the here and now and the there and then. These displacements are not only geographical but also cultural and social, revealing the legacies of colonial histories, the internalization of racialist and sexist positions, the problematic of how to live the multi-locationality which is at the heart of diaspora. In this it is the *child* of the diaspora, the second generation, upon and by whom the effects of diaspora are played out, for she is the one for whom displacement is the dominant or only experience, raising questions of identity and belonging which are very different from those faced by the parental generation.

Multi-locationality as identity

The question of how to live the multi-locationality of diaspora haunts, quite literally, Zindika's play 'Leonora's Dance' which 'traces the pattern of Leonora's illness from agoraphobia through to final mental breakdown – where her negativity takes on a life of its own in the shape of the spirit Medusa' (76). Leonora's negativity, as Zindika puts it, is occasioned by her leading a diasporic life in a postcolonial culture. Zindika manifests this through her opening stage directions which are both descriptive and analytic of the situation that Leonora, a woman from Jamaica, and her two lodgers, a Chinese student of medicine, Melisa Chung,[2] and Leonora's niece Daphine, find themselves in:

> All scenes take place in the house. There is no clear indication of day or night. Each character will occupy a different space on stage. There is a communal space where they always meet. The communal space is dominated and controlled by Leonora. The other two lodgers must go through the communal space always to get to their own space. Each character controls their own space, they never invade each other's space uninvited. Whenever they do, something dramatic happens.
>
> (1, 1: 77)

The illusion of the single place, suggested by Leonora's house as the location of the action, is undercut by the multiple divisions of that space, and by a violent, chaotic outside, repeatedly referred to in the play, in which none of the women is able to function effectively. The disaggregated spatial location of the characters within the house – a metaphor for multi-cultural Britain and for the diasporic lives of its inhabitants but also a diasporic *mappa mundi* of sorts – not only reflects community segregations as they occur in diasporic cultures among people from diverse ethnic backgrounds; it also maps the different experiences and positions these characters inhabit vis-à-vis their colonial histories/heritages and each other. The spatialization of those differences[3] thus mirrors the dominant tenor of much writing on race and culture during the 1980s which, as indicated in the introduction, articulated the problematic of homogenizing the term 'black' and what it stood for. As Naz Rassool puts it: 'Used as a *racially* descriptive term "blackness" has historically provided a universalizing, homogenizing category in which the concept of "foreign Otherness" has been encapsulated *par excellence* in both colonial and postcolonial discourse' (1997: 187). However, 'Black people do not comprise a hermetically sealed or homogenous category: skin colour, history and culture all play a part in their definition' (Aziz 1992: 293). Indeed, Aziz states that she uses the term 'black' 'mostly to refer to people of African and Asian descent living in Britain' (293). 'Asian' in the UK does not, as it does in the United States, refer to Chinese people (Ghuman 1999: xii) who as a migrant group thus become invisible in Aziz's discourse and who are indeed in Britain in the main absent from cultural representation.[4] In that respect Zindika's play highlights an invisibility otherwise rarely remarked upon.[5] It also sets up an inter-racial and inter-cultural dynamic the problematic of which, further discussed below, is played out in the course of the performance.

In 'Leonora's Dance' geographical space and psychic location are mapped onto one another, reflecting the difficulties of leading a diasporic life in a postcolonial culture. As Sheila Allen has pointed out, 'ethnic identity is only meaningful where those of different ethnic origins are brought together in a common social context' (1994: 94). What problematizes this further is the fact that the notion of some unitary ethnic origin is itself imaginary. Leonora, Melisa Chung and Daphine are all caught in what Hélène Cixous has described in *Rootprints* as an *entre-deux*, a condition of 'a true in-between' (1997: 9), a moment of flux. Their identities are shaped by this in-between-ness, and not just along racial or ethnic dimensions. Gender, race, class, and a certain idea of origin haunt all the characters who do not want to, or cannot, make simple either/or choices. As Ben Jancovich put it: 'What happens when one's cultural self-image is out of synch with one's racial heritage?' (1993: 133).

Leonora, in fact, is of mixed-race parentage, a white father and a black mother. In the cultural imaginary of multi-cultural Britain, however, identity is identified with a unitary form of codification, with a monolithic racialized position. As Root puts it *à propos* of the US context: 'social forces complicate matters. For example, the

U.S. Census Bureau, employers, health insurance, and so on, expect racially mixed people to choose only one racial and ethnic identity' (1997: 168–9). Leonora, however, is *métisse*, to borrow a term from Jayne Ifekwunigwe (1997; 1999), 'someone who by virtue of parentage, embodies two or more world views' (1997: 131). But the socio-cultural racialist drive towards a unitary racial or ethnic identity does not allow for an easy embodiment of *métisage*; on the contrary, *métisage* posits a threat to assumed structures of classification, defying notions of singular ethnic identities.

Ifekwunigwe's work explores the issue of *métisse* identity, indexing the socio-cultural skills required to *achieve* – since it is never possible just to *be*, as Leonora demonstrates – a *métisse* identity. Similarly, Root analyses the difficulties mixed-race women face in xenophobic cultures and counsels that 'Parents should acknowledge the complex effects of physical appearance, provide direct education about the fantasies and stereotypes that people may have about multiracial people and interracial families, and teach a child psychological and verbal defenses that are empowering' (167). However, such acknowledgement is difficult, possibly impossible in a context where the 'multiracial' child is born of conflict and strife as is the case with Leonora.[6] In the pivotal Scene Five in Act Two of the play, the history of Leonora's and her mother Frieda's life are revealed. Leonora, the child of the local white landowner Marshall Croft and Frieda, one of the 'negro[es] on his land', came to her mother's aid as Croft sought to kill Frieda to prevent her from publicizing their relationship. Frieda had tried to get more money out of Croft for Leonora's school fees and dancing lessons but he refused her. In the ensuing fight, Frieda tried to stab him, he fought back to kill her, and Leonora came to her mother's aid, effectively helping to kill her father in the process. Frieda was sent to prison. Given this background, Leonora's mixed-parentage identity emblematizes, on her father's side, the colonial history of the white landowner lording it over his black slaves/servants/workers, a racialized sexual history of white men exploiting black women, and a history of men failing to take (financial) responsibility for the children they father outside state-sanctioned relationships. On her mother's side, Leonora's identity is bound up with the history of the oppressed, sexually exploited, and not valued woman whose self-determination is limited by the circumstances she finds herself in, and whose experience is one of violence and violation. The length of Frieda's sentence, fifteen years, indicates that she was jailed for murder rather than manslaughter, and that her action was not viewed as a matter of self-defence.[7] In the light of this history which relied – on the father's part – on a public denial of his relationship with Leonora's mother, and on her mother's part, on the meeting of violence with violence in her final encounter with the father, supporting Leonora's mixed-race identity in an empowering way is difficult if not impossible, making Leonora's identification with both sets of parents also difficult if not impossible.

For the producer of the play, Leonora's *métisse* status instantly raises the question of how to cast her character effectively since that affords multiple possibilities of projecting a racial cultural politics. Should she be cast as someone who could 'pass' as white, seems mixed-race, is white, or is seemingly obviously black? Each of the possible casting decisions has different implications regarding the racial politics manifested through that decision. The play itself suggests that Leonora's appearance leads her to be identified as black. She, however, rejects that heritage which comes to her through her mother, wanting to transcend the oppressed status she associates with her mother: 'I was going to soar like a bird' (2, 5: 106). While her appearance might align Leonora with her mother, her psychic identification is with her white father and what he stood for. She thus manifests a form of 'internalized racism' as discussed by Rassool (1997: 193–5) that leads her to subdue and disown her 'black' heritage in favour of her 'white' one, a procedure of psychic violation which creates the fissure that ultimately promotes her breakdown since Leonora is not accepted in the 'white' world that she aspires to belong to. That lack of acceptance is the marker of a racialized, hierarchically ordered world in which 'whiteness' connotes a superior status compared with blackness and where, moreover, identity is not a matter of individual choice but of ascription, residing in other rather than in self. Leonora cannot 'choose' to identify as 'white' since identity requires corroboration, becoming effective in the social rather than the solipsistic.[8] She embodies that '"Who I am" or "who we are" is never a matter of free choice' as articulated by Ien Ang (2001: vii). It is this as much as her unresolved relation to her history and past, expressed through her rejection of her mother, which keeps Leonora housebound, retreating into self instead of engaging with others who are unwilling to accept her self-definition as 'white'. As she, knowingly and disturbingly, puts it: 'one percent black can ruin your life' (1, 2: 85).[9]

Leonora is thus the victim of racism – she was, for instance, not able to pursue a career as a ballet dancer as that art form is reserved for whites[10] and she is not allowed to identify as such. However, she is also a perpetrator of racism; when speaking to her Chinese lodger, who was born and brought up in Britain, Leonora nonetheless carefully distinguishes between 'them', that is the Chinese lodger, and 'us', the English among whom she includes herself in the process of 'othering' the lodger, when she says to her: 'still not use to our English weather yet I see . . . You'll soon get use to it like us English' (1, 1: 78). Leonora is caught between her socially enforced identification as black derived from her mother which regulates her social existence, and her psychic identification with her dead white father who subjugated her mother. When Leonora's mother comes to visit from the Caribbean during the course of the play, she says to Leonora: 'Face realities girl. Some of us are turkeys not meant for the sky. Come back home with me. You see what happens when you stay away too long – you forget where you belong. Divided loyalties' (2, 5: 107). Leonora's mother here touches upon the *entre-deux* which constitutes Leonora's but not, importantly, her own life. Although violated by Leonora's father, the white local landowner, Leonora's mother Frieda did not move to Britain and has not endured the migratory experience her daughter has undertaken. Like the island women in Pinnock's 'Talking in Tongues', Frieda has thus not suffered the uprooting Leonora exposed herself to. She also, unlike Leonora, manifests a matrilineal identification with women which secures her sense of self. Leonora's response to her mother's demand that she return to the Caribbean is: 'But can't you see mama, this is where I belong. This is my father's land. Where else should I belong? It's my birthright.' Leonora's mother, who does not suffer from the ontological uncertainties which beset her daughter, tells Leonora: 'But it's you mother's line that is important, after all who know who your father is?' (2, 5: 107). In *Strangers to Ourselves* (1991) Julia Kristeva charts the move from the mother- or homeland to the strange place, the land of the father and the law of the father. In the struggle between the *'elsewhere'* (or the land of the father) 'versus the origin' (the domain of the mother), or to put it another way, the *'nowhere* versus the roots' (Kristeva 1991: 29), a maternally identified origin or root prevails in Zindika's play. The play powerfully suggests that displacement and a diasporic existence have psychically crippled and economically deprived both Leonora and her niece Daphine. The end of the play sees Leonora's mother intent upon taking Leonora – who has suffered a severe breakdown – back to the Caribbean, and Daphine taking on Leonora's mother's mantle as a spiritualist and healer. In this resolution the white father is erased. One could argue that that process, however, entails a renewed denial of a crucial aspect of Leonora's inheritance, affirming her blackness – on 'black' territory, i.e. in Jamaica where, her mother promises her, 'They'll roll out the red carpet, sing the national anthem' (2, 5: 107) – but obliterating her identification with her white heritage which, nonetheless, will not simply go away because it is denied. Within this play, the character of Leonora seems to come to stand for the impossibility of living as a *métisse* woman, and the need to choose one ethnic or racial identity even if one has mixed-race parentage.

Materializing the immaterial

The unsettling/unsettledness of Leonora's identity is formally encoded in the play through the invocation and construction of a spirit world which raises questions about the relationship between the material and the immaterial. Within the secular context of western theatre, there is a long tradition of such invocations, particularly and significantly in Shakespearean drama from *Hamlet* and *Macbeth* to *A Midsummer Night's Dream* and *The Tempest*, but also for instance in Goethe's *Faust*. However, the materialization of a spirit world is distinctly uncommon in contemporary western theatre where unsettled identities are pathologized and psychologized rather than attributed to the influence of spirits. The appearance of spirits on stage in a contemporary theatre piece thus queries canonical assumptions of the western world view, a querying that is cleverly reinforced in this play through the different ways in which the characters in 'Leonora's Dance' react to these spirits. Each of the female characters on stage has a spiritual other/other world to which she relates (see table).

Character	Spirit/Spirit World
Leonora	Medusa
Melisa	Mioshan; ancestral spirits
Daphine	dibi world (African spiritual heritage)
Frieda	dibi world (African spiritual heritage)

Of these a key figure is Medusa, the only spirit who actually appears on stage and who, according to the didascales, '*is a threat to LEONORA's sanity and LEONORA's loss of contact with the outside world*' (1, 1: 77). The choice of the figure of Medusa as the spirit that oppresses Leonora signals the diasporic clash between the western, African, and eastern cultures which inhabit the house. In Black Theatre Co-operative's 1993 production of the play this was reinforced by Medusa being presented with white tribal markings more commonly associated with African cultures than the Greek tradition with which the figure of Medusa is usually associated (see plate 6). Leonora's aspirations to embrace a culture that rejects her find expression in the figuration of Medusa as the 'bad' spirit,[11] who encourages Leonora to destroy herself.[12] Leonora's alienation from and rejection of her Jamaican roots is juxtaposed with her niece Daphine's much more affirmative stance towards a black heritage she wishes to claim as the antidote to the racism she is exposed to in Britain. As she says: 'I've been in this country all me life and I still feel like an alien' (1, 6: 91). Challenging Leonora's infatuation with western culture, Daphine invokes an Africanist stance:

Plate 6 Glenna Forster-Jones as Medusa and Ellen Thomas as Frieda in Black Theatre Co-operative's 1993 production of Zindika's 'Leonora's Dance'.

> DAPHINE: . . . who gave science and mathematics to the Greeks? It was us Africans. Everything in the West originated in Africa.
> LEONORA: (*Shocked*) Africa.
> DAPHINE: Yes, Miss Leonora. We're Africans . . . you and me.
> LEONORA: Don't tar me with the same brush.
> DAPHINE: It's nothing to be ashamed of.
>
> (1, 2: 81)

As Paul Gilroy (1987) puts it, 'Black Britain defines itself crucially as part of a diaspora. Its unique cultures draw inspiration from those developed by black populations elsewhere. In particular, the culture and politics of black America and the Caribbean have become raw materials for creative processes which redefine what it means to be black, adapting it to distinctively British experiences and meanings. Black culture is actively made and remade' (154). Zindika takes this process one step further, for her play features not only rituals derived from

Caribbean dibi, in particular the initiation ceremony which Frieda seeks to enact upon Leonora to make her take on/over her heritage, Frieda's socio-cultural role as dibi woman; she also portrays rituals[13] of Chinese ancestor worship and propitiation carried out by Melisa, Leonora's Chinese lodger. The suggestion is thus that Chinese and Afro-Caribbean culture share the invocation of ancestral spirits as a way of mediating between present and past, and in the presentation of both eastern and African-based ancestral spirit invocation, as well as through the portrayal of the spirit of Medusa, Zindika produces a version of what Patrice Pavis and others have described as *intercultural* theatre, a theatre which brings together elements from discrete cultural traditions, in this instance to affirm their power and significance in the characters' lives.

Both Frieda and Melisa appeal to their ancestral spirits for support and help in a world where their identities and desires are threatened (see plate 7). This is in stark contrast to the western spirit Medusa whose presence, uncalled but insistent, is destructive. When Frieda recognizes that Leonora is 'possessed' by Medusa, she invokes an entire diasporic history of her peoples to combat this 'possession': 'I shall have to call them all – no matter how far away they are; Ivory coast, New Guinea, Benin, Bermuda, and Burundi. I shall go way back, past the middle passage, to the old world, to Africa. This is one battle I cannot afford to lose. I shall call them all to this house . . . Come griots, come. Come marabouts and kings. Come sprinkle Sam-Sam for your followers. (*Sprinkle water*) Sing Tai-nai your warrior songs' (2, 4: 105). Frieda seeks to combat Leonora's colonization by Medusa, the re-enactment on the mind of her daughter of the history of colonization that she herself suffered corporeally, and that was suffered geopolitically by the countries that encompass her extended history. As Gilroy (1987) puts it: 'grounding the contemporary experience of racial oppression in the past is recognized as a first step in progress towards emancipation from the mental slavery which has remained intact even as the physical bonds have been untied' (208). In Frieda and Leonora's case, grounding the present in the past encapsulates both public and personal history since it is only through their pivotal exchange in Act Two, Scene Five that Leonora is brought face to face

Plate 7 Judy Hepburn as Leonora, Ellen Thomas as Frieda, and Glenna Forster-Jones as the intervening spirit in Black Theatre Co-operative's 1993 production of Zindika's 'Leonora's Dance'.

with the history of their joint killing of her father which has driven mother and daughter apart, but which also binds them. That personal history, in its inter-racial and class tensions, is embedded in the wider history of colonialism in Jamaica.

Gilbert and Tompkins suggest that 'traditional enactments have special functions in post-colonial societies and are often key sites of resistance to imposed values and practices' (1996: 54). This is precisely the case in 'Leonora's Dance', in which both Frieda and Melisa invoke their ancestral spirits to combat the imposition of western culture and values on the one hand, and oppressive cultural traditions on the other. Importantly, as sites of resistance these invocations do not only offer a counter-discursive stance to secularity and to western culture and values at a semantic level; they also produce a counter-discursive position in relation to the high-cultural tradition of western theatre as a secular space permitting only of particular contents that do not, conventionally, include sacred rituals based in oral folk histories and traditions.

That counter-discursivity is taken further through the play's juxtaposition between western science and medicine, and eastern and African-based spirit invocation. Leonora's state suggests, within a western framework, that she is having a breakdown. Medusa's use of words such as 'psychosis' and 'persecution complex' (2, 4: 105) seemingly situates Leonora's condition on familiar psychiatric terrain, despite the fact that the words are spoken by a spirit, an immaterial entity. The acceptance of this immaterial entity's existence within a western clinico-cultural context is predicated upon notions such as 'split personality' and 'schizophrenia' which indicate a splitting off in the unsettled identity of different aspects of the self, making Medusa an externalization of Leonora's self-destructive impulses. The 'making real' of this other or double, or fragment of Leonora's self on stage, through the on-stage presence of an actress playing Medusa, destabilizes the notion that she is 'only in Leonora's head'. However, at the same time such making manifest of the immaterial is also part of an extended western theatre tradition where, in the move from the nineteenth to the twentieth century, a belief in the spiritual and immaterial gradually gave way to a perspective of the secularized internalization and psychologization of these immaterial phenomena. What unsettles this notion within Zindika's text is the fact that Medusa is presented as part of a spiritual plane that also encompasses Frieda's ancestral spirits and Melisa's. Indeed, Melisa foresees what befalls Leonora: '(*Appears confused*) I see two women, dancing or fighting. I can't tell. One woman is in white. She's being pulled by the other woman towards the sun – or something. A very bright light. I can't see their faces. One is old – the other young . . . Oh, I don't know, it's not clear, perhaps they're both young or both old' (2, 3: 100). This prefigures the moment where Leonora, dressed in the white ceremonial robe that is meant to be part of her initiation into the state of dibi woman, rushes out into the street, seemingly led there by Medusa, as reported by Melisa who runs out to rescue her: 'I saw her. I saw her pulling Leonora into the road. I saw her. Her eyes were evil. Her face was twisted and full of anger and . . . and . . . hate' (2, 5: 109).

In seeing Medusa, Melisa is forced to understand that the spirit of Mioshan whom she has tried to invoke and with whom she hoped to set up home was not the spirit that she actually conjured up, that she mistook Medusa for Mioshan. But the parallel planes on which these spirits are believed by the protagonists to be operating sets up a striking contrast to western science and medicine as it is presented in the play. Leonora believes in western science, and takes Diazepam to combat her depression and anxiety attacks. The pills, however, do not help her since they do not enable her to deal with the underlying causes of her situation. Similarly, and despite the advances in reproductive technology she tries to talk to Melisa about, she has no children; western medicine has been unable to help her in this context, too. In the contest between western science and spirituality as presented in this play, spirituality wins out, and Frieda's final assertion that 'England needs Mother Frieda' (2, 6: 110) heralds this.

Within this complex, Melisa emerges as the most balanced person, pursuing her studies in western medicine whilst at the same time continuing her ritual ancestor worship and conjuring of spirits, albeit in modified form. For Melisa, 'ritual en-actment is a way of "possessing" the past, of finding a home within the fractures of a history marked by dislocation . . . and a present complicated by continued race/class inequalities' (Gilbert and Tompkins 1996: 71). These inequalities register in Leonora's racist attitude to Melisa, but also in Frieda's easy suspicion of her. Melisa, unlike Leonora and Daphine who have active female family connections, is all alone; her mother has died, there appear to be no other female relatives. Like Leonora and Daphine she has a problematic relationship with her father whose impositions she has rejected. Thus socially isolated, Melisa draws on the mythic female figure of Mioshan, her 'mentor' as she describes her. When Daphine finds a picture of Mioshan, Melisa is forced to explain this figure (see plate 8): 'She's a taoist princess. A woman of great insight and powers. One of the few women who surpasses men in greatness. I'm going to find her. We're going to live together at the foot of the Himalayas' (2, 1: 95). In fact, Mioshan – rather like Melisa herself – refused to marry the man selected for her by her father and stabbed her father to death. Sentenced to death, she vanished and

Plate 8 Doreene Blackstock as Daphine and Toshie Ogura as Melisa in Black Theatre Co-operative's 1993 production of Zindika's 'Leonora's Dance'.

'No-one knew the secret of her disappearance – but it is believed that she roams the earth constantly as a peasant woman, a herbalist – all kinds of disguises looking for lost souls to guide and protect . . . You could say I'm her apprentice' (2, 1: 95). The play sets up parallels between this idea of a healing woman and the dibi woman, also a herbalist. It thus projects the notion of intercultural similarities that need to be recognized as a source of mutual support for women. The play advocates matrilineage, the bequeathing of powers and money (in the form of the deeds to Leonora's house) from woman to woman. It indicates that women will come to each other's aid: Melisa helps both Leonora and Daphine, Frieda helps Daphine and Melisa; the female spiritual world does protect women. Men, within this structure, are distant, law-imposing figures whose lives and rules damage the women around them.

Leonora's, Daphine's, and Melisa's diasporic lives force them to confront their unsettled identities as women with histories of migration. Significantly, none of them was born or brought up in the house they co-inhabit in London – they have all come to it from different places within and outside Britain. As such the house symbolizes diasporic space. Medusa repeatedly, and in quasi-incantatory fashion, articulates the fragility of the diasporic structure which the characters inhabit: 'A house built on cracks, fissures, I mean . . . This is the house that Jerry built . . . This is the house . . . some come to cower, some come to hide . . . built on stilts, shifting sands . . . This is the house . . . a sanctuary full of refugees . . . This is my house' (1, 1: 78). This is simultaneously a representation of Leonora's state of mind, of the fragility of multi-cultural Britain, and of western culture, which fails to offer those who embrace it stability.

Matrilineage

As is common in a number of works by Black and Asian women playwrights, women are constructed as able to 'see' things, as having particular spiritual, presentient, and predictive powers which are often inherited through the female line. As Daphine, at first seemingly the least believing of all the characters in the play, says: 'My mother sees spirits. She says that one day I'll see spirits too . . . and my daughter Daryl she'll see spirits too – when she's older. She says it generic – but I don't know whether to believe her though' (2, 4: 104). The lure of the west, in the case of Leonora its cultural lure, depletes the culture and inheritance of Jamaica. When Frieda, Leonora's mother, comes to London, she does so in part to find out what has been happening with her daughter but also to sort out the issue of succession, of passing on her gifts as a dibi woman which she inherited from her own mother and expects to pass on to her daughter. Leonora, however, rejects that role. The play thus mirrors the problematic discussed in chapter two in relation to 'Leave Taking', namely the difficulties of a female cultural inheritance and succession within a diasporic context in which blood ties that originally secured succession are unravelled.[14] Leonora is without issue – she has no children, and is unlikely to have any since she is middle-aged and has rejected men with whom she has had very bad experiences. She also lacks sympathy for her mother's cultural roots. Daphine, in contrast, seeks to mediate her cultural alienation by harking back to African roots and already has a female child. She also – fortunately as it turns out – is a distant blood relation to Frieda and Leonora. She thus becomes the ideal woman to take on Frieda's heritage as a dibi woman. The appropriateness of her disposition for that role is enhanced by the revelation of her illiteracy (promoted possibly by being dyslexic but also, importantly, by psychosomatic responses to being ill-treated by her father for making mistakes when reading and by teachers' unsympathetic and racist responses to her in school). In consequence, and by way of compensation, she has developed what she calls her 'computer brain' – an ability to memorize everything. This makes her the ideal recipient of Frieda's knowledge, which is passed on orally rather than in written form. The final scene shows Daphine rote-learning the medicinal properties of herbs from Frieda, embarking on her future as dibi woman.

As part of this future, Frieda gives her the deeds to the house. As Frieda says: 'It seems my journey to England was twofold. I thought I was coming to initiate my daughter. But, what I found was not as simple as I thought. England needs Mother Frieda – You've been chosen – accept with grace' (2, 6: 110). Whereas Frieda's initial plan was to take Leonora back to Jamaica to take her rightful place as her eldest daughter and successor, Frieda effectively bequeaths her spiritual inheritance to England, inserting it into British culture through teaching Daphine and offering her – in the form of the deeds of the house – a secure future with a roof over her head and potential for an income. This is a continuation of Daphine's earlier line of western culture resting on an African inheritance, a recognition of the reciprocal inflections of diverse cultures within one space, contemporary Britain. It is further reinforced by Frieda's recognition that the negative spirit she – in a somewhat racist manner – associated with Melisa, whom she sought to evacuate from the house, was in fact Medusa, and not an aspect of Melisa's Chinese ancestor world.

Only the Chinese lodger, threatened by Leonora's mother with being thrown out of the house or displaced, states that 'sometimes I think tradition is a dead man's revenge on the future' (2, 4: 106) and leaves to make, yet again, a different life for herself. However, as in Leonora's and Daphine's case, that move is also predicated upon a resistance to the paternal, on a break with certain traditions. Leonora and Daphine are constructed as unable to cope with the multi-locationality into which they are forced in postcolonial Britain. But for Melisa Chung, promised in marriage at the age of four by her parents and on the run from them, that multi-locationality offers opportunities for re-fashioning the self, attempting to integrate her desires and her history. Seeking to propitiate the spirits of her parents, Melisa Chung vows in her final speech before moving out of the house: 'I know I will bring shame on you my parents, my country, my ancestors – with my selfishness. I will wear my cheongsam, celebrate Chinese New Year. I will endeavour to speak Cantonese, even wear peach blossom in my hair on special occasions – but slave and chattel I shall not be' (2, 4: 106).

The permanence of diaspora

Diasporic existence exacts a price. Melisa, Leonora, and Daphine are all socially isolated, cut off from their own and other communities. Cut off from their roots, all three are constructed as needing to find a compromise between their past and the present in order to heal the effects of the fractured diasporic identities they inhabit.

All the female characters in Zindika's play, with the exception of Leonora's mother, exist in an estranged relation both to their country and culture of origin and to the place to which they have migrated or moved. This is a common scenario in Black British women playwrights' work. It maps a diasporic rather than a postcolonial identity. But in contrast to Zindika's play, in which the central characters arrive at a form of resolution through a return to, or compromise with, the country and/or culture of their origin, in many other plays no such resolution occurs or is possible. Winsome Pinnock's play 'A Rock in Water' (1989) is a good example of a play that presents a diasporic existence as a permanent rather than a transient condition. Her heroine, Claudia Jones, is based on a real-life character credited with having started the Notting Hill Carnivals and run one of the first black presses in the UK. As such the play is part of the feminist tradition, very powerful during the 1980s, of recovering forgotten female historical figures and establishing a *her*story, a canon centring on women whose work and life does not feature in traditional histories. Elean Thomas, who – at the time that Pinnock's play was first produced – wrote a brief history of Claudia Jones' life for *Spare Rib*, reveals Jones' obliteration from 'official' history and describes her own knowledge of Jones as having derived from oral transmissions, specifically her Uncle Nathaniel who told her: 'Come my little African queen, there is another African queen you should know 'bout. She is from now. She living right now in America but she born in the other island right next door to we . . . Trinidad. And she is a great queen. She stan' up pon her foot an' fighting for we people' (1989: 18). Pinnock, too, acquired her knowledge of Jones through oral transmissions, through interviewing people who had known Claudia Jones.[15] In 'A Rock in Water' Pinnock points to the paradox of Jones' life, the juxtaposition between her 'having started the Notting Hill Carnivals' and running 'one of the first black presses virtually singlehandedly. Yet when she died in 1964 she was alone and by the 1980's had been forgotten, even by the community she had served tirelessly for most of her life' (46).

In Pinnock's play Jones' life is constructed as diasporic. Having left Trinidad at the age of nine to move to the United States, Jones early on rebels against the fate of poor Black female workers, including that of her mother. She, interestingly in some ways rather like Leonora, wants to be a dancer, but like Leonora she is told by her mother that 'the sooner you get used to washing some white woman's clothes . . . the better. Because it's what you're going to be doing for the rest of your life. Even if you pass those wretched exams' (1, 1: 49). The harsh realism expressed in Claudia's mother's words and echoed by another Black mother, also out with her daughter looking for cleaning jobs, is juxtaposed with Claudia's desire to be 'a dancer at the Apollo.' The opening scene of the play thus establishes the framing parameters of aspiration and idealism versus a certain kind of realism which will haunt Claudia Jones' life as told in Pinnock's play. Railing against her fate as an exploited worker, Jones becomes involved in trade union activities, the Black Power movement, and the communist party. Like the appositely named 'Red', a union activist and colleague of Jones' mother, Claudia seeks to improve the working conditions of her Black fellow workers, displaying a caring attitude that is established symbolically in the early scenes of the play through her nurturing of a seed[16] and of a bird that has a broken wing. In both instances, however, death occurs and her nurturing efforts are in vain. In the play Claudia thus becomes complexly and contradictorily associated both with a caring attitude and an inability to bring or sustain life in what she nurtures. She also becomes associated with death and loss. In the opening scene, as she and her mother stand on a street corner in Brooklyn, waiting for her mother to be offered work, Claudia asks 'Why don't we go back to Trinidad?' (1, 1: 48). Her mother assumed she had forgotten Trinidad, and the conversation between them moves on, signalling the impossibility of a return. In the play Trinidad thus remains only as a memory, a place of childhood of which Claudia says, 'It was better there, there were good places to play. Let's go home' (1, 1: 48) but about which her mother significantly says nothing.

Claudia's mother dies of overwork, exhaustion, and a resultant heart condition when Claudia is eleven years old, and thus the geographical displacement already enacted through the move from Trinidad is compounded by the loss of the mother, a key moment in Claudia's life that is later recalled when, on her thirty-seventh birthday, by then a famous Black union and communist activist, she makes her speech: 'On this my 37th birthday, I think of my mother. My mother, a machine worker in a garment factory died when she was just the same age as I am today. I think I began then, to develop an understanding of the sufferings of my people and my class and to look for a way to end them' (Thomas 18; 'A Rock in Water', 1, 10: 68).[17] The need to think back through our mothers, Virginia Woolf's famous injunction, as well as the recognition that the personal is the political, both important tenets of second-wave feminism, combine here to make Claudia Jones into the activist she became but also, importantly, serve to isolate her from the people she loves and becomes close to. Pinnock portrays the loss of Jones' mother as the beginning of a series of losses Jones has to endure, always conjoining the geographical with the personal, and indicating that a spatial unsettling is never achieved without a personal unsettling, too. In the course of the play Claudia loses not only her mother, but also her childhood sweetheart Ben, her father, her friend Elizabeth, comrades from her political struggles, and a sense of 'home'. Arrested and repeatedly imprisoned in the United States for her involvement in communist politics and anti-American activities, she is eventually deported from the States, not to Trinidad as she had hoped (Trinidad rejects her) but to England. When her lawyer tells Claudia that 'England has agreed to accept you', Claudia articulates the hierarchical colonial relationship that informs that decision: 'Of course. Because Trinidad belongs to England and so, therefore, do I' (2, 12: 75).

Genderizing activism

Claudia may consider herself owned by England as part of its colonial legacy but she never belongs. The black community in Britain into which she moves in 1955 has its own contradictory agendas, legacies of experiences different from Claudia's. Her arrival immediately creates tensions. One of these tensions is gender-based – the fact that she as a woman has achieved a certain notoriety and fame as a political activist generates jealousies among some of the male activists in Britain. Ned, one of the characters in the play, serves to epitomize this attitude. His constant put-downs of his wife Dina and his sexist attitudes towards women in general are not only typical of the period but have also already been played out in previous scenes that took place in the States where part of the debate was also about the place of women in political struggle. Indeed, it was in part women's disillusionment with their sexist treatment by the Left and the various civil rights movements that helped to fuel second-wave feminism both in the USA and in the UK.[18] Claudia's social isolation is thus to some extent generated by her refusal to play a conventional gender role. That isolation also marks the position of rebellion Claudia inhabits and which distinguishes her from her parents' generation. After an encounter with the police, Paulsen, a friend of her father's, tries to explain to her the assimilationist position he and Claudia's father adopted:

People like your father and myself are very vulnerable. That's why it's so important for us to fit in. Why, I remember when my papers came through. Jumped for joy. Literally. Sarah and the girls thought I must have gone mad. But it meant so much to me, you see. I felt safe, like a baby all wrapped up in cotton wool. It was all written down. It couldn't be erased. I couldn't be erased. At last felt that I belonged.

(1, 6: 62)

The construction of the state as *in loco parentis*, as guarantor of an identity otherwise under threat and bereft of belonging, is matched by Claudia's father's pride in never having been in trouble with the law and in his faith, not shared by Claudia, in the church and in God. Claudia's assertion, 'Your God is a bigot, he hates blacks, jews and women' (1, 6: 63) mirrors her resistance to institutions and hierarchies organized by powerful men who will not allow change: 'I'll never accept that this is the way things are meant to be, that I have no power' (1, 6: 63). Claudia's 'will to power' is repeatedly interpreted as attention-seeking behaviour, and her early desire to be on stage, later realized through her political activism rather than through entertainment, feeds into a position, partially endorsed by this play, that Claudia was motivated by the wish to be a 'star'. The *entre-deux* between aspiration (political and personal) and reality (building platforms for alternative political positions whilst supporting black workers and trying to keep the peace among different factions of the black community) leaves no or little space for Claudia as a private individual to develop lasting relationships. As Thomas (1989) relates it, in her political work in Britain Jones 'was supported by friends and comrades, but the adjustment was difficult as Claudia had not been a "career politician" earning a fat salary. She was almost penniless. England was different in some vital respects from the US, it was even more difficult here for a Black woman to be accorded the due respect and authority, even within "the left"' (17). This is forcefully played out in the fourth scene of Act Two when Claudia arrives in Southampton Docks, lording, or rather lady-ing, it over the comrades who have come to welcome her without any sense of their financial impecunity or lack of resources. Her final lines of that scene, 'Bring my suitcase would you? There should be a trunk somewhere. Perhaps you could find it for me' (2, 14: 81), replicate the stance any white memsahib might have adopted towards the 'natives' of a colonial country she had come to grace with her presence. In her anxiety – as she later confesses – at arriving in a foreign land, she manifests the high-handed approach which anticipates the tensions between her and Ned that become increasingly problematic in the course of the second act, leading, *inter alia*, to an alienation between Ned and Dina, as Dina becomes Claudia's supporter and secretary.

Unsettled in her own identity, Claudia unsettles others. In so doing, albeit with costs to herself and others attached, she manages to achieve some changes, improve some people's lives, fight for what she believes in. But, as the play makes clear, the costs to Claudia for this are high. She remains and dies alone, her sole consoling image the memory of a moment with her mother when she was a child, the world seemed full of possibilities, and her dream was to be a dancer. It is this moment which both opens and closes the play, thus encapsulating the development of Claudia Jones' life in historical time with the monumental time that Julia Kristeva associates with the maternal. As in many other plays by Black women playwrights, the relation to the mother and the loss of that relation figure as key moments, forever fixed in the daughter's imaginary, in the unsettling of the daughter's identity.[19] It is this moment which is constructed as the driver of Claudia's desire to achieve change for exploited labourers; it is also what is viewed as being at the core of her identity, the moment which holds her – and the play – together. Against this monumental time is set the historical development of Claudia's life, signalled not only through the chronotopical representation of her life in the stage directions and the sequential telling of her life history, but also through the consecutive numbering of the play's scenes across the two acts that make up the play, effectively Claudia's life in the USA and her subsequent life in the UK respectively. This consecutive numbering of the scenes indicates the continuities in Claudia's life, the idea of a relentless continuity, rather than a 'before' and an 'after', or a beginning, a middle, and an end. Structurally, the play thus constitutes a circle with a line through it, suggesting that in the beginning, that childhood moment with the mother, lay also Claudia's end, her destiny to be unsettled between aspiration and reality.

One key idea related to this is the play's treatment of the notion of 'community'. The inter-generational differences in attitude depicted in her aspirations compared to her mother's and father's lives and views index a wider disparity between diverse individuals and groups of people right through the play. In almost every scene the conflict between those who accommodate and those who rebel is played out. The idea of 'community' as a homogeneous group experiencing similar oppressions and being fuelled by common goals is thus presented as an illusion; instead, the play makes it clear that communities themselves bear the marks of colonial violence which fracture their cohesiveness. 'Home' for all the characters in the play becomes, as Avtar Brah puts it, 'a mythic place of desire in the diasporic imagination. In this sense it is a place of no return, even if it is possible to visit the geographical territory that is seen as the place of "origin"' (1996: 192). In Claudia's case, 'home', that mythic place of desire, is simultaneously the memory of a certain moment in childhood and the memory of a geographical homeland, neither of which she can re-enter or retrieve except in the imagination. This is the reality, and the tragedy, of her situation.

In the past two decades many Black British women playwrights have sought to address the problematic of a diasporic existence, rather than the legacies of coloniality, in their work. This has several effects which indicate why their work has been consistently marginalized in the history of theatre studies, despite their work being taken up by prestigious institutions such as the Royal Court Theatre in London. Many of the playwrights point to the racialization of cultural forms. Zindika, for instance, made her heroine Leonora dream of being a ballet dancer 'to highlight the issue of stereotyping of black people in certain jobs, careers, artforms while others remain European-preserved' (76). When Leonora tells her Chinese lodger about her inability to get into the Royal Ballet, Melisa counters: 'Well perhaps you would have been more suited to modern dance. African. Jazz. Calypso . . . oh I love

calypso' (1, 3: 84). Such internalization of the racialization of art forms
articulates, I think, one reason why Black performance art has been
more successful in eliciting theoretico-critical attention than Black
women's work for theatre. However, not only is theatre as a high-
cultural form very much a white preserve; it is also noticeable that the
Black and usually male playwrights who have been successful within
it, such as Wole Soyinka, have done so in postcolonial terms, locating
their work over there rather than here, playing out colonial conflicts
and their legacies as opposed to articulating diasporic experience.[20]
Diaspora, however, forces us to attend to the here and now, making
dissociation difficult or at least more difficult than when contemplating the sins of the fathers committed abroad. That we continue to be
uncomfortable with facing up to the diaspora which is Britain today
is one aspect in the deep-rooted, fully institutionalized racism which
continues to permeate this country.

Identity crises

Kaahini (1997) is described by Maya Chowdhry as 'a passionate and
contemporary story about a young person facing adolescence and coming to terms with their self image and personal identity'. It predates –
by a number of years – the film *Bend It Like Beckham* (2002) which
also centres on an Indian girl who is football mad,[21] producing a culturally complicated narrative of dislocation and the unsettling of an
identity at the onset of puberty. The play, in some respects the product
of the rise of queer during the 1990s, explores the inter-relationship
of culture and gender. It consists of nineteen short scenes, detailing
the history of Anishaa and Neelendra who came to the UK when their
child Esha was born, having wed against their parents' wishes. Esha,
a biological girl, is brought up as a boy since Neelendra passionately
wanted a boy, and Anishaa found it initially easy to go along with Neelendra's self-deception regarding the sex of the child. Esha grows up
seemingly as a boy to be a competent footballer and wants to turn professional. Her close friend Farooq suspects nothing but notices, with
advancing adolescence, that Esha is not interested in girls. The onset
of Esha's period and the question of her sexual/relational as well as
educational future precipitate a crisis of identity for all members of

the family who have colluded in the deception that has made it impossible for Esha to inhabit her biological identity as girl. That crisis has several dimensions. It includes, for the parental generation, the question of where the family belongs. Anishaa is desperate to return to India and reminds Neelendra that they were originally only going to come for a limited period: 'Running away from our families, because of love, having to live here with all this racism. How do you think that made me feel? . . . You said five years at the most' (11: 28). For Neelendra India is the past which has become uninhabitable, partly because of the sacrifices involved in moving to Britain, which included the thwarting of Neelendra's own professional ambitions to work in a white-collar occupation in a bank rather than on the trains, and partly because of his assumption that his ambitions for his 'son' would be more easily realized in England. Neelendra's problematic investment in his son is articulated in the opening scene in which he and Anishaa seek help from a mystic to whom they tell a nightmare Neelendra has had. Here the play suggests the importance of the psychical or spiritual dimension in determining people's lives, for Neelendra's dream is 'real' enough for him to ask for interpretive help. The mystic appears to fulfil the function of the analyst, attempting to help Neelendra understand his unconscious. His reading of the dream metaphorically and, as is typical for Chowdhry's plays, lyrically, anticipates the events of the play as it unfolds. Neelendra's dream expresses the gender anxiety which will haunt the play:

> Well I dreamt, it felt like I was a . . . woman in the dream and I
> was about to give birth. I look down to see that my belly has
> split open, I can't feel any pain but I sense a rushing sensation
> and blood surges out like a huge wave, it seems like my whole
> self is draining away . . . Then I watch a buffalo leave my body
> from the same wound, it floats up into the air and I know it's
> my soul . . . Somehow I know it is lost and searching for its
> mother.
>
> (1: 1)

The mystic tells Neelendra: 'In the dream it is you who is the mother, this represents a part of yourself you cannot face, yet you are already a father' (1: 2). Esha has not been born at this stage but Anishaa is pregnant. The mystic also tells Neelendra: 'I see that you want a son for your own life to be fulfilled, it's as if you believe you must have a son in order to live' (1: 2). The mystic articulates the over-investment Neelendra has in male succession and in a certain idea of masculinity which Neelendra comes to enact by pretending that his daughter is a son, and bringing her up as such. Anishaa goes along with the pretence, and until the onset of Esha's puberty, the pretence remains seemingly unproblematic.

The arrival of Esha's period and her friend Farooq's increasing interest in girls finally forces the interrogation of Esha's gender identity. As her parents pretend she is a boy Esha is left to figure out her situation: 'I am their son. I act like a son, speak like a son, perform like a son . . . That's the answer, I suppose' (6: 12). *Kaahini* plays on the notion of gender as performance through indexing Esha's ability to inhabit what are supposed to be masculine roles, in particular in relation to playing sports and to defending herself and Farooq physically from racist attacks by other kids, and through Esha's eventual performance as a girl when she starts to wear kamiz and dhupatta, and is courted by Farooq who 'mistakes' Esha for an Asian girl and falls in love with her.

When Esha's physical femininity forces itself upon her consciousness, she is invited – both through her parents' denial of her biological sex and through her hitherto successful 'impersonation' of a boy – to make a choice regarding her gender identity. For a while she tries to inhabit both masculinity and femininity, thus reflecting her parents' division between Neelendra's desire for a boy and Anishaa's contentment with a girl. Anishaa, who becomes aware of this, attempts to force Esha to make a choice, which Esha counters with: 'I thought you wanted a daughter. Can't I be . . . a son for him and . . . your daughter?' (13: 36). The denial of this possibility is also the assertion of the need for a unitary gender identity which regards biological sex and gender-specific roles as mutually reinforcing and exclusionary. As a girl, Esha cannot play football; as a boy, she is not allowed to wear dresses. But Esha wants both. This desire comes undone when Farooq falls in love with her and Esha is forced to inhabit both her old male self and a new female one. She names herself 'Kaahini', and entices Farooq until his commitment to her forces her to reveal herself as Esha. In an attempt to secure Farooq's attachment before revealing herself as Esha, Kaahini asks Farooq what Farooq would choose if he had to decide between family and love, and friendship and love. Farooq typically and romantically answers 'love' but also says that 'Friendship is love, there's no choice, why?' (15: 48).

However, Esha's revelation of herself as a girl generates a crisis in Farooq whose gender certainties become confused by this revelation. Following a period of crisis Farooq and Esha are eventually reconciled as Esha tries to work through her identity. In the final scene she tells Farooq: 'Maybe I'm too much of a boy to ever really be a girl, I don't know, but the lie's over . . . You fell for the girl that I was trying to become or the boy I was, I don't know which' (19: 58). Esha recognizes that conventional gender attributions do not capture her identity. When Farooq counters her statements with 'she wasn't a proper girl, it was you dressed up', Esha responds, 'That's who I am, if you loved her then you loved me' (19: 58). The idea of the 'proper girl' is here disclosed as just that, an 'idea', based upon an assumed congruity between a biological essence and a culturally determined appearance that conjoins the two in an apparently seamless fashion. Much earlier, in Scene Eleven, Anishaa, attempting to get Neelendra to accept that Esha is a daughter, not a son, said: 'You just can't change nature' (11: 28), but the play raises the question of the nature of 'nature' and the cultural assumptions that underpin our idea of 'nature'. Esha herself reinforces the idea of the dominance of 'nature' or biological essence when she says, 'My body's caught up with me, things have changed' (13: 36) and when she tells Farooq: 'My body betrayed me, took over my dreams, became my dreams. All the time I had the answer inside, it was the question I was looking for' (19: 58). She says that she 'had to see if it was even possible for me to be a girl' (19: 58) and Farooq's initial admiration of her as a girl clearly showed her that it was or is possible for her to be a girl. But through several symbolic actions by Esha in the final scene such as kicking a football around wearing a kamiz and retrieving her train set as well as an Indian doll in a sari, and in a set of parallel lyrical sequences, Esha and

Neelendra affirm the flexibility of identity. Esha questions 'How do I remember/my childhood/now?/Do I have to/rewrite it,/edit out/the train-set/the football team?/It.', and 'Who/am /I/now?/Am I/a girl/in a boy's/personality?' (19: 55, 56). These questions are mirrored by Neelendra's parallel recognition that 'Worn out garments/are shed by the body,/worn-out bodies/are shed by the dweller/within the body,/new bodies are donned/by the dweller, like/garments.' This culminates in Esha's assertion: 'Beneath my skin/a woman has been/growing./What is this male /power/that slips so easily/with my mask/and becomes ashes' (19: 56).

Esha's assumption of femininity is not as straightforward as this last sequence suggests. Retaining her physical prowess, and gradually understanding that she is both Esha and Kaahini, her final line to Farooq as he holds and kisses her is: 'You don't even know me' (19: 59). Nonetheless, the play's narrative suggests a sequential unfolding of identity in which adulthood succeeds childhood and womanhood succeeds, performatively, both boyhood and girlhood. The narrative thus replicates Neelendra's dream of being mother as well as father, of needing to come to terms with the fluidity of both masculinity and femininity.

Through its happy ending, that is both Neelendra's acceptance of Esha's girlhood and his attempts to plead with Farooq on Esha's behalf, and through Farooq's embrace of Esha, the play constitutes something of a romantic comedy which, in Shakespearean fashion, assures the temporality and provisionality of identities seemingly or actually mistaken, and reinstated at the end. However, the situating of this romantic comedy in an Indian context marks this play as both of the very recent past and as exceptional since the playing with gender that it entails is both still very much taboo in South Asian cultures and at the same time has become more prominent in recent theatre work by second-generation migrants in Britain.[22] This issue will be further explored in chapter six. Here, however, it should be noted that coincidentally with the rise of queer and the mainstreaming of homosexuality from the mid-1980s onwards, second- and third-generation migrants raised the question of gender identity as part of the general debate about identity that diaspora entails. The seeming threat to conventional gender roles that questioning gender attribution signals is augmented in a context where identities are threatened in multiple ways including through racism, the erosion of socio-cultural patterns that have been diasporized, and the consequent unsettling of notions of belonging. One might argue that the very fact of Neelendra's dream and that he seeks help from a mystic at the opening of the play is indicative of his potential openness to 'otherness', both from without and from within. It is upon this openness that the redemption of his relationship with Esha is grounded and the resolution of the play's crisis secured. The affirmation of the feminine, Neelendra's admission of his lost soul seeking its mother and Esha's coming to femininity, is the key principle which structures the play and drives its narrative. This is signalled in the play through the lyricism that accompanies moments of crisis and resolution, and through the completion of Neelendra's dream in Esha's later dream in which she kills the father and absorbs him into her by eating him (14: 40). This process of simultaneous feminizing through encorporation of the masculine and absorption of the masculine into the feminine creates less a sense of identity as androgynous than a sense of identity in process, rather like the successive shedding of bodies referred to in Neelendra's lyrical sequence in Scene Nineteen. Esha's assertion of her unknowability as the final line of the play reinforces that continuing gender ambiguity which defies nature as well as culture.

5   Culture clashes

In 1978 Amrit Wilson published *Finding a Voice: Asian Women in Britain*. Wilson's book remains a key document in detailing Asian women's lives in Britain, particularly for the period from the end of the Second World War to the 1970s. It highlights the diverse migratory paths that brought Asian women from diverse Asian communities to Britain, thus indicating the inadequacy of the term 'Asian' to do justice to peoples with very different religious, linguistic, sociocultural, and economic histories, homogenizing them as it does under the banner 'Asian'. Wilson interviewed a range of Asian women of diverse ages, backgrounds, and migratory histories, including women who were born in Britain. She argues that, their diverse backgrounds notwithstanding, Asian women in Britain share three things: their oppression as women, their experiences of racism within Britain, and their exploitation as a class of workers (168).

Family and community

One of the key experiences articulated by the women Wilson interviewed was the culture clashes they experienced in coming to Britain and living in Britain. These culture clashes were in part a function of the radically different socio-cultural norms governing British society compared to their various own ones. Chief among these differences was the importance placed on collectivism, the family, and community among many Asian cultures compared to the emphasis on individualism and self-determination in British culture. Linked to the central role of family and community among Asian cultures are the notions of *izzat* (honour) and *sharam* (shame) for which there are no equivalents in British culture. One of the major sites where these differences

138

are played out is marriage, and the plays discussed in this chapter all centre on marriages and issues arising from them that are driven by the values placed on the family, community, *izzat*, and *sharam*.

An important difference between many Asian cultures and the British one is the emphasis on collectivism versus individualism (Ghuman 1999). Collectivism points to the overriding importance attached to a person's role within the family, the kinship structure, and the community whose honour and standing is of greater importance than the desires of the individuals which 'Asians tend to equate . . . with selfishness' (Ghuman 24). Within collectivist structures, 'Marriage [is] a family concern, not a private matter between man and wife' (Ghuman 24) and 'The overwhelming majority of the first generation had their marriages arranged by their parents or "go-betweens"' (Ghuman 25). One of the key sites of cultural difference is thus the issue of marriage. Wilson vividly describes how women inhabit a key position as bearers of cultural values within these structures. She argues that their lives are governed by three concepts, 'the male ego whose nurturing, preserving and boosting is considered of vital importance' (30) and which, in Muslim communities, is linked to *izzat*, male family identity and honour; 'a sense of hierarchy . . . synonymous with the existence of the family; and finally the closeness of relationships' (30). All three concepts, which in their most intense versions diverge significantly from British sociocultural norms, contribute to the culture clashes to which Asian women in Britain are exposed and which involve questions such as what a woman can or should wear, how she should conduct herself outside and inside the home, what kind of and level of education she should have, whether or not she should work, how she should form relationships. All of these issues are central to the plays discussed in this chapter, in which contemporary women playwrights explore the culture clashes that shape Asian women's lives in Britain.

'Heartgame' (1988), devised ten years after Wilson's pioneering text, resembles that text most closely of the three plays considered here, since it is based on stories told by young Bangladeshi women who 'had been born in rural Bangladesh and had come to Britain to escape flooding and poverty' (Cooper 1990: 103). It is thus a play devised by first-generation migrant women who came to the UK either as children or as young adults during the late 1970s and early 1980s. One of the interesting aspects of this play is that it arose out of a collaboration between a white woman playwright, Mary Cooper, and the Leeds Bengali Women's Drama Group.[1] Cooper details this collaborative process very vividly, suggesting that its origin was the use of drama 'to increase the personal confidence and language skills of the young women' who had already devised one play and now wanted to write 'a play about romance' (103). Asked to tell the playwright 'about the kind of marriages they would expect to have' as a way of getting into the subject, the Bengali women produced an account of 'the perfect Muslim arranged marriage' which, however, 'was not what they understood by romance. Romance was as rule-governed as marriage but it was exciting, secret, forbidden and chaste' (103). Out of a series of workshops 'Heartgame' eventually emerged, and, like the other plays discussed in this chapter, one might argue that it belongs to the category of the issue-based play which dominated feminist theatre in the 1980s and for part of the early 1990s. It is the case that a number of devices are employed that disrupt the linearity of both time and space, such as the intercutting of scenes to foreground the simultaneity of actions taking place in different locations at the same time and the repetition of the opening scene as the final scene. However, the dominant theatrical mode is (in keeping with the construction of many issue-based plays) realist, signalling its relation to a material reality that is explored within the play. The play is thus in many respects very much of its period. It also bears traces of an oral tradition through the use of story-telling and metadiscursive intervention as a device to comment on the dramatic narrative and move it on.

Romance versus marriage

The issue at stake in 'Heartgame' is the issue of romance and marriage within the Muslim community. Reeta, one of the protagonists, is attracted to Raju. Born in Bangladesh but brought up in Britain since the age of seven, Reeta has to negotiate the contradictory demands of her Muslim background and the British context in which she lives.

Wilson, emphasizing the preeminence of males in Asian communities, describes an Asian woman's position within her own community as follows: 'Her birth is almost invariably a disappointment to her family . . . She often becomes very close to her parents, particularly her mother . . . If a Muslim, she usually marries a cousin who lives in the same village' (4). *Izzat*, the male-centred family honour, is maintained by ensuring that women wear traditional dress, do not engage with boys after the age of twelve, and have a limited education since the expectation is that girls will stay at home, most probably living within the extended family of the husband once married, and do housework. Since family honour and status hinges, *inter alia*, upon an appropriate marriage, endangering one's marital prospects through behaviour that brings shame on the family such as associating with boys, wearing inappropriate clothing etc., is considered a major concern for the family and the community. In Soraya Jinton's *An Arranged Marriage*, for instance, Lalita, the central character who is trying to avoid an arranged marriage, tells her friend Leander: 'if the boy agrees to the marriage and I refuse then the rest of the community will think my parents have insulted the other family by turning them down' (4: 7).

Knowledge of such behaviour is spread through gossip, and fear of gossip is thus extensive. The power of gossip is demonstrated in 'Heartgame' through the escalation of a rumour about Raju which begins with the assertion that he and his friends were causing trouble in the park and ends with Raju's father being asked, 'Is it true that your son's charged with assaulting a young woman in the park?' (3: 51). Despite the untruth of this rumour, Raju's father tells Raju, 'True or not, they are all talking about it. It's ruined any chance of finding you a wife here. We've booked tickets for next week. We fly from Heathrow on Monday' (3: 52–3). Gossip here becomes the motivator for enforcing the swift imposition of a suitable marriage upon the boy, demonstrating both that women and men are viewed as equally implicated in the upholding of family honour, and that both genders are expected to submit to the law of the parents and the community which acts as a regulator of the individual's behaviour.[2] The phrase 'finding you a wife' as opposed to 'you finding a wife' indexes the role of the parents and the community in determining key relationships in individuals' lives to which, despite some protest, both Raju and Reeta, as well as the third character, Anju, ultimately submit.

Whilst Reeta and Raju supposedly secretly meet in the park, and through those meetings flout the rules of their community regarding courtship, Anju, Raju's cousin, is shown, in intercutting scenes during Scene Two, as living as the family drudge 'in a small village in the Sylhet region of Bangladesh' (2: 37), helping her mother with the household chores that include doing all the housework generated by her four brothers as well as the father. Here the gender inequality that Wilson highlights in *Finding a Voice* and which is based on strict gender segregation and the gendered division of labour becomes only too visible. Anju's life contrasts significantly with Reeta's who has much more freedom than – and not as many brothers as – Anju has. That difference reveals Reeta's family's adjustment to life in Britain where girls in general enjoy greater freedom than Muslim communities would normally allow their women. However, even though Reeta has more freedom than Anju, she is intensely aware of the problem of lying to her parents about her whereabouts so that she can meet Raju. It poses a significant dilemma for her: 'It's not as if I'm messing about with all the boys. That would be wrong. The Prophet says it's right to love one man if he's good. And Raju is good. But it's wrong to lie. How can something be right and wrong at the same time? I know I should tell Mum' (2: 37). Reeta does not know how to reconcile her romantic longings with her family's expectations regarding her behaviour and decides in favour of subterfuge and clandestine meetings. When these meetings are observed, her relationship with Raju unravels as he is sent back to Bangladesh to be married off to his cousin Anju. Once Reeta's mother discovers the locket Raju has given to Reeta and confronts her about it, a moment of possibility opens up as Reeta's mother tells her that if Raju proposes marriage in the conventional way, she will not object: 'Well, if his family contact us I won't raise any objections' (11: 87). But this good news comes too late since Raju has already been taken to Bangladesh and returns to Britain as a married man. In a heart-breaking scene, Reeta has to discover this, and face the alternative to marriage with Raju, namely marriage to 'this creep from Dhaka' (13: 96) as she describes the man her parents have chosen for her should Raju's family not ask for her.

One of the most interesting points that emerges in this scene, as Reeta learns that Raju is married to his cousin and now cannot marry her, is the way in which Reeta is shown to be much more romantically or emotionally invested in their relationship than Raju.[3] Raju's explanations of his actions, including his failure to tell Reeta that he was being sent back to Bangladesh to marry, show a refusal to accept any responsibility for his behaviour. Very much still a lad, and in many respects immature,[4] he tells Reeta that 'it was all arranged' – note the passive voice used here – and that he never promised her anything (13: 97), that his parents wanted matters settled quickly (13: 97), and that he thought she wanted to continue at college rather than get married – the two being constructed as mutually exclusive – (13: 98), culminating in his assertion that 'There's nothing I can do about it' (13: 98).

Reeta's mistaken emotional over-investment in Raju compared with Raju's own emotional under-investment in their relationship had already been signalled previously in Scene Two when Raju was late for a clandestine meeting which was difficult for Reeta to arrange because of the greater degree of surveillance exercised over her as a girl than over Raju as a boy. Raju was late because a mate of his brought a video which they watched and which developed a fault. This excuse for being late, indicative of the male-centred culture which Raju inhabits, is balanced in this early scene by his gift of the locket, a gift which is a double-edged sword for Reeta since she is both meant to wear it to demonstrate her affection for Raju and has to hide it so as not to betray her meetings with Raju to her parents. It is, of course, through the locket that her mother eventually discovers Reeta's relationship with Raju. But the locket does not mean what it seems to signify – when Reeta confronts Raju in Scene Thirteen with 'But you gave me this. *(The locket.)* I thought you . . .', he quickly counters her with 'I never promised you anything' (13: 97), thus demonstrating precisely the worthlessness of romance, its meaninglessness from a male perspective.

This is also indexed in his relationship with Anju. She, like Reeta, over-invests emotionally in Raju because 'No one had ever told her and certainly no one had ever asked her but she knew that everyone had always hoped she would marry Raju' (4: 56). The expectation of this marriage leads Anju to fantasize about Raju, 'And though Anju had never met Raju she had confided all her secrets to him in the long conversations she had with him at night alone in bed' (4: 58). She has seen a photo of him but because 'he was running . . . the picture was blurred' (4: 58), a metaphoric reference to the fact that Anju's image of Raju is blurred and inaccurate. Although he is good-looking and comes from Britain, the country of which Anju dreams, 'living in London with a washing machine' (5: 63),[5] this dream is exploded when Raju, who does not really want to marry, repulses Anju and treats her in a casual and nonchalant manner which clearly expresses his lack of interest in and emotional attachment to her. Significantly, she has to learn that both the place where they will live (Leeds, not London) and the washing-machine (although present in the household, it is broken) are not what she imagined.

The blurred image, the broken washing-machine, and the geo-social dislocation Anju has to contend with all become emblematic of the fracturing of her romantic fantasies about the man she was going to marry. Instead, Anju finds herself continuing in the role of family drudge she had in her village in Sylhet. As her sister-in-law tells her about her mother-in-law: 'She's got no daughters so she's looking forward to having a daughter-in-law to help her out. I told her you were very hard-working' (6: 65). In addition, Raju rejects her: 'Last night he went to sleep on the floor. So I took some blankets and joined him. My mother-in-law says he's not used to having a wife. He's nervous. She tells me to flatter him, to wear clothes he likes, take an interest in cricket. But cricket's so boring and how am I supposed to know what clothes he likes?' (12: 90).

The intimacy with Raju which Anju conjured up in her fantasies about him dissolves as Raju, very much still 'the lad', sees his life as a male in the Bengali community confirmed. Made a partner in his father's restaurant and given a car as part of his new status as a married man, Raju continues to do as he pleases, unconcerned by the emotional deficits that agonize Anju, and expecting her to conform with their community's gendered role prescriptions. When Anju, in an effort to please him, and following but misunderstanding his mother's advice, dresses in western clothes (mini skirt and high heels), Raju is horri-fied: 'I don't want my wife to look like that. Nor would my mum. She'd kill you' (13: 94). Raju, it transpires, wants a traditional wife. To both Anju and Reeta he maintains that his decisions are gov-erned by what his mother wants. Thus he says to Reeta: 'She wants someone who could bring up the children to speak Bengali' (13: 94). Through his marriage Raju has become inserted into the male order of the Bengali community and he acts in accordance with its socio-cultural rules. These accord young women no importance beyond that of bearing children and being domestic drudges, servicing male needs and leaving no room for any form of romantic fantasy or desire. For women, any respect is only achieved at a later stage when daughters-in-law arrive in the household and take on the lowest positions within that household, thus affording the mother-in-law some power and status.[6]

Significantly, the play does not advocate either arranged mar-riages or love trysts as preferable for women. Instead, it focuses on the discrepancy between the romantic investment young women make in their relationships and the lack of emotional investment men have in these relationships. It suggests that in Bengali culture, as constituted in this play, options regarding relationships are limited for both men and women, and usually agreed through family arrangements.[7] How-ever, a man's public life and relationship with his male peers in his community is much more significant in his life than his relationship with his wife. For the women neither clandestine love relationships nor arranged marriages provide the emotional contentment they de-sire. Their freedom is severely curtailed, and their emotional wellbe-ing depends to some extent on the relationships they can build with other women in their households and communities. In cases where an arranged marriage does not work out, women are shown to come off worse than men. Raju's new status as a married male does not im-pact on his general behaviour (he agrees to meet Reeta secretly, for instance, and is only forced by her suggestion of marriage to reveal his now married status). Instead, he is given material rewards (a car and a partnership in his father's restaurant) to affirm his enhanced status in the male order. In contrast, the play makes very clear that marriage for the women means submission to a partner who is not emotionally attached to them and subjection within the household of the in-laws – the scenes in Leeds once Raju and Anju have returned from Bangladesh are punctuated by constant requests that Anju do household chores of various kinds and by her mother-in-law telling her that it is her role to please her husband. One has to assume that the same kind of life is in store for Reeta once she marries 'this creep from Dhaka' (14: 96) her parents have chosen for her.

The play offers a particular kind of intervention in the debate about arranged and forced marriages as it has occurred in the UK over the period since the 1970s.[8] That debate has been framed by British representations of arranged marriages among South Asians as economically opportunistic and driven by the desire to enable immigration into Britain from South Asian countries,[9] as frequently 'forced upon' women (which it no doubt sometimes is),[10] and as antithetical to the gender equality, individual autonomy and self-determination, freedom of choice, and liberalism that supposedly govern British culture. As Brah (1997) suggests: 'Many of the contemporary academic, political and popular discourses on Asian women . . . present them as "docile" and "passive" victims, both of archaic "traditional" customs and practices, and of domineering Asian men' (74). Her empirical research showed that the great majority of the Asian adolescents she interviewed expected their marriages to be arranged and that 'many adolescents said they were confident that they would not be forced into a marriage that they did not want' (77). The high rate of divorce among the white British population which suggests that 'love marriages' are not particularly successful unions was noted as a reason for not having more faith in that process than in arranged marriages.

'Heartgame' constructs Raju, Reeta, and Anju as having some say in the choice of their marriage partner, but that choice is curtailed, in Raju and Reeta's case, by the threat of scandal arising from rumours about Raju's behaviour on the one hand, and the detection of Reeta's friendship with Raju on the other. When Reeta's mother finds out about that friendship she says to her daughter: 'Do you want to bring disgrace on the whole family? Because that's what you have done' (11: 85). Here the family and in addition in Raju's case the community become the cornerstones of decisions made about both Reeta and Raju, namely that they each should be married, that they must choose a marriage partner. Importantly, they are not told whom to choose. Both Reeta and Raju agree to this process as a way of appeasing their families and in order to remain respectable within the socio-cultural order of their community. The play thus offers a commentary on the difference between a culture in which family and community are vital to the position of the individual, and collectivism is more important than individual desire, and another culture, the British one, in which neither family nor community can exercise significant direct powers in forcing a moment of marriage.[11] The clash between those socio-cultural expectations and prescriptions is not resolved through the celebration of one form of relationship (love marriage or arranged marriage) being constructed as privileged. The play thus confounds conventional British attitudes that suggest the preferability of the love match. Instead, the play places the two female protagonists Reeta and Anju literally and metaphorically in the same position – at the beginning and the end of the play. The opening and the closing scene, the latter a direct replication of the former, show Reeta and Anju together, waiting at a bus stop and talking to each other. Through telling each other about their situation they come to realize that they 'share' Raju and, indeed, the dilemma of a difficult relationship. One could argue that the structure of the play, its circularity as suggested by the fact that in its beginning lies its end, signals at a metaphorical level not only the similarity of the young women's positions but also the entrapment that that position – marriage to a male who is emotionally underinvested in his relationship – entails. Against that reading might be set the fact that both are going to college and attending courses, Anju determined to create opportunities for herself within British society to secure her marriage, and Reeta trying to fend off the moment of her own marriage. They are positioned outside – outside the home, on the road, on the move. A positive reading of this ending might argue that they are caught in a moment of opportunity, however uncertain their fates beyond that moment might be.

Language and diasporic space

One of the most interesting aspects of 'Heartgame' is its deployment of both English and Bengali. This is a deployment of bilingualism seldom seen in play text publications in Britain. In her afterword to the play Cooper explained that her own complete lack of Bengali and the diverse levels of English-language competence among the young women of the Leeds Bengali Women's Drama Group made bilingualism a necessity. During its rehearsed reading at the Writers' First Festival at the Sheffield Crucible Theatre in June 1988, 'some characters [spoke] almost entirely in English and others almost entirely in Bengali' (104). However, since bilingual audiences are rare (the vast majority of white British theatre-goers speak no South Asian languages and not all audiences will know English), Cooper in her final version opted for 'a highly artificial, but totally comprehensible, seamless mix of English and Bengali' (104). This move puts Bengali into a cultural frame from which that language is often excluded, namely British theatre, a form of 'high art/culture' which has a long history of monoculturalism and of homogenizing cultural expression within a particular western[12] paradigm. The insertion of Bengali into the published text of the play, an insertion that confronts white British readers with symbolic structures which they are unlikely to be familiar with, encourages the reader to recognize other cultures operating within and beyond English, not as discrete, hyphened-off entities, but as integral parts of the fabric of British culture.

More importantly, Cooper's assertion of a 'totally comprehensible, seamless mix' signals to readers of the text as much as to the theatre-going audience of the play that Bengali, and all that goes with that language, is not the expression of something that is utterly alien and incomprehensible but rather a language that exists as an integral and intricate part of British culture. It gestures towards the comprehensibility of Bengali and Bengali culture and thus exceeds those constraints that impose radical difference as the only means of understanding diasporic cultures. Thus, as Gilbert and Tompkins put it, 'the linguistic authority arrogated by English for centuries no longer prevails automatically' (1996: 172); instead, the possibility of the democratization of the linguistic space, written as well as oral, is opened up. 'Heartgame' thus reflects the 'linguistic displacements as well as physical and cultural dislocations' (Gilbert and Tompkins 173) that migration commonly involves – Anju's and Reeta's exchange at the bus stop bears powerful testimony to that – and the possibility of disrupting monolithic linguistic spaces in favour of a sharing of that space, both literally and metaphorically.[13] Anju and Reeta both find themselves at the same bus stop, going to the same college, 'sharing' the same man, sharing similar socio-cultural experiences which involve, *inter alia*, negotiating the same socio-cultural space. Their intermingling of English and Bengali, as Reeta tries to help Anju find the right English words to ask for a return bus ticket, foregrounds the co-existence of the languages as much as the characters within one geosocial frame. It invites the audience to share that recognition. It also invites the audience to recognize the dilemma Reeta and Anju face as they come to understand the similarity of their position.

Difference unto death

That dilemma – a culture clash which leads to women's subjection within marriage – is made even more forcefully explicit in Rukhsana Ahmad's 'Song for a Sanctuary' (1990), written, according to Ahmad, 'partly in response to the murder of an Asian woman at a refuge' (in George 1993: 159) and toured nationally in 1991. The murder referred to was that of Balwant Kaur, 'a young Asian woman and mother of three' (Southall Black Sisters 1992: 314) who was killed in Brent Asian Women's refuge on 22 October 1985.[14] Ahmad states that 'Song for a Sanctuary' is not 'a documentary or a biographical play' (159), but the broad outline of the play's narrative corresponds to Balwant Kaur's case. Kaur had come to the refuge in July 1985, following eight years of severe abuse from her husband. He tracked her down at the refuge and went there with two other men to murder her. When his accomplices realized that he had murder in mind (rather than burglary as initially asserted) they deserted him and warned Kaur of her husband's intentions. The refuge informed the police who came to talk to the

Plate 9 Joanna Bacon as Eileen and Sayan Akkadas as Kamla in Kali Theatre Company's 1990 production of 'Song for a Sanctuary'.

residents but did nothing further by way of protection. Several days later Kaur's husband returned to the refuge and stabbed her to death in front of their children.[15] Ahmad's play elaborates this skeleton of Balwant Kaur's history into a complex engagement with cross-cultural and gender differences. 'Song for a Sanctuary' – the elegiac title of the play foreshadowing the death of Rajinder Basi, Kaur's counterpart in the play – is set in a refuge and in Rajinder's home. Anticipating Rajinder's death, the three-act play has fewer and fewer scenes in each act as Rajinder's time runs out: the first act contains seven scenes, the second act has five scenes, and the last act has only three scenes. The effect is an acceleration in intensity of action and revelation, culminating, in the final scene, in Rajinder's murder.

Ahmad structures the socio-cultural clashes she explores in the play through juxtaposing two sets of characters in the refuge whose differences and similarities are explored: the refuge workers Eileen and Kamla (plate 9), and two of the women who are clients of the refuge: Sonia and Rajinder. These pairings, functioning as both mirrors and opposites to each other, reveal inter- as well as intra-cultural differences among the women as they portray issues of class, professionalism, and socio-cultural attitudes that impact upon relations within and across diverse backgrounds. They suggest that any assumed homogeneity based on ideas of affinity born of class, ethnic, gender, or professional affiliations is at best temporary and provisional but more likely a fiction. The play thus emphasizes both the specificity of every individual's situation and, through the tragic unfolding of its narrative, the necessity of understanding those specificities within the broader framework of the need for support which transcends that individuality. The play suggests that there are no easy alliances but that some form of accommodation of individual needs is required to afford all the women involved the protection and help they require.

The opening scene shows Rajinder settling into the refuge. She is a middle-class, Punjabi-speaking, Muslim Pakistani woman who has come to the refuge with her three children, following violence and abuse from her husband. Like Sonia, another client in the refuge who is white and working class, able to articulate the pattern of her relationship with her abusive partner Gary but unable to leave him, Rajinder has tried to leave her husband before but returned. Eileen, one of the workers in the refuge, also came to the refuge as a battered wife, and broke free from her abusive marriage following several attempts to leave her husband. All three women thus present a pattern typical for domestic violence of cycles of abuse, repeated attempts to break free, and often inadequate support from the authorities to allow the women to change their lives.[16] But whereas Eileen and Sonia are able to talk about their experiences of abuse, Rajinder is not. Her refusal to articulate and acknowledge publicly what has happened to her, which meets powerful disapproval from the 'Indian' worker Kamla, is a function of her commitment to her cultural background. She has a strong sense of *izzat* (honour) and *sharam* (shame) both of which function to control women's behaviour and sexuality. As Southall Black Sisters note: 'The notions of *izzat* and *sharam* are all pervasive amongst Asian families, irrespective of religion, caste and class' (1997: 22). If women fail to uphold the honour of their family and bring shame on it, 'they are deemed to have broken ranks with their family, and to have brought the entire family, and even their caste group or whole community, *samaj* or *biradri* into disrepute and shame . . . Because Asian communities are so close-knit, the concepts of honour and shame take on extra significance. The control of women is dependent on consensus and the collusion of the entire community in reinforcing and policing them' (Southall Black Sisters 1997: 23).

This is made evident in 'Song for a Sanctuary'. Rajinder has fully internalized her community's prescriptions of honour and shame which include, as a consequence, the notion that 'Where I come from we deal with things within the family' (3, 1: 182). Having come to the refuge already constitutes a major break with that position, and is indicative of quite how awful things must be in her home. But the workers, especially Kamla, fail to read her arrival in those terms since they themselves are not familiar with and do not subscribe to either *izzat* or *sharam*. They are thus immune to their meaning and the force they exert over Rajinder. Having come to the refuge, Rajinder is unable to acknowledge verbally and publicly what has been going on at home because she understands that to do so would be to bring dishonour to her family. Both the articulation of problems *per se* and any involvement of external authorities in such problems amount to publicizing these problems and constitute a form of dishonour. Women are expected to be silent about any domestic problems – the failure to do so, to violate the sanctity of home, family, and community, is constructed as shameful.

However, in a pivotal scene in Act One, the play also shows that dealing with things within the family means precisely, as Southall Black Sisters assert, sacrificing the individual to an ideology of honour and shame which makes women the scapegoats and victims of men's unacceptable behaviour. Act One, Scene Six shows Rajinder discussing her plight with her older sister Amrit. This reveals that Amrit, who completely identifies with the socio-cultural values of her family and community, is correspondingly unsympathetic to Rajinder's plight, showing why, ultimately, these 'things' cannot be dealt with within the family. Amrit does not want Rajinder to leave her violent husband since this will bring dishonour to the family. She interprets Rajinder's desire to leave as a form of 'western selfishness' which will impact on her daughters: 'Your selfishness will ruin your daughters, I can tell you that. They'll learn all the self-indulgent, sick ways of the West' (1, 6: 171). When Rajinder desperately asks her: 'Would you rather I set myself alight in my back garden?', Amrit answers: 'Honour is always preferable to disgrace, but the choice of course is yours' (1, 6: 171). The cruelty of this response highlights the problematic of women's collusion in ideological structures that serve to subjugate them, even unto death. Amrit is willing to see her sister sacrificed to the upholding of a spurious family honour which, as the play shows, utterly despicable actions – when carried out by a male – seemingly cannot undermine.

In terms of Rajinder's conduct within the play, it is Amrit's attitude and the force of the notions of *izzat* and *sharam* which help to explain why she refuses to discuss the physical and sexual abuse she has suffered at the hands of her husband, and why she refuses to involve the authorities even when she has finally been forced to acknowledge that her husband sexually abused their daughter Savita. To Kamla she explains her position by stating that 'the circumstances in which you have to make [choices] are often beyond your control. Like birth, or death' (2, 1: 174). The use of these similes which naturalize life choices into a quasi-biological cycle of life and death as beyond individual control articulates Rajinder's attempt to uphold some sense of commitment to her community's values despite having been served so badly by them. When Kamla attempts to involve the authorities in dealing with Savita's abuse, Rajinder resolutely refuses to allow it, saying: 'I'd like to avoid a scandal. She's got to marry one day. But then you don't know what it is to live within the community' (3, 1: 182). Rajinder tries to protect her daughter's honour in what is already an untenable situation.[17] Kamla tries to suggest to her that it is precisely 'the "privatization" of women's lives which keeps us from seeing domestic violence in a socio-political context' and that her 'story is common enough . . . It's part of a pattern of how men have used women over the years' (2, 1: 175).

Rajinder, however, is to her cost not ready to see this. Immersed as she is in the cultural values of her community, she attempts to uphold and maintain what she can of its prescriptions. She sees her children's future as firmly embedded within the community they are now at odds with and all the way through the play maintains a sense of pride in the cultural identity and values that have contributed so significantly to her misery. Thus she tries to maintain an illusion of difference between herself and her family and the other inhabitants of the refuge. She is appalled by the lack of hygiene in the refuge and by other clients' failure to respect the need to keep a kosher or hallal kitchen, i.e. separating meat and dairy products. Viewing her own habits as superior, she refuses to allow her children to be exposed to western mass media such as TV and cinema because, as she puts it, 'I'd like my children to grow up with some sense of who they are. We're different' (1, 5: 171).

Rajinder seeks to distinguish herself both from Sonia, the white working-class fellow client in the refuge who – trying to earn some money – compromises the refuge by bringing a male punter back for the purposes of prostitution, and from Kamla, the 'Indian' refuge worker (compare Kamla's and Rajinder's self-presentations in plates 9 and 10). However, as Savita tries to disclose to her mother that she has been sexually abused by her father and that she understands the abuse he has meted out to her mother, she tells Rajinder that Sonia is 'a hooker' who is 'not ashamed of it' and 'is in charge of her body' whilst 'Housewives sell their bodies too, you know. Only it's to one man . . . and they have no control over . . . their . . . bodies' (2, 2: 176). Rajinder, shocked by this analysis, hits her daughter but is also forced into confronting the parallels between her own and Sonia's situation.

The class and cultural differences Rajinder is initially able to activate in her desire to distinguish herself from Sonia do not pertain in the same way in the difference she attempts to assert between herself and Kamla. Kamla is mixed-raced and comes from a poor background but has turned herself into a professional woman with a political agenda which dissociates her from her 'Indian' background.[18] Unmarried, she is an independent, assertive woman, unfazed by the demands of any particular Indian cultural heritage. Her inability to speak Punjabi or any other Indian language proficiently sets her apart from Rajinder, as do the values she holds. Within the context of the refuge she constitutes a particular moment in the refuge movement, different from Eileen, the white worker who herself initially came to the refuge as a client and has been there for eleven years. Both

Plate 10 Simon Nagra as Pradeep and Kusum Haider as Rajinder in Kali Theatre Company's 1990 production of 'Song for a Sanctuary'.

Kamla and Eileen are paid workers at the refuge. But Eileen is typical of the initial stages of the refuge movement in Britain, inaugurated by Chiswick Women's Aid which was founded by Erin Pizzey in 1971.[19]

Herself a victim/survivor, taken on because of her commitment to the cause, Eileen is an older worker who has not only herself had the experience of domestic violence, which makes her sympathetic towards other women with similar experiences, but who has also done the work for many years and is more tolerant than Kamla is. Eileen tries to see things from the clients' viewpoints. She is not interested in imposing her views on them. She is constructed as the mediating figure within the refuge and the play. She is willing to 'bend' the rules for the clients to accommodate them and thinks they need empowerment rather than 'telling'. Eileen does not expect much by way of change and is therefore relaxed about cases like Sonia's where a client keeps going back and forth between the refuge and an abusive partner. Although she herself managed to break free from her abusive partner she does not expect all other abused women to be able to do so. Kamla, by contrast, does not have any experience of domestic violence herself and is anxious to achieve change for women. She does so from a position of 'knowing what's best'. Full of prejudice and stereotypes – she takes some convincing that Rajinder needs help, for example, since she mistakenly reads Rajinder's failure to show distress and her middle-class appearance as signs of her immunity from domestic violence – Kamla has the interests of her clients at heart but she is rule-bound, authoritarian, overly assertive, and insensitive to Rajinder's cultural needs. In consequence Rajinder finds Eileen easier to talk to than Kamla, and any assumption of affinity based on a shared cultural background is called into question by the play. As Kamla, during one of her altercations with Rajinder when Rajinder puts her Asianness in question, says to her: 'You can't deny me my identity. I won't let you. You people with your saris and your bloody lingo and all your certainties about the universe, you don't have a monopoly on being Asian. You can't box it in and contain it and exclude others. I'll define myself as I bloody well want to' (3, 1: 183).

The juxtaposition of Rajinder and Kamla reveals identity as dynamic and changing. Kamla's version of Asianness is radically different from Rajinder's. Kamla's identity is bound up with her appearance, and thus not entirely a matter of choice but also of attribution. In addition, within her imaginary, Kamla's identity is also bound up with a particular collective and personal historical past. Early on she explains to Rajinder: 'This language thing . . . it looks like an inadequacy and it isn't. Names are all they had left to them, in the Caribbean; to keep the languages going seemed a bit pointless in the end.' Kamla thus reveals that her diasporic history is different from Rajinder's since she is not from India but came to Britain from the Caribbean. She tells Rajinder: 'They struggled to make us Indian, in some sense. But it was hard; there probably isn't a lot we have in common' (1, 1: 163). This statement bespeaks the multiple histories of displacement and dispossession which shape the trajectories of some diasporic people[20] and simultaneously indicts the homogenization of 'Asians' under a unitary racial and/or ethnic banner which fails to take account of the diversity which is diaspora. It also articulates the reason for the differences between Kamla and Rajinder. 'The question of "where you're from" [here] threatens to overwhelm the reality of "where you're at"' (Ang 2001: 34); both Kamla and Rajinder in their different ways experience 'the idea of diaspora . . . [as] a disempowering rather than an empowering one, a hindrance to "identity" rather than an enabling principle' (Ang 34). Kamla registers some nostalgia for the culturally specific things of her childhood such as how to store 'good shawls', Indian songs, and Kathak dancing, but she dismisses this nostalgia with 'it was no use to me. Who cares for all that crap anyway?' (1, 1: 164). Her fractured relation to her history leads her to be unsympathetic to those such as Rajinder who want to foster continuity.

The play strongly suggests that it is not continuity *per se* which is the problem, but a continuity that validates men's oppression of women that needs to be disrupted. It shows that the characters in the play who seek to accommodate those oppressive structures, in particular Rajinder, but also Eileen, Sonia, and Savita, all become the victims of that accommodation. Rajinder's husband's ability to track down and kill her is in part fostered by the failure to involve the authorities in what has been going on. The play vividly details – through the various women's narratives – the police's limited response and unwillingness to exert themselves in cases of domestic violence. As has been variously documented, this is not just a function of the history of seeing the domestic as personal and outside of public jurisdiction but also a function of exercising multi-culturalism by assuming that Asian communities will regulate their own and that police intervention will be regarded as heavy-handed and potentially racist through 'interfering' in what is supposedly 'custom and practice', an expression of 'cross-cultural difference'.[21] However, Rajinder's resistance to an involvement of the authorities in her daughter's abuse – which would have led to the arrest of Pradeep, her husband, and would have deprived him, through imprisonment, of the opportunity to kill Rajinder – enables Pradeep to track her and the children down and to murder her. The play thus establishes that the privatization of domestic abuse and sexual violence is not conducive to the safety of its victims, and that there are contexts in which the respect, here mistakenly exercised by Eileen, of what are different cultural norms and practices can jeopardize women's lives.

Just as Rajinder attempts to act in accordance with her community's values, so her husband Pradeep justifies his behaviour in terms of those values. Rajinder is justly terrified of him: 'I'm trying to escape from a man who's cunning, and strong, and tough as a bull; he can see through curtains, he can hear through walls. I'm really frightened of him' (1, 1: 162). Her representation of Pradeep as all-powerful, a permanently looming, threatening presence who has seemingly extranatural abilities, is theatricalized in the play through Pradeep's intermittent, sudden, silent appearances (see plate 10). Those appearances render visible the fear that makes Pradeep palpably present even when he is absent. He is made real to show how real he is to Rajinder, and to visibilize her preoccupation with the threat he represents. When he finally appears in person at the refuge his appearance is thus in some respects not a particular shock to the audience, who have already come to understand his threatening presence through his silent appearances. The last scene simply makes manifest what the play has tried to persuade the audience of already, namely that Pradeep is something of an inescapable force in Rajinder's life, a more threatening and possibly more violent version of Sonia's Gary, buoyed up in his attitude by a culture that accords him ownership of his wife and children. Unrepentant in his attitude towards the murder he has committed, he states: 'This is not murder, it is a death sentence, her punishment for taking away what was mine . . . She can't leave me, she's my wife' (3, 3: 186). Pradeep does not present his behaviour as a form of honour killing, a revenge for Rajinder having brought shame to his family by leaving him and making public their domestic problems, but rather as the meting out of justice in a case of a violation of property rights. Ironically, in British law the violation of property rights often results in the most extended forms of punishment, with robbers sometimes receiving much longer sentences than killers, for example. Pradeep's assertion of his property rights over his wife and family bespeaks their objectification by him and offers that objectification as the explanation for his ability to abuse both his wife and his daughter and finally to kill his wife.

Intra-cultural dilemmas

Meera Syal's screenplay 'My Sister-Wife' (in George 1993) produces the notion of a cross-cultural clash as an intra-cultural dilemma in ways both very similar to and radically different from the two plays discussed so far. It features Farah, a young Urdu-speaking Muslim woman who has grown up in Britain and who, at the beginning of the play, runs a successful carpet business. She falls in love with a fellow Muslim man, Asif Shah, who turns out to be married. The question arises whether or not she should become his second wife, polygamy not being ruled out within Islamic law though forbidden by English law. Initially, Farah rails against this suggestion made by her mother after Asif has been to see Farah's parents: 'The old Asif Shah charm strikes again. God, whose side are you on? Well done, mum. Couldn't get me to marry the village idiots in flares your friends kept suggesting. Asif's rich and brown so he'll do . . . I'll look fab in a harem, and if my maharajah gets bored, he can always swap me for a bloody camel!' (5: 113). Farah here makes a distinction between village life and urban living, between the unsophisticated boys from back home in their out-of-date fashions and herself as a young woman who has grown up in a western environment and who rejects being palmed off to a man with traditional ideas. The fact that she points to previous suggestions for marriage highlights, as in 'Heartgame', that she has been given some choice regarding her marriage partner.

When Farah rails against the idea of becoming Asif's second wife, her mother raises the issues of family honour and of shame: 'We brought you up here. But have we left nothing of home in you? . . . Honour. Obligation. Duty to the family. Things we thought we had taught you' (5: 113). Farah's mother is concerned for her daughter who appears to be heart-broken following the discovery of Asif's marriage to Maryam and the fact that he has two daughters by her. Farah's romantic obsession with Asif leads her to yield to her mother's pacifying comments that Asif's marriage is 'An arranged match to a village girl . . . No real family besides his' (5: 113). Farah's mother suggests that 'He'd be no man in my eyes if he could forget his responsibilities towards [Maryam]' (5: 113). Although the marriage of Farah and Asif would be polygamous, it does not violate English law because Asif's first marriage was never registered in Britain. Maryam was brought over 'as his cousin'. Asif maintains 'they've been emotionally apart for years, and she has given her permission' (5: 114) to the marriage with Farah. This representation brings up the problematic of marriages which are solemnized in Pakistan and under Islamic law but are not registered within a British context. Southall Black Sisters (1997) and Amrit Wilson (1978) detail the difficulties women face who are brought to Britain from Muslim countries without being registered as married to their husbands in the UK. Not only does this situation allow for the polygamous set-up Asif proposes, but it also puts the non-registered women in a precarious position, especially at a time of crisis, since the husband can always threaten to denounce her to the immigration authorities and thus bring about her deportation. The husband's failure to register his wife *as his wife* thus becomes a way of exercising control over the wife whose disempowerment is increased through having no legal status.

In Syal's play this disempowerment is made explicit by the way in which Maryam is treated. Both Asif and Farah initially disregard her feelings and she is very obviously treated as the family drudge and servant. At one point she tells Farah:

> Asif went to England one week after we got married. For five years I lived in Pakistan waiting for him . . . Then we came here. I knew nobody. Asif would pretend I was a servant when his business people came for dinner. Then the girls were born. I did not give him a son. He was so disappointed. When I found out about the girlfriends I said I didn't mind. They were only white women, so I knew they didn't matter.
>
> (44: 133)

The misery Maryam has had to endure is made only too explicit here. Degraded by her husband, debased within a sexist, patriarchal tradition which values boys more highly than girls and in an inverted racist manner through having to suffer Asif's affairs with white women, Maryam is an extreme but – so these plays suggest – not uncommon example of the put-upon wife. In acquiring a 'sister-wife', the title of the play playing upon the two women being presented as 'sisters' when it is convenient for Asif, as well as on the idea of a sisterhood based on certain similarities between them, Maryam had hoped she would at last have 'Someone to talk with, go shopping with, cook with. The sister I never had, with one thing in common we both love' (44: 133). This idea, whilst leaving intact the patriarchal aspiration towards polygamy, introduces the notion of intra-familial female bonding as the emotional compensation in polygamous relations. It relies simultaneously on the assumption of the immutability of men's rights to polygamy and on an ideal of female bonding which is not borne out by this play.

Maryam introduces Farah to other women living in polygamous households in order to break down Farah's romantic aspiration of a monogamous marriage to Asif and to suggest instead that sharing a husband is desirable. As one of these women, Fauzia, says: 'Only the English think love is made in the bedroom. In the Koran, it says a man who will care for another wife will sit at the left hand side of

Mohammed and the right hand of God. We are both equal. Both loved. Why should we feel afraid?' (49: 135). Here the clash between the values Maryam tries to defend and those Farah holds becomes apparent. Farah who has married for love and in the belief that Maryam's relationship with Asif is over meets her match in Maryam who, whilst unable to prevent Asif's marriage to Farah, decides to fight back to keep Asif, not specifically because she loves him but because she has nowhere else to go if Asif does not support her.

The marriage of Farah and Asif is made possible by a combination of appeals to cultural and communal traditions within the Pakistani community and culture clashes between the laws of one culture (Pakistani Muslim) and those of another (Britain) regarding marriage. Maryam is the Anju of this play, set up as a contrast to Farah (functioning like Reeta) at the beginning of the play (see table):

Maryam	Farah
arranged marriage to Asif	love match with Asif
rural background	urban upbringing
from back home	westernized
housewife	career woman
confined to the domestic	participating in public life
traditional	'modern'
wearing Pakistani suit	western clothes

Maryam and Farah represent the intra-communal culture clash that results from differential migration patterns and movements. In the same way that Ranu was sent back home to find a wife there, so Asif married Maryam in Pakistan, sending for her five years later. In contrast, both men got to know their girlfriends in Britain and responded to the attraction they present as westernized women. However, both men are also steeped in the traditions of a culture that privileges males and subordinates women. That privilege depends on men's collusion with the values of the traditions that underwrite their privilege, and both men respond to the demands of those traditions by doing 'the honourable thing', that is marrying in conformity with the expectations of their communities. In this respect, Asif represents an older version of Ranu. Ranu, as a young man, still dependent on the material provisions generated by his father, is in no position to contemplate marrying a second wife, whereas Asif, as an older and wealthy man, is materially able to take a second wife if he so wishes.

Female dis/locations

The dramatic tension in 'My Sister-Wife' arises from the juxtaposition between Maryam and Farah. As Farah, desperate to realize her romantic dreams, agrees to a polygamous marriage with Asif, she is deluded into thinking that Asif, like her, desires a monogamous relationship based on romantic love. She is quickly made to realize that Maryam's submissive, domestic, traditional femininity – which Farah initially despises – holds attractions for Asif who yields to the undemanding attentiveness of Maryam as he struggles with Farah's desire for a romantic monogamous relationship. Asif becomes the simultaneously inadvertent and unavoidable judge of Maryam and Farah as they compete for his favours, Maryam in her attempt to safeguard her and her daughters' financial security, Farah in her desire to actualize the romantic dream which underpinned her consent to marriage. In order to achieve their ends, the women, but especially Maryam, begin to manipulate each other and in the course of the play a structured reversal in their roles is introduced as Farah, eager to please Asif and aware of his delight in Maryam's submissive femininity, begins to play the 'little Pakistani housewife' she so despised Maryam for being, whilst Maryam starts to wear business suits and applies for a job in Farah's business, eventually ending up running it. The reversal of this position is semiotically encoded in the change of dress and appearance the women undergo in the course of the play: Maryam, who begins in shalwar kamiz and dhupatta looking dumpy, ends up wearing a western woman's business suit, whilst Farah, initially smart and dressed in sharp western business attire, ends up being dumpy in the shalwar kamiz and dhupatta that she did not want to identify with. These contrasts are played out most spectacularly in Scene 16 and Scenes 100 and 101. Both scenes focus on Asif giving a party for business friends but in the first one Farah is presented as the wife and Maryam reduced to the role of invisible servant, whilst in the second set of scenes it is

Maryam who now occupies the role of official wife whilst Farah has become the invisible drudge.

The play does not simply present a reversal as the two women fight to retain Asif's attention. It also projects three other sets of voices that act as commentaries on the situation. They are the voices of Poppy, Farah's English friend who cannot comprehend what is happening to and with Farah; Sabia, Asif's mother who presides over the household; and the voices of two sets of Pakistani women in polygamous marriages, one real and one imaginary. Poppy inhabits a position of English incomprehension of Farah's gradual acceptance and decline. One of Farah's close mates with whom Farah initially identifies very much and in whom she confides, Poppy becomes the measure against which Farah's gradual withdrawal from a westernized perspective is judged. When Poppy comments on the fact that Asif and Maryam are not divorced and that she herself would not tolerate such a situation, Farah counters this with: 'Family, duty, responsibility . . . I've thrown so much of my past away without trying to understand. We do things differently, Poppy' (18: 120). However, understanding the past is not the same as trying to inhabit it. Farah's only way to enter into the figure of Maryam, whom she increasingly imagines to be more desirable to Asif than she herself is, is to renounce her western associations, and she eventually tells Poppy that she cannot see her any longer (83: 146).

In the course of the play both Maryam and Farah attempt a relocation of their selves from the position they originally occupy in Asif's household to that of the other: Farah attempts to become like Maryam, and Maryam attempts to become like Farah. Through the impact this exile from the self and relocation has on the two women, the play offers a complex commentary on the respective roles the women inhabit. It points, most obviously, to the performativity of these roles, stating clearly that it is possible for women to make themselves over or to relocate themselves into another role. However, the play goes beyond the assertion of performativity to signal the relative desirability of each of the two positions, Pakistani housewife and westernized working woman. As Maryam relocates herself into Farah's position she gains respect from her husband and no longer has to occupy the role of family drudge, and, most importantly within the play, she no longer feels that she has to service him or be afraid of him. Her transformation enables her to stand up for herself and gain the independence necessary to resist subjugation. Farah, on the other hand, declines in her ability to stand up for herself; indeed, the play suggests that she becomes almost paranoid in her sense of persecution from Asif's family, and that she begins to 'see' things such as the harem, as she lets go of herself, stops taking care of herself, and increasingly slips into Maryam's position within the household. Her relocation thus maps a decline, her alienation from self into Maryam's role not a source of validation but of disintegration and further dissociation from those around her. The play thus makes plain that the position of 'Pakistani housewife' is undesirable for women, imprisoning them in a situation of self-denial, abasement, subjugation, and abjection.

Having been introduced by Maryam to Fauzia and her friends, Farah tries to enter into the spirit of polygamy and to believe in the notion of female comradeship or sisterhood that it is suggested she might derive from it. Isolated from those she knew before such as Poppy, and recently bereft following her own mother's death, Farah is without female confidantes to whom she can talk about her situation. She thus becomes vulnerable to Maryam's attempts to subjugate her into the Pakistani housewife role, to the talk of Maryam's polygamous friends, and to Sabia's, her mother-in-law's, machinations. Just as Pradeep appeared to Rajinder in 'Song for a Sanctuary', an externalized presence of a looming threat, so a harem of four wives (the number allowed a Muslim man) begins to appear to Farah, as a threat as well as the potentially desirable emblem of a sisterhood Farah is unable to find within Asif's household. Standing before 'an Arabian nights display' Farah tells Poppy: 'In my mother's story, all the women together, so . . . happy. They seemed like lovers and the husband the odd one out' (35: 128).

Farah and Maryam never achieve such togetherness. Instead they remain locked into a dance of attraction and repulsion, driven by their competition for Asif who in turn is incapable of handling both women. Sabia, Asif's mother, asserts that having a son will be the determining factor in maintaining Asif's attention and affection but

Maryam has been unable to produce a son. In desperation both women turn to a fortune teller and 'witch', Mata-ji, who produces potions designed to intervene on their behalf. They also use medicines concocted by Sabia, Asif's mother. When Farah discovers that one of these medicines has killed off her houseplant she becomes deeply suspicious of the food prepared within the household. Simultaneously she begins to recognize the power of such interventions. Both Maryam and Farah begin to put potions in each other's food, with tragic consequences. Farah who becomes pregnant has a miscarriage due to such an intervention and, in a climactic scene, Asif is killed by a potion that Farah put into Maryam's water decanter to make Maryam, pregnant again, miscarry.

The final scene shows Farah and Maryam, like Anju and Reeta, stuck in the same place. As the stage directions describe it:

> FARAH and MARYAM sit together on the bed. FARAH is in
> MARYAM's arms, drained. A shaft of sunlight breaks through
> the grey and momentarily lights up their faces, now so
> similar, so beautiful. MARYAM is talking to FARAH
> soothingly as if comforting a child. FARAH closes her eyes.
> MARYAM rocks her gently.
>
> (119: 158)

As in 'Heartgame', both the arranged marriage and the marriage based on romantic love are constructed as foundering on the sexism which underlies the customs that enable both arranged marriages and polygamy. The play makes clear that Farah and Maryam are not their parents' generation and cannot inhabit the same social structures which their parents accepted as the norm. Both personal desire and social context are incompatible with the traditions according to which their parents lived. Maryam is willing to tolerate a second wife but not on terms that render her unequal and invisible. Her transformation from 'little Pakistani housewife' to an independent assertive woman is achieved through the arrival of Farah who is made to take on the burden of producing a son whilst Maryam sees and takes the chance to secure a financial future for herself through acquiring a job which is independent of Asif and any necessity to be maintained by him. As Maryam puts it to Farah: 'I'm safe with you. Two wives, more chance of a boy. I'm free Farah. I'm not scared of him any more' (97: 151).

Farah, on the other hand, has to recognize that the cost of accommodating a polygamous set-up is so great for her that it results in a physical and mental decline that is only halted by the catastrophe of mistakenly killing Asif (the potion was intended for Maryam). Whilst the imaginary harem urges co-operation between the wives, Farah and Maryam are incapable of establishing such a bond. That bond, which would serve to uphold both polygamy and the imbalance of power between women and men underlying it, emerges as a fantasy of both women and men. Asif's statement that 'My mother lived with my father's other wives for twenty years' (40: 131), offered as a justification for Asif's life choices, is made in complete ignorance of his mother's feelings on the matter. Sabia's heart, as she herself says, is 'made of stone' (25: 122–3), turned to stone by her life experiences. When their Irish Catholic cleaner Maureen comments on 'you lot' having got it right by not being 'hung up about sex', Sabia says in Urdu: '[Sex's] overrated. Give a man a son and he's yours for life' (25: 122). It is this having to please men and trying to achieve something that you cannot influence but for which you are either blamed or praised, in any event judged (namely, having the right-sexed baby), which has turned Sabia's heart to stone. As she observes the drama between Maryam, Asif, and Farah unfolding around her, she says in English: 'Throw another prawn on the barbie' (25: 123), a comment that appears at first to be a random remark picked up as she learns English. It is, however, her comment on the fate of women in her culture, a culture to which she tenaciously clings despite and because of the damage it has done her.

In the end, however, Asif is the prawn thrown on the barbie – a fire generated by the culture clashes of trying to live in a traditional manner in a contemporary context. Asif too is thus constructed as a victim of the culture clashes he has sought to transcend in his household. He is not presented as either unkind or deliberately cruel; rather, his failing is the failure to question the cultural norms he attempts to live. He never questions his 'right' to have affairs, multiple wives, a son, a household that panders to his needs. He wants his wives to be happy and he tries to treat them as equals but fails to see how this process robs them of their individuality and dignity, setting them up against each other and destroying his and Farah's relationship. It is significant that the dream sequences of the harem are always located in Pakistan in a sunny environment. Pakistan here signals the past and traditions that cannot be maintained in Britain. Intellectually, Asif, Maryam, and Farah all understand this, for they deny their polygamy in front of Asif's English business associates. When Farah, towards the end of the play, finally reveals to the assembled guests in their household that she is the second wife, Maryam scolds her: 'Some things we keep within the family. The outside world would not understand' (105: 155). She thus acknowledges the culture clashes they are trying to circumvent through denial and silence. But those clashes cannot be denied, and the tragic deaths of both Farah's baby through a deliberately induced miscarriage and Asif signal the unsustainability of customs that lack wider social peer support and therefore a validating framework.

In all three plays discussed in this chapter, and in some of the additional ones mentioned in the endnotes, Asian marriages are under scrutiny as a key site on which culture clashes between east and west are made manifest, in particular in the impact that the marriages have on the women involved. In each play the females try to negotiate, for the most part unsuccessfully, between the traditions with which they have been brought up and which insist on the primacy of the family, the community, *izzat*, and *sharam* as the guiding values for one's actions, and a western position which favours individualism, self-determination, equality between the sexes, and the economic independence of women. Significantly, none of the plays focuses on 'forced marriages'[22] as they are the objects of common critiques from western commentators. Instead, they highlight the problematic of value structures which disadvantage women to the point where either they kill (as happens in 'My Sister-Wife') or they are killed (as occurs in 'Song for a Sanctuary'). One overriding problematic is the emotional and romantic over-investment women make in their relationships with men, an investment not matched by that of their male partners. In this sense the plays are powerfully anti-romantic, arguing that the affective orders on which that over-investment is based themselves require scrutiny and revision. The culture clashes detailed in the plays are thus as much about east–west conflicts as they are about clashes between the urban and the rural, the traditional and the 'modern', and about gender – a dimension that is often ignored in discussions about culture clashes.

6   Racing sexualities

The previous chapter has already – within the context of the theatrical representation of arranged marriages – provided an account of the particular heteronormative sexual politics that emerge in some contemporary plays by Asian women playwrights. Simultaneously with the emergence of an interrogation of that sexual politics in Asian playwrights' work, Asian and Black women playwrights[1] have begun to write about divergent forms of sexuality and thus to challenge heteronormativity both within and across cultures. Given the histories of domination and submission, exploitation and subjugation which inform Britain's colonial past and which are articulated through the racism that permeates its present, all sexualities, including heterosexuality, are racialized as part of the complex interplay of sex, race, and gender as they are articulated in British society. This racialization acquires a specific poignancy when divergent sexualities are at stake. As Sagri Dhairyam puts it: 'the developmental telos of my journey from not-lesbian to lesbian is simultaneously an ironic journey from Indian and silent otherness to Western and articulated subjectivity' (1994: 26). In this chapter I shall therefore focus in the main on two plays, both by mixed-race British women playwrights, that emerged at two very different moments of lesbian and of black politics. Jackie Kay's 'Chiaroscuro' (1985; published 1987) is rooted in pre-Clause 28,[2] pre-queer days[3] and predates theories of performance/performativity. It projects the difficulties of lesbian closetedness and invisibility in an interrogation of racialized visibilities and the politics of female friendship. Valerie Mason-John's 'Sin Dykes' (1998; published 1999), on the other hand, is fully invested in the politics of sexuality as performative within clearly articulated racialized power structures that operate both inter- and intra-racially and, as I shall discuss below, re-enact as well as query the dominance-submission dynamics which echo historical forms of slavery and enslavement. The plays thus visibilize shifts in lesbian and in identity politics, replaying racial oppression in/as sexual oppression whilst querying the meaning of identity.[4]

Figuring identities

In her postscript to 'Chiaroscuro' Kay writes: 'In all of the drafts of this play I have been obsessed with naming. What do we call ourselves as lesbians and black women? How do we get our names? How do we as-sert our names? What are our past names?' (82). The quest articulated here, a quest that gained prominence in (lesbian)[5] feminist writing on both sides of the Atlantic during the 1980s through publications such as Audre Lorde's *Zami: A New Spelling of My Name* (Watertown MA, 1982; first published in the UK by Sheba Feminist Publishers, London, in 1984),[6] bell hooks' *Feminist Theory: From Margin to Center* (1984),[7] and Denise Riley's *'Am I That Name?'* (1988),[8] is particularly perti-nent in a context which is counter-hegemonic, emerges from a history of silencing, and defies the drive towards the monolithic which under-pins dominant culture. As Kay writes: 'Each of the characters tells the story of her name. She is also searching for another name. She is in flux, reassessing her identity, travelling back into memory and forward into possibility' (82). This search for a name, for an identity, gains height-ened significance, as 'Chiaroscuro' demonstrates, when identity is in question, in flux, fractured by a non-linear relation to one's history.[9] That fracturing is, in a sense, invisibilized in Jill Dolan's brief discus-sion of Jackie Kay's 'Chiaroscuro'. Dolan's comment on the play is embedded in a monograph on theatre that seeks to explore, *inter alia*, the possibilities of lesbian representation within a realist framework. Dolan identifies the play as 'a coming out story' (1993: 141) and, writ-ing from a North American perspective, she asserts: 'The four black women characters read as archetypal positionalities in a struggle for sexual and racial liberation that are often at odds' (141). Dolan simply describes the four characters as 'black' and, through assigning them 'archetypal positionalities', cements them into a place that appears to be invariant when, I want to argue, the opposite is the issue, namely how to make a space, how to affirm an identity, from a situation of instability and indeterminacy of identity. As the plays detail, that instability derives from cultural norms that prescribe particular racial and sexual figurations as dominant, simultaneously casting all forms of divergence from those norms as 'other', without history, without place, as lack.

Kay's and Mason-John's personal trajectories share characteristics which significantly impact on the plays they produce. Kay, of mixed-race descent (her father was Nigerian, her mother Scottish white) as she has movingly presented in her autobiographical collection of poetry *The Adoption Papers* (1991), was adopted by a white family as a baby. Mason-John describes herself as 'from the African Diaspora . . . born in Cambridge' (1995: xiii): she had a spell in a Barnado's home and was brought up by white foster parents as well as spending some time with her black, sadistic, biological mother (1999: 8–9). Both Kay and Mason-John thus have fractured histories in relation to their biological families, and the experience of cross-racial fostering/adoption. Significantly, another contemporary lesbian playwright and performer from Britain, Maya Chowdhry, like Kay comes from a mixed-race background. In 'Living Performance' (1998), she describes her experiences as follows:

> I was/am mixed race/heritage/parentage. From an early age I
> learnt to perform my identity following the 'Where are you
> from?' question. The performance text ranged from: 'Scotland,
> where d'you think?' to 'My dad's from the Punjab' to 'My dad
> was born in the North West Frontier state of Pakistan and my
> mum's from Kent with Scottish and French ancestry,
> McLaren's from near Aberdeen.'
>
> (10)

In Chowdhry's representation, the performance of racial identity, always derived from a position of being singled out as 'other', as in need of explanation, precedes the performance of sexual identity:[10] 'Later, when I discovered that there was a sexual identity to be had, I learnt to perform the ritual of "my girlfriend lives in Sheffield" in answer to the "Are you married?" question' (1998: 10).

Ruptured histories

That need to *perform identity* – and the vocabulary itself bespeaks the 1990s and the impact of Judith Butler's *Gender Trouble* (1990) in shaping the identity debates of that decade and beyond – is made manifest in Kay's 'Chiaroscuro', which features Opal, 'brought up in a home in Hampshire' (1: 61) and mixed-race; Beth, a mixed-race woman whose father is from St Vincent and whose mother is English (1: 65); Aisha, who comes from the Himalayas and whose parents migrated to England in 1953 (1: 62); and Yomi who is from Nigeria (1: 65). Aisha and Yomi thus share the experience of migration and a unitary lineage whereas Beth and Opal are both born in Britain and are mixed-race. The characters brought together within this play thus resemble those in 'Leonora's Dance' in terms of the diversity of racial identities they represent. They rehearse their histories of descent during the opening scenes of the play, a sign that although the Britain of the 1980s might have been described as multi-cultural, that multi-culturality did not obviate the socio-culturally dictated necessity to identify oneself if perceived as in any way different from the norm, that is from white Englishness. Performing racial identity on stage thus becomes a way of making culturally visible the daily task of those viewed as 'other' that Chowdhry described above and which constitutes an iterative process in a racist society. This daily task is made all the more difficult where individuals do not conform to essentializing discourses of familial and racial histories that demand singular explanations of origin, laminated to a biological nuclear family. In 'Chiaroscuro' racial identity performance acquires a particular significance since it occurs within a group of peers whose histories are nevertheless quite divergent. Significantly therefore, the four young women in the play reference their biological families, in particular their mothers and female lines of descent,[11] but their families never make an appearance on stage. This is quite unlike many of the previous plays discussed in this monograph, at the heart of which were inter-generational relations and conflicts.[12] In the lesbian

plays analysed here, the female protagonists exist outside that generational framework in a peer community which in lesbian and gay
circles in general frequently takes on the function of the family, not
in terms of a nuclear or extended heteronormative blood-relation-
based formation, but in terms of providing the affective, social, and
often economic structures which govern familial relations.[13] Thus in
'Chiaroscuro' the audience is presented with a network of four female
friends meeting in an undefined but private space; in 'Sin Dykes' the
context is a lesbian club in London and two characters' bedsits; in
Maya Chowdhry's 'Splinters' (1997) the action centres on a mixed-
race lesbian's sparsely indicated workplace – she is a carpenter – into
which a woman who becomes her lover ventures to order a coffin. Each
of the three plays thus focuses on the divergent peer group as the site
in which racial and sexual identities and their interplay are explored,
moving away from the issue of cross-generational conflict which is so
prominent in other plays by Black and Asian women playwrights.

One implication of that focus on the peer group is the rupture
with one's personal history which takes on racial and sexual dimensions as the various characters seek to understand themselves and
their identities. This is not the prior rupture of fostering or adoption,
of displacement from within the biological family, but a new rupture associated with the recognition of a divergent sexual identity. As
Anna Wilson, lesbian novelist and critic, describes it: 'the term "coming out" describes a movement away from the culture of one's birth
and towards a re-cognition of one's identity within a different, non-
generationally structured, group' (1992: 80). For Yomi, one of the characters of 'Chiaroscuro', it is not so much 'coming out' that demands
this mobility but her coming to terms with her friends' lesbianism.
This involves the re-assessment of her knowledge of her family, and
the remembering of stories told to her by her mother: 'I don't want
to run anymore. I was remembering something my mother told me.
She said there were these women she used to know in Nigeria who
lived with their husbands but loved each other. She said, God it surprised me so much, that it was a pity they had to hide, a pity they
couldn't just live together out in the open, if that's what they wanted'
(2: 79). Yomi's transformation from homophobe to homophile depends

in part on this reintegration into her consciousness of a history whose memory she had suppressed but which forms part of her matrilineal heritage. The affirmation of that heritage enables her to move from her position of rejection to one of acceptance of lesbianism. The idea of the matrilineal line as a source of regeneration and strength which is common in writing by Black female writers from the African and West Indian diaspora is thus confirmed, as is Wilson's point *à propos* of Audre Lorde's writings that 'The familial ties that [Yomi] takes up again are to a community that has been refashioned: the return is not to the same place' (1992: 85). The place is, in any event, an imaginary one, but it now contains lesbians and it is this that has changed it.

The connection to and with the past in the form of the personal histories of each of the four characters, a past which informs the present and exercises considerable power over the characters' imaginary, is repeatedly articulated in 'Chiaroscuro'. Both Aisha and Beth express the desire to live not in rupture from their history but in continuity with it, a continuity significantly derived from reconciling all aspects of self in public and having all those aspects confirmed within community and family. Aisha says: 'I want to travel over there/and join my past to now/be welcomed, not a stranger/for who I am and feel at home' (1: 63) and Beth states: 'Someday I'd like to be able to be all of myself to all of those close to me' (2: 73). But homophobia, assumed or real, keeps Aisha, Beth, and Opal from revealing themselves fully, leaving Opal with 'me and my ghosts' (2: 73), Beth with 'different bits of past. All the various Beths' (2: 73), and Aisha yearning for a place she cannot (re)turn to. They all grapple with histories, beginning before their own stories, of alienation. Thus Aisha describes her parents' arrival in Britain: 'In the beginning there was the dream of decency and opportunity and education. My parents came here in 1953 to work and save and work and one day return home. They were the invited guests who soon found out they'd be treated like gate crashers' (1: 62). Aisha, having been born abroad but grown up in Britain, fears her alienation from her home country: 'It makes me want to laugh when I hear them talking about *us* taking over ... They've even taken over my tongue ... sometimes I worry ... that I'd never fit in back home. That I'd stick out a mile, or worse they'd call me English!'

(1: 62). Aisha is caught between two cultures, one which she dreams about returning to, one which she inhabits. She fears the experience of reverse alienation, of no longer being accepted by her culture of origin.

The othering which being called 'English' would involve for Aisha is mirrored by Opal's anxiety regarding her lesbian relationship with Beth: 'What would they say if they all knew? Opal, sweet friendly Opal is a pervert! What does a pervert look like?' (2: 73). A parallel is thus drawn between the issue of racial and that of sexual identity, highlighting how divergence makes visible the norms to which we are subjected and without which divergence would not register, and the internalization of those norms through the fear that loosing their bonds generates.

Racializing lesbian identities

Aisha's sexual identity is not directly discussed and in the play she is not in a relationship. However, she is friends with Beth who is an out lesbian and it becomes evident that she is attracted to Yomi whom she takes on an all-women's weekend. Yomi, on the other hand, is a single mother who thinks of homosexuality as an unnatural white vice. When she is confronted with lesbian snogging at the all-women's weekend she says: 'I've never seen two women kissing before . . . And black women at that! I didn't think we produced them' (1: 64).[14] Here the racialized dimension of homophobia appears as Yomi dissociates black women from homosexuality, aligning it with white western decadence. She is also given the homophobic lines: 'Wanted for murder! For killing off the race. God says it isn't natural. God says it isn't natural. AIDS is God's vengeance on the men . . . Man and woman. Adam and Eve. That's the way it's meant to be' (1: 67). Although these words are spoken out of character, and in a moment of stylization and violence, Yomi's interactions with Beth in particular are marked by an internalization of the sentiments underlying these utterances. She sees things in black and white, and tells Beth: 'I've always felt sorry for children of mixed marriages' (1: 70).

Yomi finds divergence difficult. In the play she is identified with the attitude towards lesbians attributed to Queen Victoria[15] when she says: 'What do they do what do they do these les-bi-ans? It is easy

to imagine what men do – but women, women. The thought turns
the national stomach, stomach' (1: 67). In Yomi's latter speech lesbian
sexuality is construed as anti-national; in her previous lines it is described as 'unnatural' and as genocidal, 'killing off the race'. The play
thus suggests that Yomi's attitude is part of a cultural tradition that
equates nation and race with *hetero*sexuality,[16] endorsed by Christian
mythology and reinforced through the social collusion which enforces
silence and invisibility upon those deemed to be divergent: 'If they
want to do that sort of thing they should do it behind closed doors'
(1: 64). The power of this pseudo-liberal injunction is made evident
in the play by the fact that although the lesbian characters within it
outnumber the heterosexist Yomi by three to one, the play's central
dynamic focuses on how Aisha, Beth, and Opal can come out to Yomi.
This issue is augmented by Aisha's emotional attachment to Yomi,
which leads Aisha to 'protect' Yomi from Beth's more assertive stance
towards her lesbianism and prevents Aisha from telling Yomi that she
is in love with her, thus silencing Aisha. Interestingly, and possibly
curiously, it is thus the women who are not mixed-race – Aisha and
Yomi – who are without partner in the play, Yomi's over-emphatic
singular identity driving them apart. In contrast it is the women who
inhabit the *entre-deux*, the mixed-race women, who achieve a lesbian
relationship that eventually becomes a role model for Yomi:

> I pictured [lesbians] ugly and lonely
> That was my only bit of sympathy
> And I couldn't see anyone
> Or smiles and softness and need
> Like Beth and Opal
> Looking good together . . .
>
> (2: 79)

During the course of 'Chiaroscuro' Yomi thus undergoes a transformation which involves acknowledging that Beth and Opal are lesbians
and that this is not a threat to her: 'It doesn't happen overnight, you
know. A lifetime under these eyes. Seeing the way I saw . . . I banished
so much from my sight. Sometimes that's bliss' (2: 80). The seductiveness of denial is clearly articulated here as Yomi hints at the comforts

of conformity. But she also has to compare Beth and Opal's joy in each other with her own lack of a partner – a price she has paid for that conformity.

Yomi's conformity is made possible by her sense of an unequivocal racial identity – her sense of self as a woman of Nigerian descent is not in question and provides her with the armour to ignore what is right in front of her eyes. This is only too apparent in her exchange with Opal (1: 70–1) about Opal's mixed-race heritage in which she uses the term 'half-caste' to describe Opal. Beth is outraged: 'It's derogatory – it's just like all those other horrible descriptions: half-breed, mulatto, the lot' (1: 70).[17] These words reference eugenicist and racist discourses of miscegenation and as such express a colonial heritage which Yomi has accommodated through internalizing its values. Her transformation towards the end of the play to a recognition of the problematic of her way of seeing gestures towards the possibility of 'identity as a conscious strategy borne by the right critical thought' (Dhairyam 1994: 26) where 'right' does not bespeak political correctness but a counter-hegemonic positioning born of a critical engagement with the values, attitudes, and language systems one has inherited and participates in. Such critical engagement, however, requires the will to change, especially in a context where visibility is at issue.

Yomi's reference to her own narrow vision emphasizes the importance of appearance and of the visual in determining what one sees. Correspondingly it is what is immediately visible, the characters' racial identity, which is the object of debate in the early parts of the first act, whereas the question of sexual identity gradually unfolds in the course of the play. Both are em-bodied identities but one is inscribed on the surface of the body in ways that the other is not as a matter of course.[18] This is what makes the silencing of Aisha's, Beth's, and Opal's lesbianism possible. However, despite the seeming self-evidence of the embodiment of racial markers, both racial and sexual identities in this play require their 'outing' since neither is a stable category, as the play testifies. The process of outing, racial and sexual, is not neutral; rather, its violence – due to the differential values attributed to diverse racial and sexual identities – constitutes

a threat to 'insider' and 'outsider' alike, generating fear of rejection in
the one and fear of transgression of (effectively imaginary but taken
for real) boundaries in the other, the dominant. 'Chiaroscuro' thus invites the audience to confront, via the exchanges between the various
characters, their own racial and sexual imaginaries, and to consider
the relationship between them. It suggests that mixed-race characters
like Beth and Opal whose histories include racial mobility are more
likely to be open to divergent sexualities than characters such as Yomi
who are subjugated by an epistemic regime of racism and sexism that
puts everyone in their place and maintains the illusion of boundaries.
This is, in a sense, what both the title of the play, 'Chiaroscuro', and
its structures, style, language, and theatrical devices allude to.

'Chiaroscuro' is a painterly term, referencing the distribution
of light and dark in a picture that relies on those hues rather than
on colour for its impact. The *Shorter Oxford English Dictionary* describes it as '1. The style of pictorial art in which only light and shade
are represented; black (or sepia) and white . . . 2. The disposition of
the brighter and darker masses in a picture'. Kay's stage directions signal the visualization of chiaroscuro through the set where the floor
is a grey cloth, chairs and stools are painted in black and white, and
'*The backdrop is a montage of landscapes and odd photographs. Its
main colour is pale grey*' (1: 59). This is augmented in the play by
the use of spot lights which generate an immediate contrast between
what is highlighted and the surrounding dark, both importantly an
effect of the lighting and thus created through a single process. This
itself underlines the dialectic of exclusion and inclusion, visibility
and invisibility which structures the racial and sexual identities of
the characters on stage, making visible that seeing and not-seeing are
a simultaneous, co-dependent process. Yomi gradually learns to mod-
ify her black-and-white vision to accommodate both mobile racial and
sexual identities and to accept diversity, the grey that mixing engenders.

Revolutions in poetic language
In her afterword to the play, Kay discusses the 'unhappy combination
of realism and symbolism' (82) that was evident in previous drafts

of the play. For the published version she therefore decided to place 'more emphasis on the symbolic'. This chimed with the inclusion of poetic language in the play, the move away from 'some of the flat and heavy naturalism which sat uncomfortably in the production' (82). Like other Black women playwrights, Kay acknowledges the influence of Ntozake Shange's *for colored girls* of which she writes that it impressed her by the way in which Shange had 'made poetry work as theatre' (83). Dolan describes 'Chiaroscuro' as 'mixing poetic, choreographed, ritualized exchanges that trade in the epistemology of cultural feminism with a realist story and scenes of a woman's tentative exploration of a lesbian choice' (1993: 141). The first part of this description could, in fact, be of *for colored girls* which is, of course, also concerned with a coming to self and the finding of an identity by young black women, hitherto silenced. Kay's theatre work,[19] as much as that of Maya Chowdhry,[20] for instance, utilizes the poetic, the choric, and movement in and out of character through the use of third- and first-person pronouns to talk about the same character, in order to explode the naturalistic frame that is the bread-and-butter to this day of much mainstream theatre. Here we have the 'revolution in poetic language' heralded by Julia Kristeva which is a key component in the representation of divergent identities, in the celebration of matrilineage, and in the articulation of a certain feminized (female) voice. This would seem to confirm Dolan's view that 'realism cannot accommodate people of color, because the model it promotes reflects the social organization of white, male-dominated, middle-class families . . . The heterosexual assumption of realism also marginalizes lesbians and gay men, since the form presupposes a traditional nuclear family arrangement' (139).[21] Dolan argues that where divergent voices appear in realist drama, it is usually in dialogue with the heterosexual dominant which ultimately wins out in the domestication of divergence which this kind of drama entails.

Insofar as the heterosexist dominant appears in 'Chiaroscuro' it does so through the articulation of its values by the characters struggling to find an equilibrium in which their racial and sexual identities can exist without censure. Beth has found an equilibrium of sorts through her affirmation of herself as black and lesbian. However, her personal confidence in those identities is tested in the social where she is expected to silence and invisibilize her sense of self, denying her sexuality and adopting – relative to Yomi, for example – a position of inferiority due to her mixed-race status. Beth refuses to do so and it is this refusal to pass (as implicitly heterosexual) on the one hand, and to acquiesce in front of Yomi's ascription of a specific and derogatory racial identity to her on the other, which becomes the catalyst for change within the play. Beth's assertiveness, for instance, enables Opal to confront her racial and sexual identities, and to move beyond the fear of rejection that haunts and contains her daily life. Beth is out of the closet, celebratory of her identities, able to acknowledge her white mother and her lesbianism.

Aisha lives among women but is in the closet and isolated. Opal finds connection through opening up to Beth, and Yomi finds connection through accepting difference. All feel the need to insert themselves, from their place within the peer community of women of a similar age, into a generational one. Beth, for instance, is determined to have a child. In this desire all the characters directly contradict Wilson's assertion that 'The tradition which the lesbian fashions or imagines cannot . . . be a familial one' (80), in that the characters in the play all desire family albeit not the conventional nuclear heterosexual one. Opal, for example, tells Beth: 'You're the only family I have, Beth, the only one I can call home' (1: 67). Their initial meeting is predicated upon a notion of mutual recognition which is associated with long-term (imaginary) familiarity. Beth says: 'There's something about her that made me feel so at home' (1: 63) and Opal confirms, 'Sometimes, you just meet someone . . . and you feel like you've known them all of your life. I feel that way with Beth' (1: 63). Their affinity is partly structured around their shared mixed-race experience and partly on their openness to lesbianism. That affinity becomes the analogy on which the ideas of 'home' and 'belonging' as psychic and relational sites of stability are based. Their relationship is thus based on a mutual recognition of a similarity or sameness based on their sharing of the space of a mixed-race identity. For Opal this recognition is constructed as a coming to self that parallels her recognition of herself as mixed-race, which involves an affirmation and acceptance of that mixed-race identity. In the play Opal's dominant prop is a mirror that she repeatedly gazes into. Initially, the mirror serves to register the disjunction between Opal's imaginary self and the self the mirror confronts her with:

> My face was a shock to me. The brain in my head thought my skin was white and my nose straight. It imagined my hair was curly from twiddling it. Every so often, I saw me: milky coffee skin, dark searching eyes, flat nose. Some voice from that mirror would whisper: *nobody wants you, no wonder. You think you're white till you look in me.*
>
> (1: 65)

In Opal's imaginary, her abandonment by biological family and desired foster parents conflates with the devalued status of black and mixed-race women in a racist society to suggest that the two are interrelated. Her way of dealing with this is to dissociate mind from body, maintaining a phantasy of whiteness which prevents her from accepting her body as her self. The play thus stages a double coming to self, a coming to both a racialized and a sexualized self in which both are accepted as part of a (partial) process of healing and discovery of self-worth.

Kay's representation of coming to self both racially and sexually in 'Chiaroscuro' is marked by the discourses of lesbian feminism that were prevalent during the 1970s and early 1980s, though not exclusive to this period – rather they are recurrent and typical of the 'coming out' phase of lesbian identities.[22] These include issues of loneliness and isolation (Act One features a 'classic' narrative of the lonely lesbian schoolgirl looking for representations of herself in textbooks, falling in love with a female teacher, and eventually finding lesbian clubs (1: 66)), attendance of women-only workshops that offer practical skills sessions such as carpentry as well as sessions on exploring one's sexuality; being or not being closeted;[23] the appropriateness or otherwise of wanting a long-term committed relationship, and lesbian feminist resistance to marriage as concept and metaphor for lesbian relationships (see 1: 67). In exploring these issues, the play utilizes devices commonly employed in certain forms of feminist theatre of that period, intended to break with the realist traditions associated with bourgeois theatre, among them moving in and out of character, narrative, live music, song, and the notion of iterativity through the repetition of the beginning as the ending. Kay states in her afterword that 'time and space were not important. What is important is what is happening and what has happened' (82). This suggests the 'monumental time' that Kristeva evokes as typical of 'women's time'; it also seeks to universalize what is in many respects historically specific. As such it is expressive of the kind of 'sisterhood is global' and 'universal oppression of women' attitude which drove and for a time united feminist action and thought in the so-called second wave of feminism. However, 'Chiaroscuro' is also a play which details a particular moment in diasporic history in Britain, the moment when first- and second-generation migrants from African countries, Asia, and the West Indies were prominent in Britain's diasporic landscape. That landscape is set to change as migration patterns shift, and as successive generations of diverse groups of people live in the UK.

Queer territories

Valerie Mason-John's 'Sin Dykes' heralds a very different era from that of 'Chiaroscuro'. Its very title points to a lesbian historical period, the 1990s, when words such as 'dyke', a word that does not appear in 'Chiaroscuro', for example, had been reclaimed as part of the affirmation of lesbian and gay identities that followed the need by lesbian and gay communities to react to the onslaught of HIV/AIDS and its attendant socio-cultural backlash against homosexuals with assertiveness and pride, and an 'in your face' attitude. The title also references divergent lesbian sexuality in that 'sin' indexes the sado-masochistic activities on which the play focuses. Where Kay's play lists the characters by name at the beginning of the play[24] and has them reveal their histories to the audience as narratives within the play, Mason-John positions her characters in racialized and sexualized terms that immediately project the inter-relationship between race, sexuality, and racialized history[25] which she explores in the play:

TRUDY: a Brixton babe, African-Caribbean, aged 25;
non-specific black British accent; femme.
GILL: a scene dyke, white European, aged 32; non-specific
English accent; butch/femme on the streets, butch between
the sheets.
KAT: an afrekeke dyke, African-Caribbean, aged 33; Jamaican
accent (patois); femme.
BD: a bull dyke lesbian, white English colonial, aged 40;
English accent, with a trace of South African twang; bull
dagger dyke, closet SM queen.
CLIO: a travelled black dyke, aged 28; Cockney ('Essex girl')
accent; dominatrix, whether top or bottom, always in charge.
TRACE: an SM dyke, who sleeps with gay men, and enjoys the
role of the slave; as a slave she is submissive but butch and
adores her mistress; when not in role of slave is laddish and
cocky; when in slave role speaks only with her body.

(1999: 42)

Unlike Kay, Mason-John historicizes and locates her play: 'PLACE:
London: Diva's Bar; Trudy's bedroom; Gill's bedsit./TIME: Late
1990s.'

Mason-John's particularization of place, time, and characters is
born out of a desire to create an intervention in the sexual–racial scene
of the lesbian and gay community of late 1990s London:[26] 'Dykes are
out of the closet. Black dykes openly do SM, dykes openly sleep with
gay men. There is dialogue, debate, and outrage, but nobody is listening anymore' (41). The 'dialogue, debate, and outrage' Mason-John
references relates to the confrontations among lesbians[27] on both
sides of the Atlantic about the post-feminist lesbian sexual scene of
the 1980s and 1990s when the notion of lesbian sex as nurturing,
loving, 'vanilla', gave way to a harder-edged, more open, and more
divergent exploration of sexuality among lesbians. This broadly divided lesbians into three camps, not entirely mutually exclusive. The
first, a lesbian feminist camp, identified with particular forms of feminist politics dating back to the late 1960s and 1970s. The second
camp was comprised of lesbians who modelled themselves on the

butch-femme structures of the bar scene dating back to pre-Stonewall days and the first half of the twentieth century – including the 1950s and early 1960s when homosexuality was still extensively criminalized and the closet a common location for lesbians and gays. A third camp were lesbians actively engaged with 'queer', the new gender-bending sexual and cultural mores of the 1990s. Typically, in these debates, race as an issue was not articulated; sex took precedence over the implications of the new sexual politics for race. As Dhairyam put it: '"Queer theory" comes increasingly to be reckoned with as critical discourse, but concomitantly writes a queer whiteness over raced queerness; it domesticates race in its elaboration of sexual difference' (1994: 26). This recognition led Evelynn Hammonds to state: 'Black feminist theorists must reclaim sexuality through the creation of a counternarrative that can reconstitute a present black female subjectivity and that includes an analysis of power relations between white and black women and amongst different groups of black women' (1994: 131). This, precisely, is what Mason-John as dramatist attempts to do in 'Sin Dykes' – hence her cast of both Black and white women (Kay's play, in contrast, does not feature white women), and of black and white women who position themselves diversely in relation to the wider historical frame that constitutes their heritage. Mason-John thus repudiates essentialist notions of '*the* lesbian', '*the* Black woman', '*the* white woman' in favour of a diversity which undercuts any form of polarized or polarizing debate, offering instead a more complex and polyvocal presentation which articulates a range of subject positions that produce contradictory and not easily resolvable views. Mason-John's list of characters makes this evident. Trudy, the 'Brixton babe' with the 'non-specific black British accent' is constructed quite differently from Kat who identifies with a particular Black African and Caribbean heritage as indicated through the appellation '*afrekeke* dyke' and her 'Jamaican accent', on the one hand, and her repeated insistence within the play, on the other, that 'black girls don't do SM' (e.g. 4: 66) and that black girls should date black girls. Clio, the third Black lesbian in the play, identifies more with her sexual practices than with her racial identity, and it is this elevation of sexual practice over racial identity and a politics inflected by an awareness of a racialized history with specific black–white power dynamics that sets her at odds with Kat. When Clio tries to seduce Trudy who has come out of a relationship with Gill, one of the white women in the play, Kat says: 'Me no say you have to start dating black women but you can forget that one she's a coconut. Sistahs like her are tearing our black community apart' (3: 55).

Reliving colonial history

Kat is presented as a Black woman with a clear sense of the colonial history that has shaped black and white women's lives. For her, white women are 'the enemy' whom one may have a fling with but with whom one would not have a relationship: 'Me na boddah with pork. I don't want to wake up every morning to a face which reminds me of those kids at school, who asked, "Wogga matter? Are you all white? Ah nigger mind, go black home, eat your coon flakes and you'll be all white in the morning"' (3: 59). The racial abuse that Kat relates here, a continuation of colonial racism, shapes Kat's views that she tries to impress upon Trudy: 'Know your history, girl, white people have persecuted so many of our people. How can you hang with someone who reminds you of slavery?' (3: 59).

Trudy is the key figure in Mason-John's drama for she is the one who undergoes change in the course of the play. One might argue that the play is about Trudy's coming to self in racial and sexual terms but, as I shall discuss, that coming to self is not epiphanic and offers no resolution; instead, it positions her as a subject-in-process whose experiences and changes raise new questions rather than resolve old ones. The play thus ends with a dilemma, a point of debate. Trudy's sexual history is one of sleeping with white women. Under Kat's tutelage, she begins to review that past and, by the time the play starts, she has split up from her white partner Gill.

In a play consisting of five scenes, Scenes Three and Four become pivotal as it is in these that the racing of sexuality through self and others, through practice and perspective, is most fully discussed. In Scene Four Trudy, intrigued by Clio, visits her former partner Gill to get advice and support about her desire to experiment sexually with Clio, specifically to engage in sado-masochistic sex with her.

In Trudy's exchanges with Kat and Gill in Scenes Three and Four, the play makes clear that all forms of sexual practice are also immediately racialized. In Scene Three Kat tries to get Trudy to understand that both sleeping with white women and having sado-masochistic sex involve an engagement with (histories of) unequal power structures that replicate Black women's past of oppression. Trudy to some extent accepts Kat's views, in particular Kat's view of relationships with white women – hence her break-up with Gill. But that break-up was complicated by the fact that Gill wanted to introduce sado-masochistic games and sex toys into their relationship and that Trudy was staunchly resistant to this. As in Kay's play, the coming to racial identity here in a sense prefigures the coming to sexual identity, for although Trudy decides to give up Gill in part because she is white and in part because she did not want to have sado-masochistic sex with her, Trudy gradually becomes interested in sado-masochistic sex, and as a novice is both excited by and fearful of it. This explains her visit to Gill because – unlike Kat, for instance – Gill is willing to be supportive about doing sado-masochism. She has no in-principle objection to sado-masochism. In the list of characters she is described as 'white European' with a 'non-specific English accent', thus simultaneously dissociating her from the Englishness that would align her with British colonial history and contrasting her with BD who is represented as 'white English colonial . . . English accent . . . with a trace of South African twang', a description that frames BD's sexuality in both national and colonial terms and explains her desire for debasement. As Trudy tells Gill: 'One night she hauled me into her office and broke down crying. Blabbering how sorry she was that things in South Africa hadn't seemed to have changed. She asked me to whip her as much as my ancestors had been beaten by her people' (4: 73).

Gill is not invested in a similar history. As a white European she inhabits a more general history of white people's oppression of Black people and it is to this that Trudy responds in refusing to engage in sado-masochistic games with her. In attempting to get Gill to understand that refusal, Trudy says: 'I don't trust your conditioning. I don't trust what thoughts you may have in your head if we played together. I don't trust that you wouldn't get carried away while

acting out a fantasy' (4: 68).[28] Trudy here suggests that Gill's embeddedness in certain histories, as indeed her own, militate against
the trust required to make oneself vulnerable to the other within a
sado-masochistic scene. Importantly, she links the history of slavery
('every time I thought of you and I experimenting, I could hear my
black sisters screaming, "Remember slavery"' (4: 68)) with contemporary histories of police brutality against Black people in Britain ('When
I fantasize about you handcuffing my hands, all I can think of is the
police beating Michael White, gagging Joy Gardner to death and shoot-
ing Cherry Groce. The images, flashbacks and memories are endless'
(4: 69)), thus establishing the continuities of racist behaviour which
shape relationships between Black and white people. Trudy justifies
her interest in experimenting sexually with Clio rather than Gill by
pointing to their shared racial history, Clio's experienced status as a
dominatrix, and her 'ownership' of a white female slave, Trace, which
she sees as a sign of Clio having 'all the power' in her relationship to
the white woman.

Racing sexual practices

In its exploration of mixed-raced (sexual) relationships, 'Sin Dykes'
raises questions about both whom to have sex with and what kind
of sex to have. Where Kay's 'Chiaroscuro' is concerned with young
women finding their racial and sexual identities and exploring the possibilities of lesbianism, Mason-John's play almost literally has moved
ten years on, is immersed in contemporary urban lesbian (sub-)culture,
and discusses the 'queer' debates of the 1990s[29] around lesbian/queer
sex with gay men (which Trace engages in) and sado-masochism.
Mason-John's characters do not question their lesbian identities; as
lesbians they are not in the closet, but in their relation to their sexual
practices they are less certain. Thus BD allows herself to be supposedly secretly whipped and degraded by her Black workers in the bar
that she runs. Kat, the 'afrekeke dyke' has a strongly politicized view
of sexual relationships that incorporates a proud alliance with African
history – hence the 'afrekeke' reference – and a lesbian feminist rejection of sado-masochism as an inappropriate and demeaning form of
sexual practice. However, being short of money she is also persuaded

to indulge BD's sado-masochistic fantasies, and this pragmatism undercuts her right-on lesbian feminist stance. It thus raises the question of what kind of sexual activity it is appropriate or otherwise to engage in and, more complexly, what is the meaning of the sexual activity engaged in for the individual. Kat, for instance, refuses to go along with BD's desires beyond a certain point; thus she dons the handcuffs but refuses to wear the lingerie BD had procured and refuses to whip BD. When Trudy finds out about Kat's behaviour, her question, 'Is that supposed to be politically aware?' (4: 81) is the question the audience is also asked to engage with.

The fact of Kat's economic need and her lack of personal pleasure in the process of semi-accommodating BD's sexual desires, her half-executed performance of an s/m scenario as opposed to an immersed participation, lend a seemingly different quality to Kat's activity compared to that of the other characters. However, significantly she is also shown to have only limited control over the situation; BD '*throws a roll of notes on the floor*' (3: 62) in response to Kat's demand to be paid, which means that Kat will have to bend over to pick the money up and, more humiliatingly, BD takes away the keys to the handcuffs, thus leaving Kat to be uncovered with the handcuffs on, exposing her activities. In addition, Trudy finds out that Kat borrows Gill's s/m equipment and this undermines Kat's political correctness even further. A gap opens between her talk and her actions which bespeak a dishonesty that encourages Trudy to go her own way, rather than continue to listen to Kat.

Where a certain politics might de-individualize and de-privatize sexual activities in favour of a shared, collective position, 'Sin Dykes' reveals that the gap between Kat's rhetoric and her sexual actions leaves a space in which, in true 1980s and 1990s fashion, everyone is out both for and by herself, acting in accordance with the individual private desires that fuel her fantasies and promote the enactment of those fantasies. Thus Trudy's fall from grace, if one might describe it as such, is prefigured in Scene Four where she is instructed by Gill how to strap on and use a harness and dildo.[30] Refusing Kat's assertion that 'Black women don't / do SM' (4: 79) and her historicizing analogies of s/m replaying the master-slave structures of oppressive regimes,

Trudy side-steps any political arguments in favour of a conservative, individualized, de-politicized stance: 'All I want to do is play. Explore pleasure, desire, fun. And if strapping a dildo on, wearing fetish gear, or playing with Clio is SM, so be it' (4: 79). Desire here overrides politics.

This stance is momentarily aborted when Clio in Scene Five appears with BD in the slave position, spits in BD's face, and gets BD and Trace to lick her boots. Trudy is horrified by these degrading activities. Trudy recovers her politics ('I was christened a womanist and Zami when I met you' (4: 78)) as she tells Clio: 'That was repulsive, it's no different when the roles are reversed either' (5: 83). But Clio's line about her relationships with Trace, her white slave, and BD is that 'there's sex and sex' (5: 83), and that she wants to 'make love' to Trudy. One could argue that Clio here replicates Kat's line about not having relationships with, that is emotional investments in, 'the enemy' or white women but reserving that investment for her relationships with Black women. However, Trudy's abhorrence in the face of Clio's degradation of Trace and BD might well be viewed sympathetically by an audience that agrees that any form of degradation of anyone is not acceptable. Kat's line, 'You'll never convince me that SM is not violence' (5: 86) would also resonate with that same audience. The question thus partly becomes how to deal with violence and with the desire for violence. And this is the question which remains unanswered within the play.

Boundaries of desire

A key aspect of the s/m debates as raised within 'Sin Dykes' is the question of power and control, of who is in charge and what that control means within racialized histories, not merely of sexuality.[31] Thus Trudy does not trust Gill not to get carried away in enacting her sexual fantasies, but one of the revelations of the play, and indeed its apotheosis in the final scene, is that Trudy gets carried away by enacting a s/m scenario. Trudy, excited by and afraid of s/m, agrees to 'play' with Clio, stating: 'the same thing which turns me on, is the same thing which scares me. You push my boundaries, press my buttons, and I just hate being out of control' (5: 88). But Trudy had already indicated

that she fantasizes about being out of control when she told Kat: 'do
it behind closed doors like you? . . . Collude with the myth, pretend
I don't like being overpowered, restrained, tied up?' (4: 80). Clio's interest in Trudy thus speaks to Trudy's sexual desires and fantasies,
and Clio manages to persuade Trudy to try s/m through suggesting
sexual games that do not immediately threaten Trudy's sense of self.
Her play with hankies (the colour of the hankies signalling preferred
sexual activities), not understood by Trudy who is constructed as sexually innocent, draws Trudy into interaction with Clio, and as Clio encourages her to articulate her fantasies Trudy begins to enact famous
couples: Tarzan and Jane, Romeo and Juliet, King Kong and Sleeping
Beauty. In all these scenarios she maintains the 'male' role, thus indicating her seeming control, but as she relaxes into these games they
shift to 'Tom and Jerry', cartoon figures famous not just for the differential power structure that underpins their relationship but also for
the violence of their interaction. The Tom and Jerry fantasy activates
the violent s/m dimension in Trudy and Clio's 'play'. As they play,
wordlessly, the stage directions indicate that Trudy '*becomes intoxicated by [the whip's] power . . . [and] becomes excited, dangerous,
out of control, unsafe, going beyond boundaries. She begins to crack
the whip at cLIO and becomes more and more excited and carried
away*' (5: 90). The accumulation of words used to describe Trudy's
increasingly unsafe behaviour alone signals the escalation of that behaviour and Trudy's inability to exert control over herself. One might
argue that by giving in to her desires and deciding to enact them,
she has already lost some control and that this loss is merely exacer-
bated in the enactment. However, Trudy's loss of control is also juxtaposed with Clio's retention of control, verbally encoded in the stage ·
direction, '*cLIO remains sexual in her whipping style, while TRUDY
becomes excited, dangerous*' (5: 90). Clio's sexualness is thus contrasted with Trudy's submission to the seductiveness of power and the
dangers of that submission. The difference between the two women
might be one between novice and experienced 'player' but it might also
be a case of Trudy simply being an unsafe player, someone who becomes intoxicated by power and does not know when or where to stop.

As Trudy succumbs, Clio uses the safe word 'Stop!' and there is '*Instant blackout*', marking the end of the play – but not necessarily the end of the scene.

The play leaves open the matter of whether or not Trudy is capable of stepping back from her spiralling out-of-control behaviour, whether or not she will respond to the demand for cessation. This is the dilemma the audience is left to contemplate as difference is established in both inter- and intra-racial terms. All the characters are shown to be equally incapable of resisting the enactment of their sexual fantasies and desires. Any ideological consideration of the problematic of power dynamics across and within racial groups is swept aside by the urgencies and necessities of the moment, whether these be sexual or economic. Desire emerges as a more powerful force than ideological dispositions; conscious consideration is not necessarily capable of acting as a restraint on individual behaviour. The narrative arc of the play thus operates on several levels simultaneously: on the one hand, the play tells the story of Trudy's falling from grace through shifting from her Zami, womanist position into a player in the s/m field, from sexual innocence to sexual experience, from a position of conscious consideration to one of succumbing to the enactment of desire. On another level, the play offers an increasingly complicated and complex narrative on the politics of sexual desire and sexual practice, moving from the opening considered set positions of the various characters, through a complication of those positions in Scenes Three and Four as they come under discussion and attack, to a climax in Scene Five through the enactment of a same-sex s/m scenario between two Black women which suggests that fantasies of domination/submission might not just govern relationships between Black and white women but might also arise within same-race scenarios. The potential for violence between Black women, already previously raised in a conversation between Kat and Gill (5: 86) in which Gill reminded Kat of her violent relationship with her previous partner, surfaces at the end of the play in Trudy's escalating violence and the uncertainty as to whether or not she will stop when Clio utters the safe word. The play thus '*puts the sting*', as Mason-John puts it, not just into '*the story*

of black and white relationships' (41) but also into relationships between Black women. It thus 'confronts difference within the category
of black lesbian . . . [acknowledging] a multiplicity of identities [and]
subject positions for black women' (Hammonds 1994: 130).

'Sin Dykes' presents a very different kind of diasporic reality
from 'Chiaroscuro'. The lesbian s/m scene set in Diva's bar represents
a displacement from mainstream culture in which the imaginary relation to a past history and culture (of colonialism, of racial oppression,
of lesbian feminist politics) that is different for each of the characters
shapes their positions and the nature of their engagements with the
s/m scene. The imaginary relation itself is structured by contemporary realities of racism and sexism; Kat's description of her brothers'
experiences in racist Britain ('Three behind bars, and the fourth is
in a psychiatric unit' (3: 59)), augmented by a more sustained narrative of the exclusion and stigmatization young Black people in Britain
experience, significantly influences her rejection of white women as
possible partners. BD's imaginary relation to colonial history in South
Africa, on the other hand, propels her towards relationships with Black
women, creating a split between the dominant persona she represents
as the owner of the bar who employs Black women to work for her
(expressive of the persistence of racialized inequalities) and the submissive, masochistic personality she projects in her sexual games with
the same Black women.

The play both explores and subverts racist sexual stereotypes
by ridiculing the notion that 'lesbianism is a white disease' (4: 79) and
rejecting Kat's line that Black women do not do s/m. It explodes a certain sexual naïvity as Trudy's reminiscence, 'I remember thinking I've
never seen two black women flaunt their sexuality so publicly . . . I've
only ever seen two white women, or one black woman with one white
woman, be so passionate in public' (2: 45) gives way to the reality of
the final scene which shows two Black women, Trudy and Clio, engaged in a lesbian sex scene. It thus, like Kay's 'Chiaroscuro' which
has no white characters, undermines the notion of a white lesbian experience as *the* lesbian experience in which Black lesbian experience
is invisible or silenced. Omosupe argues that

White lesbian culture, or the white lesbian, has become the quintessential representation of lesbian experience, of the very concept 'lesbian'. Given the Black lesbian's social/racial positioning and the charged political clime around Black lesbian identity issues, it is no wonder that the Black lesbian's self is 'embattled' – battered by the systematic oppressions that work in orchestration to erase her total self.

(1991: 108)[32]

Omosupe relates that embattlement to the lack of home which Black lesbians experience, their diasporic situation: '"Home" and a "lesbian Sisterhood" for Black lesbians and other lesbians of color among white lesbians is not a reality, but it is not an impossibility' (107). Both 'Chiaroscuro' and 'Sin Dykes' reflect the difficulties of finding that home in a community bound by sexual rather than by blood ties.[33] Here racial sameness becomes a more important signifier of the possibility of 'home' than sexual sameness although it is sexual sameness that has created the 'community' in the first instance.[34] Mason-John argues: 'What is clear is that there is no one static identity of a black lesbian (or any lesbian). In fact, it seems harder to identify the black lesbian among the crowd. The stereotype belongs underground on the night life scene . . . And the scene with its multifaceted identities only caters for the tiny minority who dare to go out and rave and be visible' (1999: 39).

7 Sexploitation?

On Saturday 10 August 2002, the BBC World TV news programme reported the final laying to rest of Sarah Bartmann, the so-called Hottentot Venus, whose 'private parts' had been de-privatized through their display in Paris and elsewhere during her life-time and after her death in 1815 when Georges Cuvier 'presented to "the Academy the genital organs of a woman prepared in a way so as to allow one to see the nature of the labia"' (Gilman 1992: 180). On 11 August 2002 the *Observer* featured an article on a 'pygmy show' in Belgium: 'Although the exhibition in the grounds of a private zoo is ostensibly raising money for the pygmies, anti-racism activists say it is degrading and voyeuristic' (Osborn: 19). Though the two exhibitions are separated by nearly two hundred years, their shared characteristics of the display of the supposedly physically exotic – in the Academy and the zoo, both sites where 'strange bodies', human and animal, are subjected to specularization – bespeak the history of the European exploitation of 'other' bodies to satisfy scopophilic desires through the former's exhibition, initiated through forced migration and displacement. That exhibition, in the case of Sarah Bartmann quite literally, is one of the backgrounds against which the sexploitation of Black female bodies has to be read and understood. For one of the recurrent themes of plays by Black women playwrights is the body as a site through which young Black women interrogate and (are led to) negotiate their sense of identity and socio-economic positioning. This has been apparent both in the previous chapter and in chapters two and three in this volume in particular. In this chapter I shall explore this issue further by focusing on three plays, two from 1984 and one from 1996, to analyse how that use of the young Black female body figures within the specific contexts of the two decades respectively, and how that use is racialized within those contexts.

Economic borderlands

Jacqueline Rudet's 'Money to Live' (plate 11) centres on a young Black woman, Charlene, who decides to become a go-go dancer or stripper in order to make a living both for herself and for her family. Rudet herself in her afterword to 'Money to Live' described the play as 'a story about hard times' which should not be treated as a '"black" play' specifically (1986: 180). However, in the opening scene the play articulates the historical basis of Charlene's present when Judy, her friend who is already a stripper and who encourages Charlene to take up the job, counters Charlene's reservations by saying: 'our great-grandmothers got used to a lot worse things' (1: 155). Judy views her job as a form of counter-exploitation in which the racial lines are clearly drawn: 'I work with white people, my boss is white, all the owners of the pubs are white, but only a few of my friends are white. I make good money in the white man's world' (1: 154). The racialized labour market hierarchy and exploitation articulated here are mirrored in Charlene's job situation: she counts herself lucky to have a job at a time of high unemployment, recognizing the discriminatory role that her colour plays in the labour market: 'At least I'm not one of the three million. I don't have a lot of choice plus, I'm black, that doesn't count as an extra 'A' level, you know' (1: 155).

Charlene's job at the bottom of the labour market, which leaves her not in abject poverty but barely able to make ends meet, mirrors the situation of Black women more generally on the British labour market, willing to work and with higher levels of employment than their white counterparts but frequently in lower-paid, lower-status jobs.[1] Here white men are bosses, Black women are workers. Judy understands Charlene's moral qualms about becoming a go-go dancer but also takes a cool look at what 'money *to live*'[2] as opposed to merely 'survive' means:

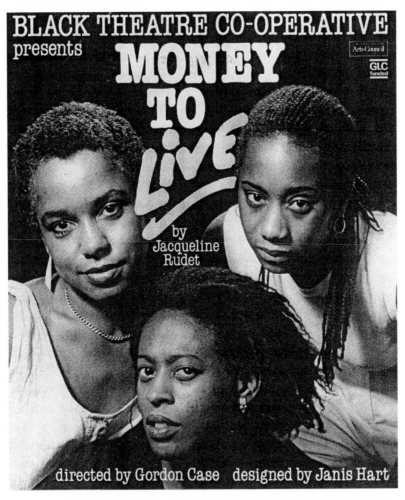

Plate 11 Poster for 'Money to Live'. Photo courtesy of Black Theatre Co-operative (now NITRO).

You think of poverty as rats and dry rot, that's *extreme* poverty but, because of the simple fact that we're now going to spend half an hour trying to dress you up . . . that means you're living on less than you would like. You've got heating, hot water, a phone, a stereo, that's true, but that's the *least* you should have!

(1: 156)

The play thus partly focuses on the socio-economic conditions that promote women's decisions to become sex-workers. It articulates women's entitlement to more than the bare material minimum but simultaneously indicates that attaining that 'more' in contemporary British society can demand ideological compromises which raise questions about women's sexploitation, women's exploitation *because of* their sex and women's exploitation *through* their sex, that is their genitalia. The conflation of those two is evident in Judy's description of the focus of men's desire in watching go-go dancers: 'all they want is to see what I've got between my legs. They don't care about any other part of my body, they just want that image for their fantasies' (1: 155).[3] The metadiscourse which Judy develops about her strip performance and which she uses to persuade Charlene to take up the job is knowing and rationalist in its understanding of the combination of racism, sexism, and economic exploitation which informs the 'job opportunities' generated by men's desire for women as specular objects of sexual gratification. Refusing to be, or to see herself as, exploited by men, Judy assumes, and encourages Charlene to assume, the position of subject, taking control of her situation, and becoming financially and emotionally independent from men. In this she views herself as a feminist, 'very concerned with sexism in society', wanting her own money and not wanting to be a housewife and dependent (6: 166). Within this logic, the paradox of taking money from men to be(come) independent of men remains unresolved. One could argue that this constitutes a realistic – rather than an aspirational – portrayal of women's economic situation under patriarchal capitalism, and is the necessary step (that is, taking money from men, not sex-working *per se*) for women to acquire the capital necessary to support themselves as well as other women.

Ideological stakes

The question of the economic logic of Judy's and Charlene's professional decisions is imbricated in the ideological debates which the play voices, predominantly – though not exclusively – through the character of Jennifer, Charlene's sister, constructed as a feminist who hangs out with white people and, according to Charlene, seemingly does not 'want to know about her people' (1: 154) any more. The structural device of juxtaposing two sisters, one 'successful', 'serious', educationally and/or economically ambitious, focused on the family, the other unable to 'make it', is a very common feature of plays by Black and Asian women as well as by other women playwrights.[4] In 'Money to Live' it takes on a particular form as each of the sisters inhabits complex and potentially contradictory positions which defy easy identification. Jennifer disagrees strongly with Charlene's choice of job as a stripper as she regards that job as perpetuating the notion that women should be viewed as sex objects and that every woman continually signals sexual availability to men. She sees it as women's role to resist that sexual objectification. Her stance is lent credence in the play in the final scene when she arrives at Charlene's flat late at night, bleeding after having been attacked by a man whose advances she refused. The fact that Jennifer is given the final lines in the play ending with the questions: 'Why do all men think that all women are just waiting to be approached? What, have I got an entrance sign over my head?' (13: 179) invites the audience to ponder *her* questions and relate these back to Charlene's position. Simultaneously, these lines reiterate the notion of the woman's body as a site to be invaded, a space to be terrorized as Jennifer's wounded head quite literally embodies.

However, the play also shows that Jennifer's position is bought at a cost. In a heated debate with Judy, in which Judy points out that Jennifer lives off others because she cannot find a job that coincides sufficiently with her ideological desire not to be exploited, Judy produces two arguments that Jennifer finds difficult to refute. One is that Judy is in a position to give actual material support to other women: 'We can both offer our voluntary services to a woman's organisation but only I can make a donation' (6: 167); the other is that she counter-exploits the men seeking to exploit her: 'I exploit every man that watches me. I'm a confidence trickster. People pay good money to see what I've got between my legs . . . how could I feel exploited?' (6: 167). This argument has already been made in the opening scene where Judy pointed out to Charlene that sexual intercourse with men is not wonderful and that if you have to use your genitalia in interactions with men, you might as well get paid for it. The context here

was the emotional and sexual exploitation of Black women by their
(Black) male partners. The play is very clear in its line that Black
men offer no support to Black women either economically or emotionally, and that their main interest in women is women's utility as sex
objects.

The impact of that exploitation is evident in Charlene's behaviour. Obsessed with cleanliness from the beginning of the play,
Charlene is eventually revealed to have become thus obsessed and to
have turned into a bit of a recluse following an abortion after becoming pregnant by her boyfriend Jeffrey, a man who tellingly does not
appear in the play since his absence is one of the keys to Charlene's
transformation. Indeed, the only two male characters who appear on
stage in this play, Charlene's father and her brother, are intermittent
presences, signalling precisely the position Black men in this play
are constructed as occupying in Black women's lives – intermittent
presences. This is reinforced by the narratives about all three male
characters who have multiple relationships with women and in all
three cases father children for whom they fail to assume responsibility and who – in the case of Charlene and of her brother's girlfriend –
are aborted by the distraught women. The gender lines are thus, in
a sense, clearly drawn regarding sexual behaviour: men act irrespon-
sibly, having sex (their seed)/money to spend, and consume women
irrespective of the consequences; women sex-work to provide.

In this world of irresponsible, absenting males, female net-
works become critical for women's survival. When Olive, Charlene's
mother, reveals that she has worked as a prostitute in order to provide for her children, the importance of female networking, already
asserted through Charlene's relation with Judy, is reinforced. Olive
tells Charlene that she entered prostitution through a neighbour; the
two women supported each other by looking after each other's children while they took it in turn to work. It is due to this history that
Olive understands her daughter Charlene's choice, even if she does
not condone it in absolute terms. The very fact, however, that both
Olive and Charlene enter sex-working, raises questions about the relationship between migration, diaspora, and sex-working among women
from female migrant groups and their female offspring. This is highly

pertinent in the contemporary context where women, in Italy for example from Nigeria, in other western European countries from eastern European countries, are forced and/or encouraged into migration for the purposes of sex-working. The links between poverty, material aspiration, and sex-working are made clear in Rudet's play and, although Jennifer is attacked by a man, this does not occur during sex-working, suggesting that women are the objects of men's aggression simply because they are women and not specifically because of sex-working. In this respect, the play supports the line taken in white playwright Sarah Daniels' 'Masterpieces' (first produced in 1983) in which women are also constructed by men as automatically sexually available to them.

Rudet's 'Money to Live' constitutes a raced intervention in the sex-working debates of the late 1970s and early 1980s which were variously fuelled by increasing feminist critiques of the so-called sexual liberation on the one hand, and the pornography debates on the other. In the UK these debates were given a particular inflection through the hunt for the Yorkshire Ripper[5] who attacked both prostitutes and women not working as prostitutes over a prolonged period, leading to 'Take Back the Night' and other campaigns by feminists who resented the impact of his murders on women's lives more generally. In temporal terms, Rudet's play sits squarely between two other plays – in this instance by white women playwrights – written during this period which deal with women and sex-working, Sarah Daniels' 'Masterpieces' (1983)[6] which engages with the pornography debates, and Kay Adshead's 'Thatcher's Women' (1987; published 1988). The latter's action takes place in 1985 and centres on women from the increasingly materially destitute north of England migrating to London to work as prostitutes. Both plays, like Rudet's, highlight the material deprivation that manoeuvres women into sex-working and expose the violence from men to which women are subjected. However, unlike Rudet's play, Daniels' and Adshead's plays are unequivocal in their condemnation of the sex-working industry and the socio-economic circumstances that drive women into that industry. Rudet is more ambivalent, as signalled in her play by positioning Charlene prior to her working as a stripper in a situation where she is materially secure

if not well off. All three plays make clear links between women's experiences with men in general and women's sex-working, and none
offers a solution to the deeply ingrained gendered relations and unequal economic conditions that foster sex-working.

Racializing sex work

Rudet's play stands out for four reasons: it remains resolutely realist whilst the other two plays become increasingly non-naturalist
in their depiction of the sex-working women and the plays' actions; it offers a racialized account of sex-working whilst the white
women playwrights' work remains race-unconscious though it is
class-conscious; it registers a diversity of sex workers' attitudes towards their work; and, finally, it details the economic benefits other
women and other people in general derive from Charlene's stripping.
The race-consciousness of Rudet's play compared to the absence of
such a consciousness in white women playwrights' work is indicative of the argument, reiterated *inter alia* in research on whiteness as
colour,[7] that the dominant group (in this instance white people) do
not think that they have to take account of those marginalized in the
ways that the latter always remain conscious of both the dominant's
and their own group's status.[8]

In the afterword of the play Rudet argues that 'What critics and
theatre people seem to respond to in my work is that I'm not overly
concerned with relations between black and white people' (180). The
very need to play down that issue bespeaks its ongoing problematic.
It is reminiscent of the ways in which feminist work has been treated,
and the resultant position of some women writers to play down the
importance of the gender dimension in their work. Rudet is keenly
aware of the racism that continues to inform British culture, but she
states that 'it's time for black people to be shown as more than just
"black"' (180). This refusal to be reduced to the body, more specifically to one's skin colour, is understandable in a culture in which skin
colour equates with all kinds of associations that influence one's socio-
economic positioning. But Rudet's assertion, 'Obviously the play has
to be performed by a black cast, and the references to the West Indies are hard to translate into any other culture' (180) reintroduces

blackness and cultural specificity as an issue. Rudet's comments thus reveal the ambivalence that diasporic identity generates, the difficulty of negotiation between validation and discrimination.

That same complex response of validation and discrimination is evident in Rudet's portrayal of the go-go dancers. Unlike white women playwrights who construct sex-working as inevitably economically determined and involuntary on women's part, part of a wider, structurally embedded discrimination against women, Rudet diffuses the astringency of that position by showing that Charlene is not on the breadline, and through the ways in which Charlene and Judy discuss other dancers' performances in Scene Thirteen. Their descriptions of some dancers seeking and encouraging direct physical sexual contact with men from the audience during performances because they will 'do anything to win the crowd over' (13: 177) – a practice that they disapprove of – might be read in terms of bravado and these women's control over the male punters, or as women's desperation, or degradation by their work. The play does not make clear whether these women's performance strategies while stripping are exploitative of the strippers or counter-exploitative of their male audiences. Significantly, however, whilst Judy describes what she does on stage (1: 155), Charlene does not. In her case it is only through the socio-economic impact which her work has on her family that the audience 'sees' the job. Charlene is thus to some extent separated from other go-go dancers, presented as occupying a certain 'moral' high ground.

Achieving subject status

That high ground is associated with the benefits the play suggests Charlene, and more importantly her family, derive from her work. Thus at the beginning of the play Charlene is depressed and isolated from her family, and her mother, sister, brother, and father exist in their own various locations of material lack and socio-emotional isolation. By the end of the play, however, the family are pulling together again. Sister Jennifer and mother Olive have – as suggested by Charlene – begun a business together. Charlene has decided to resist being a housewife and mother in favour of becoming 'a citizen of the world' (she is saving to travel) but has also started to visit her family again. She has organized an abortion for her brother's girlfriend thus sorting his problems out, and father Norbert is working doing handy-man jobs for his daughter and her friends. Last, but not least, the family are planning a get-together, financed by Charlene. Rudet may take an unduly utopic view of the impact of Charlene's greater financial liquidity in her representation of stripping, but she balances this view of material provision as social glue for the family with the fact that none of the three younger women in her play (Charlene, Judy, Jennifer) wants to take up the conventional role of housewife and mother that Charlene rightly views as 'being what a woman is' (11: 174) for her mother. For the younger generation of women the meaning of being a woman has changed. They value independence, financial autonomy, and the ability to help each other, especially other women, and not becoming the maternal, financially dependent centre of their own nu-clear family. Here Rudet highlights a marked difference in aspiration between the younger women and the older generation: 'All [the latter] ever talk about is the West Indies and family scandal' (11: 174). In contrast, the younger female generation is intent upon resisting tra-ditional female roles and do not want family other than their parents and their immediate siblings. Both generations struggle to find a place they can inhabit and are displaced, psychologically, emotionally, and – in the case of the older generation – geographically. Whilst Charlene's father Norbert deals with this situation by dreaming of going back to the West Indies, that is fantasizing about the recovery of the past, Charlene's mother Olive invests in the future in the form of her chil-dren, declaring Charlene to be 'A good daughter, a good sister and a good woman' (10: 174). Jennifer realizes herself through combining her design abilities with her mother's sewing abilities and translating these into a business. Charlene wants to acquire 'worldliness' through travel, utilizing diasporic experience to become the self she aspires to. Judy likes the job and has become used to the material comforts it affords her. Since she views her work as an extension of the usual re-lations between women and men but, importantly, transformed to her own economic advantage, she has no reason to desist from performing it – except for the question of whether or not sex-working in its various forms colludes with women's sexual exploitation and objectification, and should be resisted as part of the effort of putting a brake on that objectification. This question is posed but not answered in the play, thus inviting the audience to engage with it and draw their own conclusions.

The difficulty of dealing with this issue is apparent in a production decision that Rudet takes issue with in her afterword to the play. According to her, the male director of the play, Gordon Case, cut Scene Five (165), a scene entirely comprised of stage directions which centre on Judy teaching Charlene how to go-go dance. Rudet states that this scene is important because it indicates 'how mechanical stripping becomes for a stripper' (180). The intention was clearly to counter the notion that women enjoy stripping and that performing sexual pleasure and sensuality equals having sexual pleasure and inviting sexploitation. The difficulty lies in conveying this idea in production and Case's decision may have been motivated by wanting to remove opportunities for voyeurism from the performance. Creating a performance that offers a metadiscourse on that particular performance as it might be viewed if performed in another context (from theatre to strip joint and back again) is quite an achievement. It relies on the simultaneous signification of the multiply split subject into performer, performed character, performed character performing, and the rendition of that signification within one performance. As such it is, in fact, a particularly apt way of presenting 'woman' in this play, which is concerned with establishing the sex-worker as split subject, as 'good daughter and good woman' as much as sex-worker, as in some respects non-identical with the performance she engages in. As Rebecca Schneider puts it: 'Defined *as* split . . . and then defined *by* that split, "woman" in/as representation appears to invite one in and in and in as infinitely recessive, never quite attainable – the essence of commodity in display, ultimately silenced' (1997: 127).[9] Hence the importance of the splitting of the legs in the strip performance, the embodiment of being invited 'in and in and in as infinitely recessive, never quite attainable', matched by the going from woman to woman of the male characters in the play, interminably searching for the never quite attained. The absence of dialogue in the scene renders the female characters silent although, of course, it would be possible to produce the scene with some form of dialogue. In its printed version, however, the play relies on the surrounding scenes and dialogues to provide the verbal commentary that indicates the meaning of the strip-teaching performance.

Schneider argues that the presentation of the split subject is itself a splintered project:

> On the one hand, 'woman' is exposed as constructed, shown
> to be the dream of patriarchy and ultimately a ruse servicing
> the mold [sic] of a desire determined by capital. On the other
> hand, there is the resiliently physical fact of bearing a body
> marked female [and black] and experiencing the resultant
> social reality effects of bearing those markings. On a third
> hand, even as 'outing' the masquerade appears to promise
> an end to the naturalization of femininity, the issue of the
> inhabitability, the performativity, the 'masquerade' of
> femininity rings of the historical habit of imagining woman as
> an endlessly inhabitable, impregnable, male-identified space.
>
> (127)

In this seeming no-win situation, it is perhaps not surprising that Case decided to shy away from the difficulties of producing Scene Five and engaging with 'the explicit female body in performance' as Schneider terms it. Rudet's anger at the unauthorized cutting of the scene is very evident in the afterword of the play where her discussion of that directorial decision ends with, 'What women create in life, men destroy' (180). She regards the issue as an articulation of the gender differences that are also embedded, and remain unresolved, within the play.

Maternalizing the female body

A not dissimilar position is taken in Grace Dayley's 'Rose's Story' (1984; published 1985), first produced at the Polytechnic of the South Bank whilst Dayley was still a student there. As Dayley explains in the afterword, the play is both autobiographical (79) and reminiscent of the situation of many of the female performers of its first production (80) in that, according to Dayley, 'nearly 50% of the women in the cast were unmarried mothers' (80). The play centres on the process by which fifteen-year-old Rose decides to keep her baby once she discovers she is pregnant. It is thus a play about teenage pregnancy, a subject that received considerable attention in the Britain of the 1980s and 1990s, partly because teenage pregnancies in the UK rose significantly during that period and are the highest in Europe, and partly because the decline of the welfare state resulted in much public discourse on the issue of 'lone mothers sponging off the state' and teenagers getting pregnant as a way of giving meaning to their lives in a world in which their future looks bleak due to lack of education and employment opportunities. In fact, this preoccupation goes back to the 1950s and had its first theatrical outing in the period since the Second World War in Britain in Shelagh Delaney's *A Taste of Honey* (1958/9), written when Delaney herself was still a teenager. Unusually for the period and given that Delaney is a white playwright, *A Taste of Honey* featured a Black character, the girl Jo's boyfriend by whom she becomes pregnant. But whereas Jo, and other female characters in later plays on the topic by Black women writers, are highly ambivalent about their impending maternity and/or decide to have an abortion,[10] in Rudet's play the central character Rose decides very quickly to have the baby, despite the fact that this ultimately splits her from her family and leads to her institutionalization in a home for lone mothers and their babies. Her opening line is, in fact, 'Of course I want the baby' (1, 1: 57).

The play begins with a scene in a doctor's office where Rose has her pregnancy confirmed. Unusually for British plays (though not in actuality), the doctor is an Asian man in his fifties but it is less his racial identity than his patronizing attitude that is the focus of the scene.[11] The setting thus signals a multi-cultural society and one in which cross-generational and inter-sexual differences are more significant than racial ones.[12] Rose attributes her situation, the fact that she fell for the boy next door Leroy, ran away with him from home, and is pregnant by him, to her overly strict upbringing and socio-emotional isolation: 'it was a miserable existence, nobody outside that house could understand. It was church, school, church, school, and more church, school' (1, 1: 57). Rose's situation is, in fact, very reminiscent of Brenda's situation in Zindika's *Paper and Stone*. Here too the overly religious parent, Brenda's mother, gradually drives her children away as she manifests her inability to tolerate the changed reality that constitutes Brenda's life in Britain compared to her own background and upbringing. Raped by a white man in her youth, thus alienated from her body,[13] and having left the resultant infant to its fate on birth, subsequently displaced through her migration, Brenda's mother seeks to alleviate her pain by investing in the church and in Brenda's future as a professional member of the church – a future Brenda increasingly realizes she does not want for herself. Similarly, Rose recognizes that she has to take responsibility for herself and her child as her parents' dominant response to her situation is one of judgment and condemnation. Thus, like Charlene in 'Money to Live', it is through her body that Rose begins to establish an identity independent of her parents and to come to her self. Pregnancy moves her from a reactive and self-destructive dynamic that centres on her relationship with her parents to a position of agency and self-determination. Her misery in her parents' home, graphically described in her opening monologue (1, 1: 57–8), has previously led her to contemplating suicide. But her new sense of responsibility for another, the foetus in her womb, results in Rose deciding to take responsibility for herself, even in the face of parental opposition.

Interestingly, her parents' unwillingness to take responsibility for their child manifests itself in their continuous appeal to institutionalized authority in the form of the police, social workers, and the church, culminating in Rose's father signing over his daughter to the social services to be taken into care in a mother-and-baby home. That appeal and their refusal to take care of Rose are grounded in their lack of empathy with their daughter's situation. As Rose puts it: 'Mummy and Daddy don't understand that we weren't born in the 1920's and can't relate to their norms and values' (2, 3: 72). Her pregnancy forces Rose to grow up and understand that she has to 'learn to hold [her] own' (2, 3: 72). Always already the 'quiet one' who did as she was told, Rose shows a great sense of responsibility in how she responds to her situation. As such she in a sense mirrors Charlene, also always the responsible one, who uses her situation to bring about positive change within her family. For Rose, the pregnancy constitutes a reason for living. Previously afraid of her parents and desperate, she is now 'determined to make a go of things for me and my baby' (2, 3: 73), and in that determination she puts those around her, most especially her supposedly Christian parents and her boyfriend Leroy, to shame.

Where Rose's parents regard her pregnancy as an attack on their standing in the community and on the values they hold, Leroy initially views his impending fatherhood as a status symbol, signalling his manhood. His response to the news of Rose's pregnancy is to want to go out and celebrate with his mates. Rose's repeated insistence that he needs to find a job and provide for her and the child – since he is so keen for her to have the child rather than consider abortion – is met with prevarication and outright dismissal. Leroy is in effect not ready to assume the responsibilities of parenthood, since he is still in the process of exploring what masculinity and maturity mean to him. In the afterword to the play Dayley records that *Spare Rib* (March 1984) reviewed the play critically because of the representation of Leroy as 'Black workshy'. As in other plays by Black women, Dayley's play too portrays some Black males as irresponsible, self-centred, materialistic, drug-taking, overly assertive, and both authoritarian and unsupportive towards women. As Dayley writes in the afterword about the casting of the play: 'Men were difficult to come by and proved even more difficult to keep, especially when the going got rough. This could have been linked to the actual content of the play' (80). As indicated previously in this volume, this kind of representation of Black men was very common on both sides of the Atlantic during the 1970s and 1980s, and generated, especially in North America, a furious debate about gender divisions within the Black community. However, Dayley produces a much more nuanced presentation of Black men than *Spare Rib*'s critique suggests, for Leroy is contrasted with Bertie, his mate, whom Rose dislikes and whom she regards as responsible for some of Leroy's more problematic behaviour. However, it is Bertie – unbeknown to Rose – who attempts to get Leroy to understand and take up the responsibilities that Rose's pregnancy implies. In contrast to Rose's father who invokes the Lord to condemn Rose (2, 3: 71), Bertie suggests that Jah 'has seen she it's time fe bless you wid a youth, so look after Rose, care fi her, she a go need somebody fi stan by her' (2, 2: 69). Bertie tells Leroy that Rose's parents will expect him to show that he is a man by facing them together with Rose (2, 2: 70). But Leroy – once he belatedly arrives at Rose's parents' house – is unable to assert himself against the rage of Rose's father, and his inability to act in an appropriate way leads Rose to dismiss him (2, 4: 76). Bertie, the guy whom Rose looks down upon as a bad influence on Leroy, is in fact the only male who shows any real understanding of her situation. Ultimately, though, Rose ends up alone – facing an uncertain, if institutionally supported, future in a mother-and-baby home in the community. Her final lines: 'And this is where the story *really* begins' (2, 4: 78) invite the audience to contemplate what that story might be(come).

Splitting the subject

The audience has, of course, already been offered one story, the story of how Rose deals with her decision to keep the baby once she discovers she is pregnant. The play's title, 'Rose's Story', which suggests a narrative, is realized formally through Rose's opening and closing monologues in which she explodes the play's realist frame by turning to the audience and addressing it directly[14] in monologues that self-consciously articulate their narrative function ('let me tell you how it all started' (1, 1: 57)) and emphasize Rose's perspective as the dominant one in the play: 'By the way my name is Rose and this is *my* story . . .' (1, 1: 57). The dominance of that perspective is reinforced through the specificity of Rose's prominence at the beginning and the end of the play: she is the only character given monologues that are directly addressed to the audience and she is the only character who – as she delivers the monologues – moves from an intradiegetic to an extradiegetic position. That shift enhances the notion of Rose as the controlling agent of the narrative, thus consummately contradicting the received wisdom that teenage girls are the objects, rather than the subjects, of their circumstances. Dayley uses an embedded narrative, realized through metadiscursive monologues ('As you have heard, I'm pregnant' (1, 1: 57)), to signal Rose's agency, her assumption of subject status. Rose, as narrator, becomes the split subject, divided into the narrating and the narrated self. Her sense of selfhood, indeed her assumption of subject status, depends on distinguishing her current self – assertive, independent, determined – from her past self – withdrawn, dependent, unassertive. That distinction is accomplished through the insertion of another body – that of the foetus – into her life history, and the consequent creation of another split subject: mother and child. As Rose's story resides inside her monologues, so the foetus resides inside Rose's body and, paradoxically, confirms that there is no such thing as an autonomous subject. Rather, subjects are constructed as inter-dependent: the Rose of the past was as determined by her parents as the Rose of the present is determined by the foetus she carries. External agencies such as social services play as large a role in determining Rose's assumption of an adult self at the beginning as at the end of the play. Subject status, by women often accomplished through bodily self-determination,[15] is confirmed and conferred, in this play, through a resistance to self-destructive impulses (suicide, the killing of the body) and an affirmation of the other in self, the body within the body.

The play thus raises another very important question, namely, what does bodily self-determination for women mean? What is the status of Rose's decision? To what extent is having the baby actually *her* decision? Nobody wants her to be pregnant and she has not actively sought to become pregnant, but once she is pregnant, both Leroy and her father do not want her to abort – albeit for different reasons – whilst those in authority (the doctor, the social worker) advise her to abort. One could thus argue that in keeping the baby Rose defies the authority of external agencies but succumbs to the dictates of patriarchal injunctions. However, both Leroy and Rose's father, potentially the providing males, abdicate their responsibility for making provision for Rose and her child, contrasting significantly with the maligned Bertie who does provide for the child he fathered (2, 2: 68–9). Rose's decision not to abort, whilst coincidental with patriarchal dictates, is thus ultimately not accompanied by an assumption of responsibility on the part of the males in her life. One could, in fact, argue that whilst Rose's body and life change as a partial consequence of their behaviour and decisions, nothing changes in their lives. Instead, the state, in the form of social services and a mother-and-baby home, is left to assume a paternal (or is it maternal = caring?) relation to her, as she assumes her parental role towards the baby she is expecting.

Rose is too young to fend for herself. Telling her sister Elaine about the people 'out there' she has seen, 'hussling [sic] to make a living, thieving to survive, moving from squat to squat with no permanent address' (2, 3: 73), Rose agrees to go into the mother-and-baby home not only because as a minor she has been signed over to social services by her father and thus cannot determine her own fate, but also because she understands that she needs support in order to complete her schooling so that she can provide for herself and her baby. Subject status thus emerges as associated with taking responsibility and effectively negotiating between personal needs and desires and the constraints generated through the inter-subjective axes that determine people's lives. Rose is shown to be much more adept at the latter than anybody else in her immediate environment. Neither her parents nor Leroy are ready to assume proper responsibility in their inter-subjective relations. The state is invoked to fill the resultant void. Rose takes what responsibility she can, 'And this is where the story *really* begins' (2, 4: 78). This ending signals a newly split subject, congruent with Rose's pregnant status, between the Rose of the present and the Rose of the future whose story is as yet unknown. It leaves the audience where the audience was at the beginning of the play – in anticipation, and this is synonymous with Rose's own state of anticipation of the baby.

On the surface 'Rose's Story' confirms the much vaunted prejudice that young (Black) women get pregnant because they are promiscuous and engage in unprotected sex. But Rose's background and the presentation of her character denies the notion of unpoliced female teenage roaming and engaging in random sexual encounters. Instead, it suggests that an overly strict upbringing and lack of understanding of female children can promote the estrangement from parents that makes girls vulnerable to male affection and thus exposes them to the risk of pregnancy. The play indicates, through Sister Thompson's narrative of multiple pregnancies by different men (1, 3: 61–2), ultimately and in a sense humorously resolved by turning to God instead of men (God being less likely to make you pregnant), that Rose's story is only partly *her* story. For contrary to Dayley's assertion in the afterword that 'every pregnant teenager's experience [is] unique' (79), Sister Thompson's and Rose's stories share the experience of pregnancy at an early age and abandonment by males.[16] Similarly, one reason why Charlene's sister Jennifer in 'Money to Live' associates with white people is that 'all the black girls in my school were either stupid or pregnant or both' (5: 166). Whilst Jennifer's dismissive lines may grate, they nonetheless highlight the problematic of Black teenage pregnancy – even though teenage pregnancy is not an issue confined to Black teenagers. Rose's story may thus well be unique to her in *her* experience of it, but it is also part of a wider socio-cultural pattern which signals young women's vulnerability to sexual advances by men and resultant pregnancies – a vulnerability that comes out of emotional rather than sexual needs, and that results in the sexploitation of young girls by their sexual partners, manifested in the latters' abandonment of the young women they impregnate.

The movements of sexploitation

Another form of sexploitation, genitally focused, is articulated in Winsome Pinnock's *Mules* (1996). The play centres on young women induced to act as drugs couriers between Jamaica and the UK by concealing drugs on and in their bodies. Here the scene shifts from the local to the global, with the central characters participating in the global circulation of illicit goods through the translation of their dreams – to travel the world – being harnessed to an economy that depends on the exploitation of those dreams. In this economy, migration aids the circulation of goods, and the exploitation of young women is achieved through laminating desire to utility. The ultimate symbol of this process is Bridie, a former drugs courier who recruits new 'mules'. Without home and roots, socially alienated from her 'original' family and manipulative of the girls she associates with, her life – lived in hotels and through travel – is one of constant movement, of always being *en route*.

Mules was commissioned by Clean Break Theatre Company, a long-standing women's theatre company, established in 1979 by two former women prisoners.[17] The company's background explains the focus of Pinnock's play since the company commissions 'new plays by women dramatists exploring contemporary female experiences of crime and punishment' (Rosenthal 1999) as part of an integrated artistic and education programme that articulates the company's social programme. Given the disproportionately high number of Black women in prison – the publicity for Clean Break Theatre Company's production of Black playwright Paulette Randall's play *24%* stated starkly that 'Black women make up only 2% of the overall population. The proportion of black women in prison is 24%'[18] – Clean Break Theatre Company have a history of commissioning new work by Black women playwrights to reflect that reality.[19] In turn this context fosters issue-based plays on the experiences of women who are imprisoned.

In its focus on women as drugs couriers *Mules* explores an issue which gained prominence in public discourse during the early 1990s, namely the (ab)use of women to act as drugs couriers between Africa, Jamaica, and Europe (see Stuttaford 1992). The choice of women as couriers is in part a function of the cultural invisibility of women which seemingly makes their detection – when involved in crime – less likely. Allie, one of the couriers whom Bridie, a key 'administrator' in the supply chain of drugs, recruits off the London streets, says: 'All my life I've been somebody that nobody noticed . . . People just wouldn't see me' (2, 12: 55). That invisibilization, signalled by the use of 'wouldn't' rather than 'couldn't', constitutes simultaneously a threat and an opportunity for Allie. It is a threat because she tends to get picked on (her history is one of sexual and physical victimization), a fact that ultimately makes her tough as Act One, Scene Eight demonstrates when she turns on two girls out to rob her and manages to scare them away. The resultant combination of toughness and seeming invisibility in turn makes her attractive to Bridie – her 'opportunity' – who takes Allie under her wing to groom her to be a courier.

It is the same combination of toughness or streetwiseness and seeming invisibility that attracts Bridie to Lou, the girl whom she picks up in Jamaica and manages to persuade to act as a courier. The play thus creates an interesting parallel between young Black women in Jamaica, represented by the sisters Lyla and Lou, and young Black women in Britain, represented by Allie. This is formally encoded through alternating the location between Jamaica and London for the first eight scenes which take Allie and Lou to the point where they agree to work for Bridie. The girls' invisibility is matched by their poverty, and their willingness to take on the high-risk activity of carrying drugs depends – so the play suggests – entirely on their dream to improve their lives and participate in a material world from which they are excluded by virtue of being young Black women on their own.

This latter point is important for the play offers a subtext of maternal deprivation that leaves all its young female characters vulnerable to a quasi-maternal figure who deludes them into believing that she cares for and about them, who suggests that she is willing to initiate and assist them into a better life style, and who seems to present a combination of maternal care and role model: authoritative, understanding and thus offering possibilities of identification, and nurturant (quite literally: Bridie takes her 'victims' out to eat and feeds them – even in the final scene with Lyla before she herself gets beaten up, she comes to bring Lyla food). Allie, Lou, and Lyla have all suffered maternal abandonment by mothers who though still alive have been unable to interpolate themselves between their daughters and female (s)exploitation. Allie was sexually molested, whether by her father or her mother's subsequent boyfriend remains unclear; Lou and Lyla's mother is destitute to the point of complete deprivation. As Lou tells Bridie: 'We have a mother but she sleep naked a roadside. Sometime I see her I have to turn my head away like as if I don't know her' (1, 7: 31). The absence of an appropriate mother figure leaves the young women to fend for themselves within a peer culture that proves almost wholly exploitative as each woman tries to secure her own survival, rendering all mutual support structures, such as that between sisters Lyla and Lou, and that between Lou and Allie once they are in prison, temporary and vulnerable.

Mirrors as opposites

The combination of an absence of maternal care and lack of material opportunity makes bright, able girls like Lou and Allie respond to the opportunities offered by Bridie to lever themselves out of their material deprivation into a world of shopping and material comfort if not security. Bridie, in fact, is constructed as an older version of Lou and Allie – the 'ideal mother', both the same and positively different, the embodiment of what Lou and Allie might become. She herself articulates that similarity when she tells Lou: 'I know what it's like to have no one, nothing. We come from the same place' (1, 7: 31) and 'You're so like me' (1, 7: 32). The mirror image she offers to Lou and Allie suggests the possibility of imitation, leading Allie, for instance, to say: 'One day I'll be like you' (2, 10: 46). Bridie seems to embody the trajectory from rags to riches, from exploitation to control, that the girls strive for. Bridie's pledges of opportunity and support ('If there's anything you need, anything bothering you, just come to me' (1, 7: 33); 'I won't lie to you, Allie . . . you'll always know where you stand' (2, 10: 48)) answer to Lou's and Allie's desire to be taken care of and have their lives transformed.

Bridie, as the mirror image of the girls, seems to have her own history of maternal abandonment: 'My mother abandoned me when I was a child. I've been fending for myself since I was fourteen years old' (2, 10: 48). However, throughout the play it remains unclear whether or not Bridie ever tells the truth. As she attempts to ensure that Lyla, Lou's sister, will not denounce her to the police, she tells her a story of carrying drugs (2, 14: 58) – which she maintains she herself still occasionally does. That story mirrors exactly the narrative Allie had produced about her first experience of carrying drugs (2, 10: 44). Through this incident in particular the play indicates that Bridie's skill in recruiting 'mules' lies in her ability to manipulate others to suggest actual and potential sameness between them and herself. Simultaneously, it calls into question all her assertions of similarity, arguing instead that simulation is the key to Bridie's position. Bridie's ability to simulate sameness and insert herself into the girls' lives may well depend on her ability to generalize from her own history to that of other young women and, in a sense, to give them what she understands, on the basis of her own experience, they desire.

However, the cost of maternal abandonment – as evidenced in Bridie's behaviour – is the inability to trust and to sustain any non-exploitative relationship. Bridie becomes the 'bad mother' as she, the audience eventually discovers, cynically 'sacrifices' some of her drugs couriers, including Allie and Lou, for the sake of getting the others through customs. The girls' fate – which they assumed rested on their own ability to signify normality – was never theirs to determine; instead it was sealed before they ever boarded the plane. However, and similarly, Bridie's seeming control – which signalled her difference from the other drugs couriers – is exploded in the second act when she is found by her colleagues Sammie and Rog, roughed up (2, 16). As Rog, constructed as the more naïve of the two, attempts to understand why Bridie has been beaten up, Sammie, her 'savvy' colleague, effectively dismisses the event as part of their life style in which 'Life isn't all cause and effect', it is 'best not to ask questions', and beating up someone is regarded as a 'good way of motivating your staff' (2, 16: 65).

Rog, who – like Lou and Allie – had wanted to be like Bridie, is unmoored by seeing her done over as it raises questions about Bridie's identity. If she is not the poised and in-control character she seemed to be, what is she? Sammie implies that Bridie has no core identity: 'Take away the false passports, the clothes, the hair extensions, nails – what have you got left?' (2, 16: 66). This lack of identity corresponds to Bridie's lack of a home – she lives in hotels and chooses not to have a 'fixed abode'. Rootless, she has made herself over. Having revealed to Lou who thought she was American that she too is from Trenchtown, Jamaica, Bridie tells her: 'The accent started as an affectation when I was a child and later became part of my character. As for the ghetto . . . it isn't ingrained, you know. You can wash it off' (1, 7: 32).

Bridie is a woman living in a global, late-capitalist culture, rootless and always *en route*, in flight, not least from herself: 'I suppose if I settled down I'd have to establish some sort of relationship with myself. I can't say I particularly want to' (2, 11: 50). Lacking a core to which she can relate she translates that lack into movement, travelling between Jamaica and London, a perpetual migrant in a world that lacks both the idea and the ideal of 'home' – certainly for women. Her and the couriers' pastime and temporary fulfilment is shopping, the assuagement of desires that can never be satisfied as their excess of consumption makes clear.

Gendering migration in a global economy

Mules suggests that maternal deprivation and the absence of a core identity as well as a 'home' in its ideal sense are a function of women's structural position in the gendered capitalist culture which constitutes the world of the late twentieth century. Males are absent presences in this play in which their influence – in the form of sexual and physical violence – looms large and in which, as owners of capital and assets, men ultimately act as the puppet masters pulling the strings that make women move. Few men are even mentioned in the play. Allie's abusing father and her mother's equally problematic boyfriend signal the splitting of the mother-daughter dyad through the insertion of the male. The male, in the form of the 'owner' of home and land, then initiates the migration of women on which his accumulation of capital rests. He is rooted, the females are uprooted, *en route*, migrating as the carriers of capital they do not own. In that sense 'Practices of displacement', as James Clifford puts it, 'emerge as *constitutive* of cultural meanings' (1997: 3), here specifically as constitutive of the meaning of gendered positions. Significantly, Clivenden, the drug baron, for example, whose story of threatening a drugs courier (2, 11: 50–2) indexes his capacity for violence and intimidation, is the only one who lives in a house – which is 'all classical music and antiques' (2, 11: 51). His rootedness and at-homeness depends on the roaming of the women he employs and exploits. They become synonymous with the circulation of drugs, the movement that generates the capital on which his pretensions to middle-class culture and to rootedness rest.

The mirror image to Clivenden in Britain is the landowner in Jamaica on whose ganja fields Lyla – and finally Lou – end up working.

Jeremy Kingston maintains that 'The play has an oddly old-fashioned crime-does-not-pay feel to it' (1996: 33). That reading completely ignores the gendered economy of the play in which it is not crime but being a woman that does not pay. Thus in the pivotal Act Two, Scene Nine, structurally at the centre of the play, Bridie graphically details the death of Olu, an illegal Nigerian immigrant into Britain, from an overdose as a result of the condom holding the drugs in her vagina bursting. No male is held to account in this play – on the contrary, the two best-situated people, Clivenden and the Jamaican landowner, are males making a living out of exploiting women. The play is thus concerned not with the vicissitudes of crime but with the vicissitudes of being a female in a certain globalized economy in which women 'live like a mule, die like a mule' (2, 9: 43).

Through the symmetries she sets up between the fates of Allie and Lou, on the one hand, and Clivenden and the Jamaican plantation owner on the other, Pinnock establishes a gendered image of the world which constructs men as owning and exploiting, and women as shopping or consuming and exploited. In this world location in spatial terms is less significant than gender – women, the play states, get fucked over by men. This line is reinforced through the collapse of the differences between Bridie and her couriers at the point when Bridie is found beaten up. 'She's nothing but a mule' (2, 16: 67) Rog says, an exploited animal unable to alter her situation. Contrary to the teleological narrative of self-improvement and increasing material standards suggested by Bridie's self-presentation in Act One, the play utilizes the brutalization of Bridie and the imprisonment of Allie and Lou in Act Two to signal the provisionality of any such change, its dependence on men who are beyond the reach of the women thus victimized. These men's absence and invisibility on stage effectively theatricalizes the notion of power at a remove – theirs is not the invisibility that stems from insignificance and makes women ideal couriers, but the invisibility of a power that need not be present to be effective. Women's submission to this power is constructed both as arising from their deprived economic status and from the habitus, to use Pierre Bourdieu's phrase, of femininity. Bridie, for instance, early on asserts: 'Women don't mutiny. They ask permission first' (1, 1: 4). Later on, when Allie revels in her first successful drugs carrying and says, 'I want to be good', Bridie responds with, 'Don't we all? It's the female condition' (2, 10: 47).

The desire to be good, to please, ultimately to find acceptance and avert abandonment, structures women's behaviour in this play which also reinforces the notion that not only is any transgression, any failure to 'be good' (and 'being good' here means being good on men's terms), found out and punished, but also that 'being good' and 'asking permission' in themselves do not act as guarantors of any improvement in women's situation. It remains, for instance, unclear why Bridie gets beaten up, and 'being good' (= doing as they are told) does not save Lou and Allie from being shopped to the customs officers. Women, the play suggests, are in a no-win situation in which their goodness or otherwise does not improve their agency or economic independence from men. They remain trapped. Hence the somewhat obvious metaphor of the bird, Allie and Lou's fantasy of flying away from prison. The bird, significantly, is a 'he':

> LOU Where he taking us?
> ALLIE . . . the flight seemed purposeful.
> *The women's movement suddenly stops.*
> Then he stopped, hovering over a vast expanse of ocean. And that's where we stayed.
> LOU For three days and three nights.
> . . .
> ALLIE The colour of the water changing . . .
> LOU . . . Changing, changing and always the same.
> ALLIE We hovered for three days and nights . . .
> LOU And then we understood.
> ALLIE Everything.
> *Sound of a succession of heavy prison doors clanging shut and keys turning in locks.*
>
> (2, 15: 64–5)

The notion of flight as liberation and escape is revealed to be a fantasy, the flight's seeming purposefulness obliterated by being stuck above an abyss in which one might drown and where the key revelation, rather as in the Bible signalled through remaining in one space for a specified number of days and nights, is the understanding that nothing changes and that imprisonment is the reality of the women's lives. Movement *per se* does not effect change. Bridie's assertion that 'When I stop travelling, I still feel like I'm flying' (2, 11: 50) does not signal successful escape but the inability to achieve roots and lasting change. Migration thus emerges as a forced movement that keeps women in their place within the patriarchal capitalist economy in which they play their role as mules on a treadmill keeping the machinery and machinations of male owners going.

Covering a three-year period, *Mules'* opening and closing scenes show the sisters Lou and Lyla attempting to eke out a living in Jamaica. From selling wares they have shifted to selling their labour, making too little money to improve their situation. Things have simultaneously changed and not changed for them. Lou has had her spell in prison; Lyla has had children, a man, and is working. But the work, generated through Bridie's mediation, is still in the drugs industry, and where at the opening of the play the two girls were independent if ineffectual actors, by the end of the play they have become dependent on work given to them by men. At best their situation remains static; at worst it constitutes a decline in autonomy. The sexploitation they have suffered on account of being women and through being forced to carry drugs in their vaginas has not improved their condition.

One of the striking aspects of the three plays discussed in this chapter is the ambivalent note on which they end. All three plays portray sexploitation, women's exploitation by men as a function of their being women and through the (ab)use of their vaginas in the sex industry, through unwanted pregnancy, and in carrying drugs. All three plays focus on young women whose exodus from home occurs under circumstances that alienate the women from their homes and simultaneously suggest that home and roots are an achievement, almost unattainable for women, rather than a past left behind and nostalgically remembered. Maternality itself is compromised through sexploitation and female subjugation. In 'Money to Live' Claudette's mother has had to work as a prostitute to maintain her home. In 'Rose's

Story' her mother sides with her father and male-dominated institutions in handing Rose over to social services. All the mothers in *Mules*, with the exception of Lyla towards the end of the play, abandon or are forced to abandon their female children.

These female children in turn are unable to escape their exploitation. Claudette intends to give up go-go dancing but this is not achieved within the play; Rose does not know what her future will hold but one terrifying vision she has is of the women on the streets; Lou and Lyla see no future for themselves beyond having their labour exploited by men. The women who act as 'symbolic mothers'[20] or mentors to the young women, mediating between the parent generation/men and the young women's generation, are themselves deeply compromised in their actions and in hock to the men and institutions they represent. Judy, Claudette's friend who initiates Claudette into stripping, is unable to give up the comforts derived from go-go dancing and sees no virtue in the exploitative heterosexual relationships that might offer an alternative to sexploitative work. Miss Pickford, the social worker who deals with Rose, is imbricated in structures of male authority. Bridie is herself vulnerable to the violence of the drugs industry and has no allegiance to any of the girls she recruits on behalf of the drug barons.

As issue-based plays these three plays offer no solution to the problem of women's sexploited status. At the end of each play it is unclear what and how things might change for the central female characters. This unresolved problematic finds its disastrous resolution in Kara Miller's *Hyacinth Blue* from 1999 in the simultaneous suicide through hanging of the three female inmates that are the central characters of the play, also commissioned by Clean Break Theatre Company. Indulging in fantasies of liberation, reconciliation, and affirmation, the play gradually delivers the recognition that the women – one of whom, like Lou and Allie, has been imprisoned as a consequence of carrying drugs – are preparing to kill themselves. Charlie, the white psychotic inmate, paints a 'dream place [*sic*] in spring' (49) onto the wall of their shared prison cell and, in line with the economy of late patriarchal capitalism as discussed above, it is not the 'fruit' – women – hanging from the tree which is part of this dream place that is strange, but the dream place itself which is the background against which the women kill themselves. The shocking literalization of women's entrapment from which – no matter where they come from and what age they are[21] – they are unable to escape except through death constitutes an indictment of the racism and sexism that destroys their lives.

8   Living diaspora now

Since the very late 1990s, a new figure has emerged in the work of Asian women playwrights in Britain, the refugee and asylum seeker.[1] This figure occupies a different position in the history of migration and diaspora from the ones that dominated plays by Black and Asian women playwrights during the 1980s and until the second half of the 1990s, since – as the plays discussed below indicate – that figure occupies a space of extreme abjection, made distinct by the history of a violent past, lack or absence of citizen status and all the rights that this, at least in theory, confers, loss of community and all socio-emotional connections, complete disempowerment and objectification in the present, and uncertainty or a tragic ending governing the future. What this figure bespeaks is the changing reality of migration histories and diasporic experiences, for the refugee or asylum seeker is unlike the economic migrant who does not necessarily suffer the memory of a history of violation during war or political conflict, and who has the right to seek employment and make a life for herself. The refugee or asylum seeker has no such right; stuck, quite literally, in a confined space, the detention centre, her abjection consists, *inter alia*, in having to wait, becoming the object of processes the outcomes of which are uncertain (see Barkham 1999). Through the plays the audience is drawn into that experience of uncertainty, humiliation, invasion of privacy, and process of abjection that the refugee/asylum seeker undergoes.

The figure of the refugee or asylum seeker as depicted in Amrit Wilson's *Survivors* (1999)[2] and in Tanika Gupta's *Sanctuary* (2002) bespeaks a contemporary reality and conflict within British society that concerns Britain's position – as a state – as a country of immigration and its policies on asylum seeking and refugees (see Garrett 2002), on the one hand, and British people's reception of such figures on the other (see Dodd 2000). *Survivors* and *Sanctuary* address the issue from somewhat different positions. As the foreword to *Survivors* explains, Wilson's play is based on 'a real event which occurred in 1996' when two brothers from Pakistan tried to enter Britain by stowing away in the undercarriage of a plane. One of the brothers died of hypothermia: 'The body of the brother who died fell in Richmond' (Foreword). In drawing on an actual incident, the tragic death of an individual under circumstances of persecution and harassment, Wilson continues one of the traditions of Black and Asian playwrights' work in Britain – that of transforming real-life events for the stage.[3] Importantly, by staging the play at the Orange Tree Theatre in Richmond upon Thames, a geographical space that lies in the flight path to the approach to Heathrow, Wilson took the play to the community which had 'received' the body of the dead brother who had fallen from the plane, a community that is virtually entirely white and one of the richest in the UK. The play thus confronted that community not only with an aspect of its own recent history but also with a group of people who are not part of Richmond life and whom many from Richmond would probably only ever have seen in photos in the newspapers or on television as part of reports about riots in detention centres or debates about the now closed Sangatte camp in France from which for several years people tried to migrate, often illegally, to the UK.

Since press reports on refugees and asylum seekers often veer between reporting the individual case whose 'deserving-ness' is in question and representations of refugees as a mass phenomenon, plays such as *Survivors* have a critical role to play in problematizing the political debates on asylum seeking and the issue of refugee status. As such they fall within the socialist-realist tradition of theatre-making, designed to intervene in issues around which change, social, political, and legal is sought. Playwrights such as Amrit Wilson write as advocates, as women who understand and live the struggle to gain subject status, to '*achieve presence*' as Jatinder Verma called it (1994: 55), in a culture which continues to deny that presence. It is out of this struggle that certain forms of socialist-realist theatre are born and within that struggle that such forms of theatre persist.

Gendering asylum seeking

Both *Survivors* and *Sanctuary* tell a gendered narrative of asylum seeking and refugee experience. In both plays the asylum seekers or refugees are men. The centrality of male characters in these plays is a new phenomenon in that women writers in the past have tended to focus more prominently on female characters.[4] However, that centrality reflects the fact that in political conflict and war males are constructed as agents and women and children become part of the battleground on which those conflicts are carried out. The harrowing narratives which the central male characters are gradually forced into revealing, of the rape and murder of women and children, their own wives, mothers, sisters, children, and friends, rapes and murders which they witnessed and were unable to prevent, lay bare the gendered specificities of war and, simultaneously, testify to the emasculation of men through violent political conflict and the attendant attacks on their families as a way of destroying the latter as well as communities (see Price 2002). Both plays thus proclaim an indictment of regimes that foster violation. In particularizing those experiences, humanizing them through the portrayal of individuals and their stories, the plays force basic questions about the right to live to the front.

Forcing that question – *Survivors* ends with the line 'I want to live' – foregrounds ethical considerations in both plays. *Survivors* and *Sanctuary* produce complex histories of guilt and implicatedness in politically motivated violence that seems to set aside all consideration for the humanity of those made to suffer. Both plays refuse a simple opposition of a racist Britain on the one hand seeking to keep out unwanted foreigners who are the innocent victims of political turmoil on the other. Instead, degrees of innocence become synonymous with degrees of guilt and implicatedness, as individual characters seek to extricate themselves from the morass of conflicts they are unable to govern. Their history and past, which has motivated their escape from their country of origin and encouraged them to seek refuge in Britain, haunts them as they seek to establish themselves in Britain.

In *Survivors* this haunting in part takes the shape of the ghost of the dead brother Dilip coming to life.[5] That ghostly brother, together with their uncle Jaspal who is resident in Britain and who seeks to support the surviving brother Satnam in making his asylum application, gradually forces Satnam to remember the family's history, in particular the fact that Satnam's and Dilip's father, a police officer, had boys supposedly suspected of terrorist activities – among them friends of his sons – imprisoned, tortured, and killed. When Dilip, the younger son who was politically active, tried to organize an independent investigation into these murders and thus brought to public attention that his father was implicated in these murders, their whole family was killed in a horrendous manner in front of Dilip's and Satnam's eyes, and their own lives became endangered. During the course of the play Satnam is made to confront the reality which was his father, not a famous man respected in the community as he had fantasized, but a bullying murderer who victimized his wife as much as those that were taken prisoner. He is also made to recognize that Dilip, in an act of atonement for having brought down the family so to speak – even if in the cause of justice – gave him the space in the aeroplane's undercarriage that would secure Satnam's life whilst putting his own in danger.

Survival in context
Satnam's 'celebrity status' as a survivor of a particular physical ordeal, hanging on in the plane at sub-zero temperatures for hours on end, is poignantly juxtaposed with an impassioned speech his uncle makes, addressing the pilot of the plane who thinks of Satnam as an extraordinary individual who has 'stretched the limits of human survival': 'Survivors! You don't know nothing about survivors! We are the survivors. Here in England! Black bastard, Paki that and Paki this, that's what I face at work in the factory – then suddenly they don't want you anymore! You are redundant! Survival! We need our dignity to survive! We need an income to survive! That's when I beg and borrow money and open this shop. That's how I survive, on the edge, but I survive!' (Scene 3, n.p.). As the pilot tries to extricate himself from this conversation, arguing that Jaspal's experiences of racist attacks have nothing to do with the refugees, Jaspal retorts: 'It's got everything to

do with it! You are telling us who is a good Asian, who is bad! Who is a real refugee and who is illegal' (Scene 3, n.p.). This is at the nub of Jaspal's argument. In his juxtaposition of the refugee who becomes a celebrity case and the dailiness of racist assaults that he has to suffer in his shop,[6] Jaspal points to his continuing marginalization and in-visibilization in a culture that refuses him no matter how long he has inhabited it. As Peter, the detention centre officer, tells him: 'You can be here a hundred years mate, this can never be your home!' (Scene 7, n.p.). Jaspal's experience of Britain is that of continued harassment, continued denial of his subject and citizen status, of being made a perpetual refugee. The idea that coming to Britain would be the end of all discrimination, the beginning of a better life, the making of the migrant, is proved wrong through Jaspal's experiences. He in a sense prefigures Satnam's future, one in which the moment of escape and the period of detention are the beginning of a life where the status of refugee and migrant cannot be shaken off. Satnam's acceptance of the truth about his family's history, in particular his parents' relationship and his father's guilt, and Jaspal's and Satnam's final joining together in a pact to fight for Satnam's right to stay with his uncle, are the only optimistic notes in the play[7] in which the fight for survival, on all sides, is a fight for an always already compromised identity.

Compromised identities

Sanctuary presents an equally problematized interrogation of iden-tity, refugee status, survival, and the right to live. Unlike Wilson's play which offers a bi-cultural focus,[8] *Sanctuary* creates a diasporic space in the graveyard and church grounds which act as the site for multi-cultural encounter, simultaneously exploding any idea that the experience of war and violation is specific to one nation, one site, one history, and suggesting that the displacements generated by polit-ical conflict create new and fragile micro-communities which remain haunted by their diverse pasts. The list of characters identifies an 'Asian man', an 'African man', a 'middle-aged Afro-Caribbean man', a 'mixed-race girl', and two other female characters whose national and racial identities are not revealed. The thus unmarked female charac-ters belong to the dominant cultural group – their lack of marking signalling as much. They also, interestingly, embody dying British institutions associated with the state, namely the colonial foreign service on the one hand, and the church on the other. Both institutions prove inadequate for the protection of those whom they seek to govern – they are effectively unable to discipline the bodies over whom they seek dominion. This is made evident in the events which occur during the play.

Kabir, the Asian man who works as a groundsman in the graveyard, Michael, the African man who visits the graveyard, and Sebastian, the Afro-Caribbean man who also regularly comes to the church grounds, all have been witnesses to terrible political conflict, and to the rape, murder, and mutilation of people they knew, including their loved ones. Kabir was forced to witness the rape and killing of his wife Nusrat under horrendous circumstances. Michael is a Bantu from Rwanda who as it turns out not only holds racist attitudes towards the Tutsis who were murdered in their thousands during the Rwandan wars, but was instrumental in extremely brutalized killings of Tutsi women and children *in his role as a pastor to the local community* who trusted him and whose trust he betrayed. Sebastian was a photographer who travelled the world taking pictures of disasters and wars. He has tracked Michael down, hoping to bring him to justice. But before he is able to do so, Kabir hacks Michael to death as he recognizes that Michael is fundamentally unrepentant about his crimes, continuing to justify his brutalities and murders in terms of his racist views of the Tutsis: 'We had to be seen to show no mercy. The Tutsi women were part of the problem – they had used their feminine wiles to dilute our Bantu blood. They had to be dealt with, punished, humiliated . . . We were at war. And in war, gang rape is more effective than any military weapon' (2, 3: 104).

Michael is able to live with his past in ways that Kabir cannot. Where Michael uses his ideological position, his racist prejudices, to exculpate himself from his deeds, Kabir is haunted by his failure to help his wife as she was raped and murdered, even if it was to save his and his little girl's lives. Desiring to atone, anxious to prove to himself that he could be the father he should be, he even suggests to Ayesha, the mixed-race girl, that he will adopt her, recreating the

family he lost back in Pakistan. Kabir, guilt-ridden and destroyed by
the destruction of his family, is horrified to discover that Michael has
no sense of guilt regarding his deeds. When he realizes that Michael
thinks his actions towards the Tutsis were justified,[9] he kills him,
hacking him to death with a machete in an act of revenge for all those
whom Michael killed and, symbolically, as an act of atonement for
having failed to protect his wife. He does unto Michael what Michael
did unto others and what, in a sense, was also done to him.

The fact that this murder occurs in the graveyard – symbolically the site that is the legacy, and in this play contains the remains,
both of the colonial empires and of the church as an institution[10] –
underwrites the play's assertion that state institutions cannot and do
not protect the individual, the institutions' death in part a function
of that very impotence. In the face of the impotence of institutions to
maintain and/or do justice to those they seek to govern, Kabir takes
a humanist line, his act of killing transformed into a form of absolu-
tion, delivered by a friend to a friend. This is how he explains what
happened to Sebastian whose painstaking search for Michael in order
to bring him to justice is subverted by Kabir's action: 'He was being
my friend. Only I could be punishing him' (2, 4: 110).

The play juxtaposes Kabir and Michael as two characters who
have had similar experiences of political conflict and violation but
whose responses to those experiences are radically different. Kabir is
constructed as redeemed by his sense of guilt and repentance; Michael
is beyond redemption since he shows no regret for his deeds. In the
protection of Kabir by the white female representatives of dying British
institutions following Michael's murder, Kabir's action is condoned,
exonerated by the position which prompted him to commit it. The
play thus affirms a faith in the judgment of the individual, in the ethics
of an individualized and in some respects quasi-instinctual morality
which institutions as embodied through their members on the whole
are judged to lack.

The play, which opens with the three male characters occupying
the stage, ends with the space being left to the mixed-race girl, about
to set off on a tour of the world. This seems to suggest the end of a
certain world order, one epitomized by the men who dominated the

beginning. It also re-writes the idea of home and belonging. One reason why the mixed-race girl comes to the graveyard is that she does not feel 'at home' at home – a sentiment understood by Kabir who as previously indicated offers at one point to adopt her. The play has already decreed the triangle of home, belonging, and safety an illusion; women and children were not safe in their homes during periods of conflict and never will be. The provisionality of home, belonging, and safety, dramatically portrayed in this play, is signalled through the evacuation of all living beings from the graveyard, a stage returning to silence as the players desert it. Ayesha, on the threshold of adult life, embodying the exuberance of new beginnings, leaves the audience poised as she is to see how things will move and change – indeterminate but hopeful. Ayesha represents a new generation of migrant figures for whom diaspora is a permanently lived reality, for whom travel is an option rather than a necessity, who wants to see the world, not flee from it. She is the tourist, able to indulge her fantasies of other worlds, as yet unmarred by experiences such as the other characters in the play have undergone.

Re-figuring identities

The figure of the mixed-race girl signals the end of a world divided along racially clear lines as notions such as 'interculturality' suggest. More than that, that figure comes to emblematize the end of family as it is conventionally conceived of. The central characters in both *Survivors* and *Sanctuary* have lost their immediate families; Ayesha's family has been destabilized through her father's death and the arrival in the household of her mother's new boyfriend. Indeed, she refuses family when offered a version thereof by Kabir ('the last thing I want right now is tie myself down with yet another family' (1, 4: 64). Family is in question in many of the plays discussed in this volume, which articulate the ways in which family functions as a site of oppression, is vulnerable to the effects of diaspora, displacement, and migration, and ultimately is sustained more effectively, and sometimes devastatingly, in the imaginary than in reality.

The issue of family and belonging attaches, metaphorically, to the question of the place of the work of Black and Asian women playwrights on the British stage. As indicated in the introduction, and despite Michael Billington's (2000) article on the 'crisis in black theatre in Britain', the 1980s and 1990s have spawned a new generation of such playwrights whose work is performed in key British theatre sites. Black and Asian women playwrights speak from within. They have become, as Tanika Gupta's residency at the National Theatre loudly proclaims, constitutive subjects of British theatre as much as of other cultural arenas such as film, music, television, and dance. Moreover, through this work they have also asserted themselves as constitutive subjects in some of the key political debates and issues which contemporary Britain faces. These include, in their recent manifestations, issues of migration, asylum seeking, and refugee status, but also, much more generally, the matter of race politics, if I can put it in those terms, in Britain.

One question all the plays ask is: what does it mean to be Black or Asian in Britain today? As Tanika Gupta has put it: 'When I first started writing I was adamant that I was not going to write about being torn between two cultures. I thought, "It's so passé and boring." But inevitably, everything you end up writing is about trying to get that character to search out their roots. It's always about confusion and identity crisis' (Interview in Stephenson and Langridge 1997: 117). This is evident in Winsome Pinnock's *Water* which was premiered – in a double bill with Alice Childress's *Wine in the Wilderness* – at the Tricycle Theatre in London on 12 October 2000. *Water* centres on two young black professionals, a successful female artist and a male journalist who comes to interview her about her work. The play focuses on the issue of authenticity, of 'true' and 'false', 'acquired', 'ascribed', and lived identities. Sarah, or Della Williams as she turns out to be called, has appropriated the life of a poor black girl in her art, becoming successful as a consequence of painting a series of images depicting the latter's life and passing it off as her own history. The paintings, in fact, recall the life of a girl who grew up with Della and whose life took a downward trajectory, a life that Della, as she points out, might have ended up leading but did not.

As Della's life is juxtaposed with the girl's life, so Ed the journalist's life is contrasted with that of his brother Cliff, a black man of the streets who overdosed on drugs and died. The classic juxtaposition of a life made good and a life gone bad in this play highlights intra-racial divisions as post-migration generations growing up in Britain begin to divide into diverse social groups. That issue of intra-racial divides is of course a consistent theme in the work of the women playwrights discussed here but what is new is the recognition of the marketability of racialized stereotypes, the possibility of commodification inherent in Della's decision to create a series of paintings around the rags-to-riches narrative of the black street-living drug abuser made good through the therapeutic transformation of her life into art. The play thus raises the question of the constitutive role of art in British race politics and its collusion or otherwise in the perpetuation of racialized stereotypes. It ends with a pact between Ed and Della. One part of the pact is to further each other's careers; on Ed's part through not revealing the 'truth' about Della and her work; on Della's part through giving Ed interviews. The other part of the pact is that when Della has 'done as much as [she] can with her' (24), that is the girl she depicts in her work, Ed will debunk that work, an act that will serve him as a journalist and will fulfil the political purpose Della ascribes to that debunking:

> The pictures are the same. It's you who's changed and that
> was what I was aiming for. Their meaning has changed
> because your understanding of them has altered, but they
> can't change. When people realize what I've done, when they
> find out what the project is all about, then they will change
> too. When their prejudices have been exposed they'll have to
> change the way they see the girl they thought had executed
> those paintings. They will change the way they see me.
>
> (25)

Della's rationalization points to the importance of 'reading', of interpreting a work, and to the role of context in coming to text. The text may stay the same but as context changes so does our understanding of text. That historicity is in a sense the guarantor of change. It is within that that we need to understand the work of the playwrights discussed here. Their plays articulate the changing realities of the lives of very diverse groups of Black and Asian women, but not only women, in contemporary Britain. These include, as the examples of playwrights Ayshe Raif and Rani Drew indicate, the making of a theatre that does not require synonymy between the identity of the playwright and the characters depicted in her work. Ketaki Kushari Dyson, for instance, spoke at length to me in our interview about the problematic of self-exoticization, the issue of the implicit demand in Britain that people from diverse ethnic backgrounds assert their divergent identity through a gimmickification of 'Indian-ness' or 'Asian-ness', for instance, that she saw exemplified in television series such as *Goodness Gracious Me*. She was very aware of the commodification of certain stereotypes and asserted, against that trend: 'I don't do anything for exotic effect' (2001: 23).

Part of that discussion centred on cultural differences among regions of India and its surrounding countries. Kushari Dyson identified *Goodness Gracious Me*, and indeed *East is East*, for example, as a 'very Punjabi' form of entertainment, stating that 'No Bengali would write like that' (2001: 31). This is an important issue, for her own work is based very strongly in a Bengali cultural tradition, on Sanskrit and classical Indian literature as she describes it. Her play *Night's Sunlight* (2000) has been criticized for its ideas-based nature, its focus on language as an object of exchange, of debate, all of which she regards as very typical of the traditions within which she writes. These traditions which are more logocentric than spectacle-based resist, in some respects, the theatricality and specularization that has accompanied much intercultural theatre and performance, for example.[11] This can make it difficult for a writer to gain entrance into the theatre scene, and one of the problems Kushari Dyson has experienced is that of how to insert herself into British theatre culture. In Bengal she is a well-known and respected writer; in Britain she exists on a cultural margin without that reception. She told me the story of an immigration official in Bengal who recited some of her poetry to her as she passed through customs. Negotiating between acknowledgement and denial is clearly one of the most difficult things that Black and Asian women playwrights in Britain face. Even as a significant number of them have managed to profile themselves in key theatre sites, a discrepancy

continues to exist between the regularity with which their work is performed and the absence of any sustained critical and scholarly reception of that work. That reception also entails the acknowledgement
that Black and Asian women playwrights *are* constitutive subjects
both of the political reality of contemporary Britain and of the art
world that shapes that Britain.

Re-thinking the work of Black and Asian women playwrights in Britain

As the previous chapters have shown, Black and Asian women playwrights working for the British stage are thoroughly invested in contemporary Britain and in life within a multi-cultural environment
in which the debates about identity, difference, belonging, and unbelonging have lost none of their poignancy. It is possible to identify
thematic trajectories which their work has charted and which reflect
different historical moments of migratory and diasporic experience in
the lives of diverse Black and Asian communities in Britain. These include, for Black writers in particular, the actual moment of migration
from the West Indies or a particular African country such as Nigeria
to Britain, and the impact that decision had both on the migrating
individual and her family, those who left and those who remained
behind; the struggle to achieve presence in Britain for the second generation, those who came to Britain as young children or were born
here; the tensions between migrants and their children, especially between mothers and daughters, as a function of the issue of how to deal
with cross-generational differences in socio-cultural and economic experiences and values; the impact of racism in Britain on young Black
women's opportunities and life styles; generational differences in attitude towards a racist Britain, pacified through assimilation or rejected
through a proud-to-be-black and assertive stance that demands inclusion rather than relying on acquiescence as a means to achieve such
inclusion; the relative importance of tradition and community in an
individualized, secular culture. Asian women playwrights, similarly,
theatricalize the issue of how to make a life in diasporic Britain but
their portrayal of family and community is marked by a history of the
problematic dominance of males in the household rather than their

absence as is often the case in plays by Black women playwrights. In Asian women playwrights' work, too, the issues of cross-cultural and cross-generational clashes regarding values and traditions are frequently much more forcefully articulated than in the work of Black women playwrights. In the staging of this work, the dominant markers of migrating and migrated cultures are not only the very Asianness or Blackness of the actors, but also the use of specific linguistic markers such as patois on the one hand, and particular modes of dress, gesture, and interior decorating on the other. Work remains to be done on how the staging of the plays inscribes cultural specificity whilst challenging hegemonic theatrical practices.

There is also, to date, no significant published research on the audiences which attend the plays discussed. One of the effects of producing work by Black and Asian women playwrights on stage has, without doubt, been the drawing into the theatre of Black and Asian audiences that were not much visible in British theatres before the 1980s. In analysing those audiences factors such as stage location and type of venue need to be considered. Tanika Gupta's *Sanctuary*, when toured by the National Theatre in 2002, had a virtually entirely white audience when I went to see it at the Lawrence Batley Theatre in Huddersfield – yet West Yorkshire is an area with one of the greatest concentrations of diverse Asian communities in the UK. The West Yorkshire Playhouse in Leeds, on the other hand, always has significant Black and Asian audiences when it puts on plays by Black and Asian writers. The same is true for the Tricycle Theatre in London, though much less so for the Royal Court Theatre, for instance. *Bombay Dreams* at the Victoria Apollo in London – a venue associated with popular music and musicals more than with theatre – played to a very largely Asian audience, arriving in family groups and groups of friends, when I saw it in the summer of 2002. Simultaneously, it is still the case that plays by white playwrights fail to draw Black and Asian audiences. One might argue that in the context of theatre, a certain cultural segregation still exists. There is then a great deal of work yet to be undertaken about the audiences that attend the productions discussed, about the impact these productions have on those who view them, and about the achieving of presence both on stage and in the audience.

Part of this process involves the recognition that, as theatre, the plays analysed in this volume do not on the whole belong to the post-colonial, intercultural, or world theatre fora which have emerged since the 1980s as sites of critical debate. They are concerned, as products of and performances in contemporary Britain, with the articulation of Britain as a diaspora space and with being centred, even if problemat-ically, in that culture. Travels to parental sites of origin, for instance, are always constructed as temporary, as significant but impermanent interludes in lives that ultimately, but possibly not finally, need to be lived in Britain. To call such work 'migrant' or 'immigrant' drama, as discussed in the introduction, fossilizes that work on the one hand in a specific historical moment, that of migration, and on the other assumes that a perpetual migrant status attaches to the playwrights who produce that work and its content. These playwrights, however, whilst leading diasporic lives, are not perpetual migrants or immi-grants – the majority are British born and are constitutive subjects of a changing Britain.

Notes

1 Introduction

1   Yvonne Brewster's introduction to *Black Plays*, vol. 2, provides details of the rise of Black playwrights prior to the 1980s. However, it is noticeable that all the playwrights from the earlier period she refers to are male (e.g. Errol John, Derek Walcott, Barry Record, Wole Soyinka). This is indicative both of histories of migration, with many black men preceding women's migration into the UK, and of women's differential access to public cultural spaces.

2   Examples include Nandita Ghose, Tanika Gupta, Meera Syal, Zindika, Winsome Pinnock, Jackie Kay, Maya Chowdhry, Rukhsana Ahmad, Amrit Wilson, and Trish Cooke.

3   This is the case, for instance, regarding Meera Syal, Zindika, Winsome Pinnock, Patricia Hilaire, and Paulette Randall. The latter two, together with Bernardine Evaristo, founded the Theatre of Black Women in 1982 whilst at Rose Bruford College for Speech and Drama.

4   Individual playscripts published singly or accessed in manuscript form appear in italics in this volume, playscripts published in anthologies in inverted commas.

5   This is played out particularly powerfully in the context of writings on English literature (see, for instance, MacKenzie 1984, Ashcroft *et al.* 1989, Childs 1999).

6   Plays such as Ayub Khan-Din's *Last Dance at Dum Dum* (1999), set in Calcutta in 1985, offer pertinent commentary on this.

7   See Phelan and Lane (1998) for a discussion of Turner and Schechner's influence in Performance Studies.

8 See Turner's *The Anthropology of Performance*.

9 In the theatre this has taken the form of the thematization of racialized violence in plays like Michele Celeste's 'Obeah' (1989), which takes place in the context of the so-called Brixton riots in south London in 1981; Richard Norton-Taylor's *The Colour of Justice* (1999), an edited version of the Stephen Lawrence inquiry into the institutional mishandling of the racially motivated murder of a black teenager in 1993; and Rani Drew's *Bradford's Burning* (2001).

10 The race-related tensions that led to the race riots of the early 1980s, the murder of Damilola Taylor, racist behaviour in the police force, and racist attacks on Asian shops, for instance, are not unique to the UK. From the Clarence Thomas/Anita Hill trials to the Rodney King incident, the LA riots, and the O. J. Simpson case, similar incidents are reported in the US, as indeed in other western countries. However, when such events occur in the UK, they take on forms and meanings which are particular to British culture.

11 Black and Asian people had, of course, migrated to Britain before that time. For discussions of those earlier migrations see Visram 2002 and Solomos 1993.

12 Selma James' edited volume (1985) provides vivid testimony of this in its documentation of a conference held in London in 1982 on 'Black and Immigrant Women'.

13 These two examples may articulate clichés but they also feature repeatedly in plays by Black and Asian women playwrights.

14 Rani Drew's plays can be found in the Theatre Collection of the Drama Department of Bristol University. Her plays frequently deal with topical political issues such as the BSE crisis (*B for Beef: Buy British*); the events of Tian'anmen Square, Beijing, China in 1989 ('The Play that Never Got Done'); or the race riots in Bradford (*Bradford's Burning*).

15 There are a few, rare exceptions such as Shelagh Delaney's *A Taste of Honey* (1959) which features a 'Boy' who is black, Aileen Ritchie's *The Juju Girl* (1999), Caryl Churchill's *Cloud Nine* (1979), and Sarah Kane's 'Skin' (2001) which have black characters

but, significantly, these plays explore colonial histories and their impacts, or, as in Delaney's play, construct the black character as a fleeting presence.

16 On the failure of white people to manifest awareness of their colour see for example (charles) (1992), Ware (1992), Frankenberg (1983), Morrison (1993), Dyer (1997), and Hill (1997).

17 Such referencing of other plays that form part of the traditional western theatrical canon is not unusual. Rani Drew's *Caliban* engages with Shakespeare's *The Tempest*, for example. Nandita Ghose's 'Ishtar Descends' (1986) is on one level a re-write of the Orpheus and Eurydice myth. Trish Cooke's *Gulp Fiction* (n.d.) references a contemporary 'classic', Quentin Tarantino's film *Pulp Fiction*. The play is a spoof, featuring Ronnie and Reggie Diss as a parody of the infamous Kray brothers from the East End of London.

18 It is worth noting here that most of the reviewers of the 1996 production of Pinnock's *Mules*, performed though it was at the Royal Court Theatre Upstairs, commented on the fact that only three actresses were employed to play twelve roles (e.g. Bayley, Curtis, Murray, Gross). This had a detrimental impact on the play.

19 See Michael Coren (1984) for a history of the Theatre Royal, Stratford East, which makes some reference to the plays by Black playwrights that this theatre helped to promote from the 1980s onwards (98–100). In his policy document for the theatre of 1983–4 Philip Hedley stated: 'We can boast the largest black audience of any theatre in Britain in 1983/84' (in Coren 99). Coren highlights the importance of the theatre's location 'in the middle of an immigrant area' (99) as a reason for the programming of plays by Black playwrights. He also asserts that 'The staging of two black plays in such a short space of time [in one season] was seen by some as a negative approach: the appeal to black audiences, it was suggested, should have been carried out in a less direct manner' (99). This argument replicates the exact line taken in relation to plays by women in the 1970s and indeed the 1980s when

programming theatre seasons, where the production of a single play by a woman or a women's theatre group was viewed as having done justice to that demand/need.

20 See the work of Floya Anthias, Nira Yuval-Davis, Heidi Mirza, Hazel Carby, Lola Young, Paul Gilroy, Stuart Hall, and Kobena Mercer.

21 No such volume can be comprehensive but playwrights such as Maya Chowdhry, Valerie Mason-John, and Maria Oshodi do not feature in this volume on women playwrights, indicating quite how much work remains to be done.

22 It is worth noting that Winsome Pinnock, for example, has attributed interest in her work to the interest in Black American women writers in the UK: 'There was a lot of interest in my work when I first started because it was at a time when the black woman writer was sexy. There were a lot of black, American women novelists and they had become very successful and fashionable. And there was an upsurge in women's writing anyway . . . So I guess all of that enabled me to do quite a lot of work' (in Stephenson and Langridge 1997: 46).

23 For a discussion of the issue of cultural identity and subject construction see Hall 1992.

24 Anjona Roy is a PhD student at the University of Hull, working on Asian women activists in voluntary organizations. Her research involved interviews with these women, and the quotation is taken, with Anjona Roy's permission, from one of her interviews.

25 In an interview in 1991 with Lizbeth Goodman, Yvonne Brewster in her capacity as artistic director of Talawa Theatre Company told Goodman that they were about to produce their first play by a woman, Yazmine Yudd's *Unfinished Business*, in fact. Brewster emphasized Talawa's focus on 'epic theatre' and the rewriting of classic texts, saying that 'we never did find an appropriate play by a woman which would fit our working style' (362). This has changed over time. In 2002 Talawa toured *The Key Game* by Pat Cumper.

2 Diasporic subjects

1   See for example Sandra Yaw's *Zerri's Choice*, Jacqueline Rudet's 'Basin', and Zindika's 'Leonora's Dance'.

2   It is worth noting that this distinction between 'deserving' and 'undeserving' migrants, or genuine and bogus asylum seekers, replicates an earlier distinction between the 'honest, deserving' poor and the scrounger, a rhetoric endlessly repeated in contexts of state and welfare dependency, and in the context of the begging cultures before state structures to support poor people were in place (see Hüchtker 2001). See also Kay Adshead's play *The Bogus Woman* (2001).

3   See Amrit Wilson's *Finding a Voice* (1978: vi–vii) for a map of the patterns of emigration of diverse Asian groups to the UK. We might usefully compare these movements to the UK with the prior emigration by people from the UK to America, to Australia, and to what are now described as the former colonies.

4   The first two numbers in brackets indicate acts and scenes, the figures after the colon page numbers. Not all plays discussed in this volume have both acts and scenes.

5   Broderick makes fun of Gullyman by recounting 'English. An' he was always correcting people – remember Enid? (*Imitating.*) "Don't say wartar, man, say worter"' (1, 2: 152). Gullyman's ultimate inability to transcend his difference is articulated through the way in which, as Enid says, 'Now he can hardly talk broken English' (1, 2: 152).

6   Enid's household is the kind of 'three women household' Deborah E. McDowell (1989) discusses in her analysis of Black American women's writing. That kind of household or play for three females also features in a range of plays by Black British women playwrights, including Tanika Gupta's *Inside Out* (2002), Kara Miller's *Blue Hyacinth* (1999), and Zindika's *The Day Mother Took Us to the Seaside* (n.d.) and her *Paper and Stone* (1989).

7   However, whereas in the West Indies people might pay with chattels such as fowl, in turn used for parts of the obeah ceremonies, in England Mai demands money, the dominant currency of economic exchange.

8   Another play which highlights this is Michele Celeste's 'Obeah', which draws parallels between the Maroon uprisings in the West Indies and the Brixton riots. The British Library holds several unpublished playscripts by Michele Celeste.

9   In this context Gilbert and Tompkins take issue with Schechner's and Turner's position of collapsing ritual and drama into an evolutionary whole whereby drama succeeds ritual as performance moves from presentation to representation (55–6).

10   For an interesting and oppositional reading of the meaning of spirituality – in this instance in African-American women's writing – see Shaw (1997).

11   It would be wrong, of course, to assume that only diaspora impacts on ritual. Change is a function of time and as such ritual, like everything else, is the object of change. But the nature of that change depends on circumstance, and that is different in the West Indies from England.

12   In 'African-American Women's History and the Metalanguage of Race', Evelyn Brooks Higginbotham asserts: 'race impregnates the simplest meanings we take for granted. It makes hair "good" or "bad," speech patterns "correct" or "incorrect"' (1992: 255).

13   Both Enid and Mai repeatedly articulate that problematic. As Mai puts it: 'There was nothing for a woman – no job, nothing but babies. Mother had her first child when she was fourteen' (2, 2: 178).

14   *Black Macho and the Myth of the Superwoman* was first published in 1978. Wallace subsequently revised some of the views she expressed in this volume (see her 'Introduction: How I Saw It Then, How I See It Now' in the 1990 edition of the text).

15   This text is part of a much wider discussion within Black Caribbean and Afro-American communities about Black women's treatment by Black men. Inaugurated in the USA by Ntozake Shange's famous play *for colored girls*, this debate was fanned in the USA by the publication of works by Black (feminist) writers such as Alice Walker, Paule Marsha, Toni Morrison, and others. In the UK, writers such as Joan Riley in *The Unbelonging* have detailed similar problematics. For a critical account

see McDowell (1989). For an earlier non-literary account of the problematic see Beale (1970).

16 Marsha Norman's 'Night, Mother had won the Pulitzer Prize for Drama in 1983. Closer to home, Charlotte Keatley's My Mother Said I Never Should was first performed in 1987, the same year as Pinnock's play.

17 For contemporary documents on this issue see Zindika Kamauesi and Natalie Smith (2002).

18 It was in the context of Italian feminism (see Milan Women's Bookstore Collective 1990, and Kemp and Bono 1993) that the notion of the 'symbolic mother' as the female supporting and empowering another female first emerged. The phrase 'symbolic mother' is therefore used in this chapter both in its common-sensical sense of a woman who is not the birth mother of the person she nurtures and in the sense in which certain Italian feminists use the phrase.

19 On one level it is a quotation of Toni Morrison's The Bluest Eye (1970; London: Chatto and Windus, 1979) in which the desire to be blue eyed leads to the eventual breakdown of the little Black girl Pekola who is unable to love herself because there is no cultural investment in little girls like her.

20 In an interview I conducted with her in 2001, the playwright Zindika talked of this trauma and the difficulties of being re-united with parents and siblings one did not grow up with as a teenager.

21 Many texts on diaspora both fictional and non-fictional bespeak the impossibility of return. One particularly harrowing account occurs in Joan Riley's The Unbelonging, in which a young girl's glorious memories of Jamaica which support her through terrible experiences of abuse and degradation are destroyed when she returns to the island as an adult, only to find that her memories were fantasies she herself had created to sustain herself in an intolerable reality.

22 At the Theatre Royal, Stratford East, an area of London with a population from many migrant communities.

23   See Upton (1998) for a discussion of that issue in the French-speaking Caribbean.

3 Geographies of un/belonging

1   Ghuman (1999) vividly describes the dilemmas facing second- and third-generation adolescents of South Asian background in locating themselves between the demands of their own culture and those of their British contexts.

2   Milton Shulman produced a rather vicious review of the 1991 production of this play which indicated his inability to deal with the inter-racial dynamics of the play. Much more sympathetic and race-sensitive reviews were produced by Harry Eyres, David Nathan, and Helen Rose.

3   See, for example, Sandra Yaw's *Zerri's Choice*, Winsome Pinnock's 'Leave Taking', 'Leonora's Dance' and *Paper and Stone* by Zindika, *Inside Out* by Tanika Gupta, and many others.

4   In this play an older generation is invoked in passing rather than physically present. The impact is to suggest that the young people in the play have to find their own way and need to establish their sense of self within a peer community rather than through inter-generational exchange. This is quite different from other plays by Pinnock, including 'Leave Taking' and 'A Rock in Water'.

5   The notion of the throwback baby, a form of disparagement of the black person, drawing on a notion of a reverse evolution and thus theories directly implicated in certain racist ideologies, is interestingly and worryingly echoed in an account by the light-skinned black American writer and (performance) artist Adrian Piper of an encounter with a colleague who 'attempted to demonstrate his understanding of my decision not to have children by speculating that I was probably concerned that they would turn out darker than I was' (1998: 83).

6   The topic of socio-economic mobility and the pressures of being successful have been raised by women playwrights in Britain since the 1980s when Thatcherite conservative values and the

fluctuations of the economy created the yuppy (young upwardly mobile person). It found perhaps its most famous expression in Caryl Churchill's play *Serious Money* (London: Methuen 1987), which itself had precursors such as her *Top Girls* (London: Methuen, 1982).

7   In *Skin Trade* (1996) Ann DuCille offers a poignant analysis of the 'deep play of difference' as materialized through the manufacture and advertising of racially and ethnically differentiated Barbie dolls. Claudette's question underlines the persistence of whiteness as one of the prime signifiers of what a Barbie doll should look like.

8   During the 1970s and 1980s, and beyond, there were major public debates among black American women and men about their inter-relationships. Writers such as Michelle Wallace, Ntozake Shange, and Alice Walker stood accused by black men of racially selling out for presenting black males as exploitative and dismissive of women of their own race. A similar debate did not occur in Britain.

9   Significantly, the didascales state that 'Irma can be played by either a male or a female performer' (172).

10   The reference is to *A Room of One's Own* (1929; Frogmore: Granada, 1977), in which Woolf argues that 'we think back through our mothers if we are women. It is useless to go to the great men writers for help' (76).

11   The history of whiteness not being constructed as a colour as one of the roots of racism has been documented in various texts that began to problematize whiteness and its colour status during the 1990s (see Ware (1992), Frankenberg (1993), Dyer (1997), for example).

12   The cutting off of hair as a gesture of disempowerment has, of course, a long history, including the biblical story of Samson and Delilah.

13   In an interesting article on 'The Hair Trade' (1994; rpt in Shohat 1998) Lisa Jones describes the contradictions in racial politics thrown up by the hair trade through the sources of hair for hair extensions and wigs.

14 One of the curios of western culture is that from watching advertisements for tampons and panty liners one might think that menstrual blood is blue since the fluid used in such ads to signify blood is always blue. When Jalaarnava says to Kavitaa, 'Don't be so ignorant, you watch too much telly' (1, 2: 57), she alludes to one cultural site which perpetuates that taboo. When Kavitaa later repeats the notion that in India you have to bleed menstrual blood into a bucket, which Jalaarnava instantly dismisses, the mystification of menstruation is made only too manifest as a global phenomenon designed to erase certain aspects of female experience.

15 For a discussion of menstruation as abject see Julia Kristeva's *Powers of Horror* (1982), which contains a chapter on 'Those Females Who Can Wreck the Infinite', and also Mary Douglas' *Purity and Danger: An Analysis of the Concepts of Pollution and Taboo* (1966).

16 Jalaarnava is thus presented as typical of her generation and peer group, for, according to Ghuman, 'Nearly half of the Asian girls aspire . . . to a professional career in medicine, science, computing or journalism' (1999: 105).

17 Ghuman provides an interesting account of the educational aspirations and attainments of second- and third-generation migrants' children in the UK. He indicates that women's opportunities for educational attainment tend to be more restricted than men's but points to both the high educational aspirations and high levels of attainment among adolescents from South Asian backgrounds.

18 In the play Jalaarnava writes to her sister Kavitaa: 'I'm sorry you felt pissed off with me about coming here alone. I needed time, it's not easy to forget Tony. It's been hard keeping it all in and not being able to tell anyone. I didn't want to say anything before, in case you told mum' (3, 4: 65). The fear of the mother being told suggests that the relationship may have been illicit because with a partner considered unsuitable, e.g. an English boy.

19 This secrecy is not surprising. Rustom Bharucha talks of sexuality as 'one of the least interrogated elements in the

conceptualization of identity in contemporary India', stating
that: 'This is one construction where not even lip-service is given
to the nationalist mantra of "unity in diversity", because sexual
diversity as such has yet to be acknowledged as a viable reality'
(2000: 86). Bharucha discusses representations of both homosexuality and lesbianism in illustration of his statement. Asian cultural production disseminated in the UK has a developing tradition of engaging with homosexuality. From films such as *My
Beautiful Launderette* to the more recent *Bend It Like Beckham*
(2002), *Bombay Dreams* (2002), and Ash Kotak's play *Hijra* (2000;
performed at the West Yorkshire Playhouse in 2002), homosexuality, often in the context of inter-racial relations, has been explored in a number of cultural productions that remain yet to be
analysed in these terms as a body of texts.

20   I use the neologism 'en-propped' to signify the deliberate construction of a theatrical geosocial and geocultural space, the en-
dowment of the performance space – through props – with specific socio-cultural meanings. See Aston and Savona for a related
discussion of theatre space (1991: 111–16).

21   The significance of putting women centre stage has been extensively and variously discussed in feminist theatre criticism.
See for example Case (1988), Austin (1990), and introductions to
Griffin and Aston (1991 vols. I and II; 1996). That significance
is heightened in the case of women from diverse ethnic backgrounds who are considered doubly marginal to mainstream culture not just because they are women but because of their colour,
sexuality, or religion, for example.

22   See the introduction to the play by Maya Chowdhry (in George
1993: 56).

23   The kiss has a particular and poignant history in lesbian cultural
representation since it has figured as the symbol for lesbian sex
(see Stimpson 1981). Where many texts, especially of the first half
of the twentieth century, confined themselves to the kiss, this
play moves beyond that inaugurating sexual move to describe
lesbian intercourse, albeit poetically.

24　Kristeva is a Bulgarian who moved to France. Her work has been extensively preoccupied with the issue of migration, displacement, and otherness as evidenced in *About Chinese Women* (New York: Marion Boyars, 1977), *Language The Unknown* (London: Harvester Wheatsheaf, 1989), and *Strangers to Ourselves* (New York: Columbia University Press, 1991). Roland Barthes wrote of 'the force of her work. *Force* here means *displacement*. Julia Kristeva changes the order of things . . . what she displaces is the *already-said'* (in Toril Moi, ed., *The Kristeva Reader* (Oxford: Blackwell, 1986) : 1).

25　Use of and differences in punctuation from the first to the second verse, as well as variations in use of capital letters from one to the other, are as in the original.

4　Unsettling identities

1　All forms of theatre rely on particular conceptions of the relationship between actress and character, between the embodier and the embodied. This may be in terms of a notion of identification between the two, or of non-congruity or deliberate distantiation. However conceived, this conceptualization always rests on an understanding of a difference between performer or subject and performed or object.

2　The co-habitation of a Jamaican and a Chinese person within one space is countermanded by the spatial separation between these communities which is more commonly the case (see Ghuman 1999: 17). In this play the effect of the constellation of Leonora, Melisa, and Daphine is to highlight the complex diversities of the diasporic situation.

3　It is useful to compare Zindika's use of theatre space here with Shange's use of performance space in the stage directions of *for colored girls* where disaggregation serves the opposite function from that which it serves in 'Leonora's Dance'. In *for colored girls* difference in position does not amount to difference in experience since the narrative presented is that of the 'every-black-girl' position.

4   In British culture Chinese feature in very specific delimited ways: as brilliant classical musicians, as the Chinese State Circus, in rare plays such as Bertolt Brecht's *The Good Person of Szechwan*, and as (often female) writers who chronicle their families' histories from the empire through the Maoist regime to the present day. Such representation relies on segregation, and the other as other.

5   Ang-Lygate (1997) has conducted research with Chinese and Filipina in Britain. She, too, highlights the invisibility of Chinese people within discourses figuring race/ethnicity in Britain (175–6).

6   A useful comparison is the play 'The Body of a Woman' by Matei Visniec which details the rejection by a Bosnian woman of her pregnancy as a consequence of having been raped in the inter-ethnic war in Bosnia. See also Griffin (2003).

7   Countless texts have documented the differential application of the law to black and white people, highlighting the law's preferential treatment of whites.

8   The difficulties of having continuously to negotiate *métisse* identity are vividly illustrated in Ifekwunigwe's case studies (1999).

9   The problematic of the racialization of individuals as a function of their appearance is vividly described in the work of artist and philosopher Adrian Piper, in particular her installation *Cornered*.

10   The racialist politics underlying culturally specific forms is articulated in Melisa's comment when Leonora tells her of having been rejected by the ballet world in London: 'Well, perhaps you would have been more suited to modern dance. African. Jazz. Calypso'. Leonora agrees that 'There were reasonable cabarets around. I could paint my face white. (*Chuckle*) I thought I was white enough' (1, 3: 84). This references both the earlier history of Josephine Baker and of black-and-white minstrel shows (see Archer-Straw 2000). In his review of the play Nightingale disavowed the issue of race in culture in favour of the assertion, 'but have not zillions of white dancers been similarly afflicted?' (1993: 133).

11 In contrast to this use of Medusa, much feminist writing has involved the reclamation of vilified female figures from the past (mythic or otherwise) such as Medusa – see, for example, the first scene of Caryl Churchill's *Top Girls*, or Michelene Wandor's *Gardens of Eden* (London: Journeyman, 1984).

12 For a radically different representation of the figure of Medusa by another Black woman playwright born in Britain, Dorothea Smartt, see her 'Medusa? Medusa Black!' which reclaims Medusa as a 'Blackwoman'. There are, of course, many other readings of the figure of Medusa, including Dempsey and Millan's (2000).

13 Gilbert and Tompkins provide a useful and apposite definition of ritual within the context of postcolonial drama (1996: 57–8).

14 This is an issue that was not recognized in the reviews of the 1993 production of the play by Nightingale, Feay, Jancovich, or Woodis.

15 The most sustained use of interviews as a basis of performance has perhaps been undertaken by Afro-American playwright and performer Anna Deavere Smith whose works *Fires in the Mirror: Crown Heights, Brooklyn, and Other Identities* (New York: Random House, 1992) and *Twilight: Los Angeles, 1992* (New York: Random House, 1994) reproduce the narratives of African-American citizens living through moments of high racial tension in the USA.

16 Signifying 'nurturing' through growing plants is a metaphor repeatedly used by women playwrights. Shelagh Delaney, for instance, uses it in *A Taste of Honey* where the protagonist Jo has some bulbs she intends to grow but, prefiguring her difficulties in accepting teenage motherhood, the bulbs die.

17 A number of Claudia Jones' speeches are reproduced in her biography *I Think of My Mother: Notes on the Life and Times of Claudia Jones* by Buzz Johnson (London: Karia Press, 1985).

18 See, for example, Sebestyen (1988), Rowbotham (1992), and Smith (2000).

19 One of the most poignant examples of this is Zindika's *The Day Mother Took Us to the Seaside*, a harrowing play about the impact on the lives of three little black girls of their mother leaving

them shortly after taking them to the beach for a day. The play never resolves the mystery of what happened to the mother; its focus is entirely on how the vanishing of the mother shaped the daughters' lives.

20   In her review of the 1993 production of 'Leonora's Dance' Woodis noted that in the Black Theatre Co-operative 'In the early eighties, it was black male writers who predominated . . . like Edgar White, Caz Phillips and Mustapha Matura. Now with a new woman director, Joan-Ann Maynard, the emphasis may well be shifting' (133).

21   The issue of an Asian girl participating in sports being viewed as unseemly is given another twist in the account of a Punjabi woman who grew up in England from the age of ten and wanted to be a PE teacher, a desire that was met with horror in her school: 'They had never had an Indian woman who wanted to be a PE teacher. PE teachers always assumed that once Indian girls reached the age of puberty they were not going to participate in recreational activities, though they felt that West Indian girls were born to be sportswomen' (James 1985: 108).

22   In 2002 West Yorkshire Playhouse, for example, put on Ash Kotak's *Hijra* about which the author wrote in the introduction to the play: '*Hijra* became a comedy because this was the perfect genre in which to highlight the taboo subject of homosexuality within the Asian community, both in the Sub-Continent and in the new countries we have made our homes and to which we have imported our culture as well as its prejudices' (n.p.). Significantly, Anishaa tells Esha at one point that she's 'dressed up like a hijra' (13: 36), a role model Esha rejects as part of her reclamation of her femininity. Indeed, Maya Chowdhry's work of the 1990s always featured lesbians and gender issues.

5 Culture clashes

1   This is interesting since Wilson suggests that 'Asian women are very reluctant to talk to white women about their inner feelings. There are two main reasons: first, that they think white women wouldn't understand because they don't come from the

same background; and the second reason is that Asian women are aware of living in a very racist society, and this casts a shadow over their relationships with white people' (1978: 167). This is undoubtedly true. Cooper's example, however, shows that in dialogic exchange, understanding and some trust can be generated.

2   This is also theatricalized in Jinton's *An Arranged Marriage*, in which the protagonist's mother, Mrs Parmer, in particular keeps asserting the right of the parents to determine their daughter's life course, the expectation of respect children should show their parents by submitting to their will, and the importance of the community in policing, sanctioning, and condemning individual behaviour.

3   In 'Ishtar Descends' Nandita Ghose produces a similar narrative but with much worse effects for the girl, who has a nervous breakdown as she is rejected by her boyfriend. The play inverts the Orpheus and Eurydice myth by showing the descent into the hell of despair by Ishtar once she is dumped by her boyfriend Tammuz.

4   A similar character to Raju is Chumpa's boyfriend Ashok in Dolly Dhingra's *Unsuitable Girls*. He is also constructed as a lad who lacks emotional attachment to the women he dates but is incapable of acknowledging this. Like Raju he does not take responsibility for his actions and it is Chumpa who is left to reveal to their parents that they do not want to marry.

5   The presence of a washing-machine is, of course, of primary importance in a context where a woman is expected to do all of the family washing which, done by hand, can take enormous amounts of time and energy.

6   Even the precariousness of that status should not be underestimated. Wilson offers the distressing account of an older woman who was born in Tanzania and then migrated via Kenya to Britain where she was going to be supported by her two elder sons. This caused frictions, predominantly with her daughters-in-law, and ultimately she was forced to move out. Eventually she was able to gain economic independence from her family through the Ismaili Welfare Society (1978: 162–5). Her narrative highlights

the permanently precarious position in which Asian women can find themselves.

7   Another play which explores this problematic, albeit with a happier ending, is Dolly Dhingra's *Unsuitable Girls*, in which the heroine, Chumpa, has a limited time during which to find a husband, following her revelation that she does not want to marry her long-term boyfriend Ashok.

8   For a commentary on this phenomenon see Brah (1992; 1996), Afshar (1994), and Modood *et al.* (1997: 318–19).

9   In contrast, this play shows that Raju's and Reeta's parents' respective and identical decision to marry their children off to a partner from Bangladesh is not driven by the desire to facilitate someone else's immigration but by the socio-cultural rules which govern their community and which make it difficult to marry a child to whose name some form of scandal is attached to a partner from the community already resident in the UK. This factor, however problematic, is not taken into account in the white British position frequently adopted by those who argue that arranged marriages with partners from elsewhere are about the exploitation of economic and migration opportunities.

10 In *Domestic Violence and Asian Women* Southall Black Sisters detail harrowing cases of Asian girls being married off to violent, unsuitable partners from whom they find it difficult to escape.

11 It is important to note that heteronormativity and the pressure to marry at a certain age are nonetheless very strong in white British society in which much popular media attention is focused on encouraging marriage through projecting particular role models. The media publicity around both the marriage of Prince Charles and Lady Diana Spencer, and that of the footballer David Beckham and the pop star Posh Spice have, for example, exercised and reinforced such a coercive push.

12 I use the term 'western' here in recognition of the fact that there is a long, and certainly a twentieth-century, history of integrating European theatre work from countries such as Germany (e.g. Bertolt Brecht), France (e.g. Molière; theatre of the absurd), Scandinavia (August Strindberg, Henrik Ibsen), and the

USA (e.g. Arthur Miller, Tennessee Williams) into the British theatre canon. However, the same cannot be said of work from the Asian continent, for example. Historically, 'interculturalism' as now promoted by writers such as Pavis (1996) and critiqued by, for example, Bharucha (2000) has been confined to the appropriation of particular, predominantly 'western' theatre-textual and performance models.

13 There are a number of plays that focus semantically and linguistically on questions of language and the translatability or otherwise of diverse cultural customs from one language to another, the use of diverse languages or otherwise within one linguistic space, etc. See, for example, Dyson (2000) and Sengupta (2000).

14 For details of the case see Southall Black Sisters (1992).

15 This is not the only case of Asian women suffering domestic violence and death at the hands of brutal partners and male family/community members. Subsequent to Kaur's murder, the case of women such as Gurdip Kaur Sandhu (Southall Black Sisters 1992), Vandana Patel (Farnham 1992; Southall Black Sisters 1997), and Kiranjit Ahluwalia (Griffin 1995; Southall Black Sisters 1997) received a certain amount of public attention, but as Southall Black Sisters rightly claim, such cases receive neither enough public attention nor, frequently, the appropriate public measures in terms of protection etc. that they deserve and need to effect proper long-term changes.

16 Southall Black Sisters (1997) detail the reasons why women do not leave domestically violent partners (12–15).

17 Southall Black Sisters describe the case of a woman who was raped. They state that 'Under Pakistani law . . . it is virtually impossible to prove rape and if a woman is unable to do so, she is automatically charged with "Zina" (unlawful sex)' (1997: 55). Southall Black Sisters make clear that any form of sexual violation is virtually automatically viewed as the woman's fault, making her a potential or actual outcast in her community. As a consequence, sexual violation of women, including assault by strangers and incest, is frequently not made public or in any way prosecuted, thus effectively condoning such behaviour. In recent

years there has been a rise in representations from within the various Asian communities of such violations. Relevant representations include the film *Monsoon Wedding* (Dir. Mira Nair, 2001), and the plays 'Lights Out' by Manjula Padmanabhan and 'Mangalam' by Poile Sengupta.

18 I use 'Indian' in inverted commas when referring to Kamla because that is how it appears in the play: Kamla's Indianness is always in question.

19 Pizzey wrote an account of her experiences, *Scream Quietly or the Neighbours Will Hear*. Jan Pahl (1985) provides an account of the ideology of the refuges run by Women's Aid which indicates how closely the experiences represented in 'Song for a Sanctuary' map onto those experiences. Ahmad's own introduction to 'Song for a Sanctuary' shows that she talked to women and workers in refuges when she researched her play.

20 Ien Ang's *On Not Speaking Chinese* (2001) offers a vivid account of this multiply displaced form of diasporic identity and the problematic of living it.

21 For a contemporary discussion of the issue of Asian and Black women's experience of domestic violence, and the police and other authorities' responses to that violence, see the chapters in Part 1 of Christina Dunhill's *The Boys in Blue* (1989).

22 In Jinton's *An Arranged Marriage*, the only play I have read that comes close to portraying a 'forced marriage', the issue is happily resolved through the discovery that the intended bridegroom Rajesh has already fathered a child with an English woman whom he loves. The female protagonist's discovery of this enables her to put pressure on Rajesh to affirm that relationship. Significantly, the pressure takes the form of threatening to disclose his disgrace to the whole community.

6 Racing sexualities

1 This is not confined to contemporary *women* playwrights. See, for example, the work of Hanif Kureshi, Michael McMillan, or Ash Kotak.

2   Clause (or Section) 28 is part of a Local Government Act in Britain which was introduced to prohibit local authorities from the 'intentional promotion of homosexuality' and, in particular, forbade the teaching of the 'acceptability of homosexuality as a pretended family relationship'. The introduction of this Clause led to widespread campaigning among lesbians and gays during 1988 to have the Clause revoked. Ultimately, although the campaigns did not succeed in this aim, the effect of the government's initiative and the campaign that resulted was a much greater visibility of lesbians and gays.

3   The rise of 'queer' theory as a way of describing divergent sexualities and identities beyond the homosexual/heterosexual binary is a phenomenon of the late 1980s which gained almost instantaneous prominence and credence with the publication of Judith Butler's *Gender Trouble* (1990). For a discussion of the moment when 'lesbian feminism met queer' see Ardill and O'Sullivan (1989) and volumes 4 and 6 of the journal *differences*.

4   Paulette Randall's *Fishing* does the same but in a much more understated, suggested manner than either 'Chiaroscuro' or 'Sin Dykes'. It features two female friends, both married, who meet to go out on the town. The first act finishes with them going to bed together at the end of the night out; the end of the second act also sees them vanishing into the bedroom. The play only hints at the possibility of their lesbian relationship but could be played to suggest that the women have a long-term relationship which they are trying to make reality.

5   Lesbian appears in brackets here because this quest was not specific to lesbians.

6   The impact of Lorde's book in Britain can be seen in the fact that the first national Black lesbian conference in the UK, which was held in London, was called 'Zami I'; in April 1989, 'Zami II' was held in Birmingham (see Mason-John 1995: 11–12, and Mason-John 1999: 34).

7   Although an American publication, hooks' work was highly influential in Britain in opening up the debates around differences among women, and shifting that difference debate from its

initial focus on class to an exploration of oppression that included race as a crucial factor in women's differential socio-economic positioning.

8   Importantly, the title of Riley's text was inspired by black abolitionist and freed slave Sojourner Truth's address to a convention in 1851 where she asserted her identification with the term 'woman' against a view of female slaves as tough workers and as lacking womanhood.

9   See also Dahl (1995) for a related reading of the play.

10   A similar trajectory is charted by Sagri Dhairyam when she writes: 'I stumbled across my attraction to women through the intricate worlds of an educated, upper-class, Catholic-Hindu, third-world, Indian woman before I consciously came to name myself a lesbian' (1994: 25).

11   That female genealogy is a persistent trope in feminist writings of all kinds including feminist theatre.

12   For a comparison see Rosemary Curb's 'Core of the Apple: Mother-Daughter Fusion/Separation in Three Recent Lesbian Plays' (1990).

13   See Anna Wilson's essay on 'Audre Lorde and the African-American Tradition' (1992) for a discussion of the role of the biological family versus the lesbian and gay community in shaping lesbian characters' identity.

14   There is an extremely interesting parallel between this scene and an interview Amina Mama reproduced in *Beyond the Masks* (1995), in which one of her research participants describes being invited to *Spare Rib*'s all-women tenth anniversary party (183–4).

15   See Jeffreys 1985: 102–27.

16   For a discussion of the invisibilization of Black lesbians in Black communities and the attribution of lesbianism as a degraded form of sexuality to white and mixed-race women see Silvera (1996).

17   For a discussion of the experience of mixed-race people in contemporary Britain see Ifekwunigwe (1999) and Alibhai-Brown (2001).

18   See the National Lesbian and Gay Survey (1992) for a discussion of the (in)visibility of sexual identity.

19 See, for example, *Every Bit of It*, 'Twice Over', and 'Twilight Shift' for the use of the poetic in plays by Kay that deal with mixed-race and lesbian/gay identities.

20 See 'Monsoon', *Splinters*, *Kaahini*, and *Appetite for Living*, all of which employ poetic language and other devices designed to break away from a realist mode.

21 For a recovery of realism from its position as the maligned dominant see Diamond (1997).

22 The suggestion here is not that these issues are specific to that period but rather that – as I shall demonstrate in the second half of this chapter – different issues, strongly reflected in Mason-John's work, gained prominence in lesbian cultures during the later 1980s and 1990s.

23 Eve Kosofsky Sedgwick's *Epistemology of the Closet* (Berkeley: University of California Press, 1990) textually marks a shift in the meaning and location of the closet in lesbian and gay lives as that space itself comes under interrogation.

24 It is worth noting that in the premiere of the play by Theatre of Black Women at what was then Soho Poly Theatre in March 1986, Beth was played by Bernardine Evaristo, another Black lesbian writer and performer. Similarly, Valerie Mason-John featured as Clio in the first production of the play at the Oval House Theatre, London in January 1998, and in white British woman playwright Sarah Kane's film script 'Skin' (first transmitted on Channel 4, 17 June 1997) Neville was played by Nigerian playwright Yemi Ajibabe.

25 For discussion of the more common separation of debates about race and debates about sexuality see Hammonds (1994), Dhairyam (1994), and Calhoun (1996). Sarah Kane's film script 'Skin' offers a different but related take on these debates.

26 Reviewing the play Maddy Costa described it as 'a very accomplished, confrontational yet unaggressive challenge to the assumptions of its mostly white female audience' (1998: 115).

27 For brief discussions of these debates, see France (1984), Ardill and O'Sullivan (1989), the special issue of *Feminist Review*

entitled *Perverse Politics: Lesbian Issues* (1990), Omosupe (1991), Creet (1991), Smyth (1992), Lewis (1994), and Hammonds (1994).

28 Omosupe makes a similar point, asking the fundamental question of whether the histories of inequalities between Black and white women 'delimit our possibilities of experiencing each other as equals in lover/partner relationships?' (1991: 104).

29 These debates go further back in American history than in British history. They started in the late 1970s but came to the fore in Britain during the 1980s, experienced a racialization in part through the hugely commercially successful but also controversial film *She Must Be Seeing Things* which featured a lesbian relationship between a mixed-race and a white woman, and generated significant arguments and divisions among various lesbian groups.

30 The use of the dildo among lesbians was one of the controversial issues within the lesbian sex debates of the 1980s and 1990s. Its status as a quasi-penis and penis-substitute has been viewed as both an indication of lesbians' lack and need for sublimation within a sexual scenario devoid of men, and as a re-appropriation of phallic power.

31 Calhoun (1996) argues that s/m is a form of tabooed sexual practice imported into lesbian relationships to recover the 'outlaw' status of the lesbian in the face of her mainstreaming through feminism.

32 The whiteness of the lesbian s/m scene referred to above is made evident in Reina Lewis' article on 'Dis-Graceful Images: Della Grace and Lesbian Sado-Masochism' where all the images are of white women, and the central focus is on sexual practice and censorship.

33 This is not to reify blood ties but to suggest that whereas the notion of 'home' frequently naturalizes blood ties as the basis on which 'home' is socially constructed, in the case of sexual ties – where these are not heterosexual – such a 'home' has to be achieved.

34 For a discussion of Black lesbian experiences in the British lesbian community see Mason-John (1999: 11–40).

7 Sexploitation?

1   See, for example, Jenkins (1992), Mama (1997), Modood *et al.*
    (1997: 83–149), and Modood (1998).

2   In her afterword to the play, Rudet indicates that she wrote the
    play to understand 'why women sold their bodies in order to make
    money to live' (180). She mentions a friend who sounds rather like
    Charlene, a 'respectable' woman doing a job which enables her
    to support herself and her family financially.

3   Gilman's (1992) discussion of the exhibition focus on Sarah Bart-
    mann's genitalia and the role this played in the socio-cultural
    and medical imaginary throughout the nineteenth century pow-
    erfully captures the antecedents to Judy's understanding of the
    role her genitalia play in her stripping performance.

4   See for example Paulette Randall's 24%, Jacqueline Rudet's *Take
    Back What's Yours*, Rukhsana Ahmad's *River on Fire* and 'Song
    for a Sanctuary', Roselia John Baptiste's *No Place Like Home*,
    or Yazmine Yudd's *Unfinished Business*. Another version of this
    phenomenon is the juxtaposition of girls who are peers but who
    represent 'the sober' and 'the wild' as in Zindika's *Paper and
    Stone*, Nandita Ghose's *Bhangra Girls*, or Maria Oshodi's *The
    'S' Bend*.

5   For contemporary discussions of this case see Ward Jouve (1986)
    and Cameron and Frazer (1987); in 1995 Sarah Daniels wrote a
    play about the Yorkshire Ripper entitled *Blow Your House Down*.
    This was based on the eponymous novel by Pat Barker (London:
    Virago, 1984).

6   See Griffin (2000) for a discussion of that play.

7   See, for example, Ware (1992), Frankenberg (1993), and Hill (1997).

8   A good indicator of this is the absence of Black and Asian char-
    acters in white people's writings for theatre.

9   For an interesting discussion about the relation between race,
    gender, and the explicit female body in performance see Schneider
    (1997: 126–52) and Lewis (1999).

10 See, for example, Patricia Hilaire's *Just Another Day*, or Trish
    Cooke's 'Back Street Mammy'. For a different but related play,
    which deals with the abandonment of three young girls by their

mother who cannot cope with her situation, see Zindika's *The Day Mother Took Us to the Seaside*.

11 It is worth noting that the reverse, i.e. an Asian girl seeking medical help being portrayed as visiting a Black doctor, is very unlikely in contemporary theatre.

12 This requires modification insofar as the context that promotes Rose's situation, her parents' strictness and the significance of the church in their familial interactions, is much more commonly articulated in plays by Black women than in comparable plays by white women. This is a function of the relative importance of religion in the lives of (first-generation) migrants from the West Indies compared to those of their white counterparts in Britain.

13 In this respect *Paper and Stone* (1989) prefigures Zindika's later play 'Leonora's Dance' (1993), discussed in chapter four, in which the eponymous heroine's mother is also the victim of rape by a white plantation owner.

14 This is particularly emphasized in the stage directions of the final scene where 'ROSE *walks back and stands talking to the audience'* (2, 4: 78).

15 Bodily self-determination as expressed through the right to abortion on demand has been one of the key tenets of feminist campaigning during second-wave feminism and beyond.

16 This is also the experience recorded in *A Taste of Honey* and in *Back Street Mammy*, for example.

17 The Theatre Museum, Tavistock Street, London holds a company file with Clean Break Theatre's mission statement, handbills from various performances, and critical material. See also Goodman (1993: 205) and Rosenthal (1999).

18 See the company file at the Theatre Museum, London.

19 In a somewhat patronizing manner Jeremy Kingston's review of the play states: '[Pinnock's] play sounds authentic though less so when taking flight into lyrical, visionary stuff' (1996: 33). The latter is a reference to Act Two, Scene Fifteen, in which two of the characters, Lou and Allie, fantasize about an escape from their imprisonment.

20 The notion of the 'symbolic mother' is derived from Italian feminist theory which attempts to account for and mediate power differences among women through the installation of the 'symbolic mother' as a source of female empowerment (see the Milan Women's Bookstore Collective 1990). I use the term ironically here to highlight the illusion of mothering inherent in the role of the female mentor mediating between male power and female subordination.

21 The protagonists in this play are Patience (twenty-three years old, black, from South East London), Abina (thirty-nine, black Nigerian), and Charlie (fifty-six, white upper-middle-class English).

8 Living diaspora now

1 This figure has also emerged more widely in plays by women. Examples include Kay Adshead's *The Bogus Woman* (2001), Timberlake Wertenbaker's *Credible Witness* (2001), and Caryl Churchill's *Far Away* (2000).

2 This play was first performed on 8 April 1999 at the Orange Tree Theatre, Richmond, London.

3 Among the plays that accomplish the same transformation are Rukhsana Ahmad's 'Song for a Sanctuary' discussed in chapter five, Rani Drew's *B for Beef: Buy British* (1996), and her *Bradford's Burning* (2001).

4 Talawa's production of *The Key Game* by Pat Cumper (2002) featured an all-male cast. In the programme notes she wrote: 'Having for many years written plays with black women as their central character, I wanted to write something about men. As a mother, sister and daughter, and having been wife and partner, I thought I had earned that right.'

5 Here Gupta uses another ghostly figure, as discussed in the introduction, as a catalyst for change in the living. As she has explained in an interview, the use of ghosts in her work is autobiographically linked both to the history of her father's death and to the history of political activism in her family, resulting in the hanging of her great-uncle at the age of nineteen by the then still ruling British (Stephenson and Langridge 1997: 118–19).

6   The reality of racist attacks on shops owned by Asians was graphically and distressingly illustrated in a documentary programme made by British television in 2001 in which an Asian woman reporter ran a corner shop for a period of several weeks, recording the daily harassment to which she was subjected.

7   In this respect the play is different from both *Credible Witness* and *The Bogus Woman* which feature asylum seekers who are sent back to the countries they have fled from.

8   In fact, the detention centre is a multi-cultural site but in the play this is alluded to rather than enacted. *Credible Witness*, which also takes place in a detention centre, foregrounds that multiculturality, and indeed its dynamics and problematics, much more directly.

9   Act Two, Scene Three of *Sanctuary* references the truth commissions that were set up in South Africa to begin the process of post-apartheid healing. Kabir wants Michael to confess his deeds and in so doing to repent them; Michael, however, is only capable of post hoc rationalizations and attempts at excusing his behaviour. Unchanged in his fundamental attitudes, he proves to be incapable of repentance, raising the question of whether or not he deserves to live under such circumstances.

10   Significantly, her grandmother says to Jenny, the vicar: 'You've wasted your life marrying yourself to a dying institution' (1, 2: 30).

11   The English-Language performance I saw in Swansea in 2000 had some very spectacular, visually powerful moments which, as Kushari Dyson acknowledged in the interview we had, worked very well against the foreground of the debates that are at the logocentric heart of her play, lending it a certain physicality which is necessary for theatre.

Bibliography

PLAYSCRIPTS

Adshead, Kay. 'Thatcher's Women.' Mary Remnant, ed. *Plays by Women*. Vol. VI. London: Methuen, 1988. 13–50.

Adshead, Kay. *The Bogus Woman*. London: Oberon Books, 2001.

Ahmad, Rukhsana. 'Song for a Sanctuary.' In George 1993. 159–86.

Ahmad, Rukhsana. *Black Shalwar*. 1998. Playscript ms 8638. British Lib., London.

Ahmad, Rukhsana. *River on Fire*. 2000. Playscript ms 9397. British Lib., London.

Ajibabe, Yemi. *A Long Way from Home*. 1990. Playscript ms 4877. British Lib., London.

Ajibabe, Yemi. *Parcel Post*. N.d. Playscript ms 608. British Lib., London.

Bancil, Parv. 'Made in England.' In Nkrumah 2000. 90–131.

Baptiste, Roselia John. 'Back Street Mammy.' In Considine and Slovo 1987. 67–79.

Baptiste, Roselia John. 'No Place Like Home.' In Considine and Slovo 1987. 141–55.

Brewster, Yvonne, ed. *Black Plays*. London: Methuen, 1987.

Brewster, Yvonne, ed. *Black Plays: Two*. London: Methuen, 1989.

Brewster, Yvonne, ed. *Black Plays: Three*. London: Methuen, 1995.

Buchanan, Wayne. 'Under Their Influence.' In Nkrumah 2000. 236–309.

Celeste, Michele. 'Obeah.' Barrie Keeffe, ed. *The 1988 Verity Bargate Award-Winning New Plays*. London: Methuen, 1989. 43–84.

Chowdhry, Maya. *Appetite for Living*. 1996. Playscript ms 7694. British Lib., London.

Chowdhry, Maya. *Kaahini.* 1997 (rehearsal draft). Playscript ms 8025. British Lib., London.

Chowdhry, Maya. *Splinters.* 1997 (rehearsal draft). Playscript ms 8398. British Lib., London.

Chowdhry, Maya. 'Monsoon.' In George 1993. 56–75.

Churchill, Caryl. 'Cloud Nine.' 1979. *Churchill Plays: One.* London: Methuen, 1985. 242–320.

Churchill, Caryl. *Far Away.* London: Nick Hern Books, 2000.

Churchill, Caryl. *Top Girls.* 1982. London: Methuen, 1984.

Considine, Ann and Rovyn Slovo, eds. *Dead Proud from Second Wave Young Women Playwrights.* London: Women's Press, 1987.

Cooke, Trish. 'Back Street Mammy.' Kate Harwood, ed. *First Run 2.* London: Nick Hern Books, 1990. 38–95.

Cooke, Trish. 'Running Dream.' In George 1993. 187–227.

Cooke, Trish. *Gulp Fiction.* N.d. Playscript ms 7376. British Lib., London.

Cooper, Mary. 'Heartgame.' Mary Remnant, ed. *Plays by Women.* Vol. VIII. London: Methuen, 1990. 31–105.

Cumper, Pat. *The Key Game.* First performed at the Riverside Studios, London, 3 October 2002.

Daley, Tracey, Martin, Jo, and Josephine Melville. *Shoot 2 Win.* London: Oberon Books, 2002.

Daniels, Sarah. 'Masterpieces.' 1983. Rpt in Sarah Daniels, *Plays 1.* London: Methuen, 1991. 159–230.

Davis, Jill, ed. *Lesbian Plays.* London: Methuen, 1987.

Dayley, Grace. 'Rose's Story.' Michelene Wandor, ed. *Plays by Women.* Vol. IV. London: Methuen, 1985. 55–80.

Delaney, Shelagh. *A Taste of Honey.* 1959. Rpt London: Methuen, 1982.

Dempsey, Shawna and Lorri Millan. 'Mary Medusa.' In Goodman 2000. 247–57.

Dhingra, Prabjot Dolly. *One Night (When Love and Desire Became a Sin).* 1996 (1st draft). Playscript ms 7777. British Lib., London.

Dhingra, Dolly. *Unsuitable Girls.* London: Oberon Books, 2001.

Dhingra, (Prabjot) Dolly. *Unsuitable Girls.* N.d. Playscript ms 9342. British Lib., London.

Drew, Rani. 'The Play That Never Got Done.' *The Making of A Chinese Play*. Cambridge: Cambridge Poetry Workshop, n.d. 81–188.

Drew, Rani. *B for Beef: Buy British*. 1996. Bristol University Theatre Collection.

Drew, Rani. *Myself Alone/Asia Calling*. 1996. Bristol University Theatre Collection.

Drew, Rani. *Bradford's Burning*. 2001. Unpubl. ms, courtesy of the author.

Drew, Rani. *Caliban*. n.d. Unpubl. ms.

Dyson, Ketaki Kushari. *Night's Sunlight*. Kidlington, Oxon: Virgilio Libro, 2000.

George, Kadija, ed. *Six Plays by Black and Asian Women Writers*. London: Aurora Metro Press, 1993.

Ghose, Nandita. 'Ishtar Descends.' 1986. In Gray 1990. 85–110.

Ghose, Nandita. *Bhangra Girls*. 1989. Unpubl. ms, 3rd draft, courtesy of the author.

Gideon, Killian M. 'England is De Place for Me.' 1987. In Gray 1990. 13–66.

Goodman, Lizbeth, ed. *Mythic Women/Real Women*. London: Faber and Faber, 2000.

Gray, Frances, ed. *Second Wave Plays: Women at the Albany Empire*. Sheffield: Sheffield Academic Press, 1990.

Griffin, Gabriele and Elaine Aston, eds. *Herstory*. 2 vols. Sheffield: Sheffield Academic Press, 1991.

Griffin, Gabriele and Elaine Aston, eds. *Pulp and Other Plays by Tasha Fairbanks*. London: Harwood Academic Publishers, 1996.

Gupta, Tanika. *Skeleton*. London: Faber and Faber, 1997.

Gupta, Tanika. *The Waiting Room*. London: Faber and Faber, 2000.

Gupta, Tanika. *Inside Out*. London: Oberon Books, 2002.

Gupta, Tanika. *Sanctuary*. London: Oberon Books, 2002.

Harwood, Kate, ed. *First Run: New Plays by New Writers*. London: Nick Hern Books, 1989.

Hilaire, Patricia. *Just Another Day*. N.d. Playscript ms 1655. British Lib., London.

Jinton, Soraya. *An Arranged Marriage*. N.d. Playscript ms 3802. British Lib., London.

Kane, Sarah. 'Skin.' *Sarah Kane: Complete Plays*. Intro. David Greig. London: Methuen, 2001. 247–68.

Kaur Bhatti, Gurpreet. *Besharam (Shameless)*. London: Oberon Books, 2001.

Kay, Jackie. 'Chiaroscuro.' Jill Davis, ed. *Lesbian Plays*. London: Methuen, 1987. 57–83.

Kay, Jackie. 'Twice Over.' Philip Osment, ed. *Gay Sweatshop: Four Plays and a Company*. London: Methuen, 1989. 121–46.

Kay, Jackie. *Every Bit of It*. 1992. Unpubl. ms, courtesy of the author.

Kayla, Lisselle. 'When Last I Did See You.' In Considine and Slovo 1987. 97–107.

Keatley, Charlotte. *My Mother Said I Never Should*. London: Methuen, 1988.

Khan-Din, Ayub. *East is East*. London: Nick Hern Books and the Royal Court Theatre, 1997.

Khan-Din, Ayub. *Last Dance at Dum Dum*. London: Nick Hern Books and the Royal Court Theatre, 1999.

Kotak, Ash. *Hijra*. 2000. Rpt London: Oberon Books, 2002.

Lakshmi, C. S., intro. *Body Blows: Women, Violence and Survival – Three Plays*. Calcutta: Seagull Books, 2000.

Mason-John, Valerie. 'Brown Girl in the Ring.' In Mason-John 1999. 99–112.

Mason-John, Valerie. 'Sin Dykes.' In Mason-John 1999. 41–90.

Mason-John, Valerie. *Brown Girl in the Ring*. London: Get a Grip Publishers, 1999.

McMillan, Michael. 'Brother to Brother.' In Nkrumah 2000. 132–75.

Miller, Kara. *Hyacinth Blue*. 1999 (4th draft). Playscript ms 8871. British Lib., London.

Nkrumah, Afia, intro. *Black and Asian Plays Anthology*. Compiler. Cheryl Robson. London: Aurora Metro Press, 2000.

Norman, Marsha. *'Night Mother*. 1983. London: Faber and Faber, 1984.

Norton-Taylor, Richard. *The Colour of Justice*. London: Oberon Books, 1999.

Oshodi, Maria. 'Blood Sweat and Fears.' In Brewster 1989. 93–142.

Oshodi, Maria. *Here Comes a Candle*. N.d. Bristol University Theatre Collection.

Oshodi, Maria. *The 'S' Bend.* N.d. Playscript ms 2301. British Lib., London.

Padmanabhan, Manjula. 'Lights Out.' In Lakshmi 2000. 1–54.

Pinnock, Winsome. 'A Rock in Water.' In Brewster 1989. 45–91.

Pinnock, Winsome. 'Leave Taking.' Kate Harwood, ed. *First Run: New Plays by New Writers.* London: Nick Hern Books, 1989. 139–89.

Pinnock, Winsome. 'A Hero's Welcome.' In George 1993. 21–55.

Pinnock, Winsome. 'Talking in Tongues.' In Brewster 1995. 171–228.

Pinnock, Winsome. *Mules.* London: Faber and Faber, 1996.

Pinnock, Winsome. *Water.* 2000. Playscript ms 9296. British Lib., London.

Raif, Ayshe. 'Caving In.' Mary Remnant, ed. *Plays by Women.* Vol. VIII. London: Methuen, 1990. 125–60.

Raif, Ayshe. 'Fail/Safe.' Cheryl Robson, ed. *Seven Plays by Women.* London: Aurora Metro Press, 1991. 185–221.

Raif, Ayshe. *I'm No Angel.* 1993 (final draft). Playscript ms 5997. British Lib., London.

Raif, Ayshe. *Café Society.* N.d. Playscript ms 1469. British Lib., London.

Randall, Paulette. *24%.* N.d. Playscript ms 4974. British Lib., London.

Randall, Paulette. *Fishing.* N.d. Playscript ms 1654. British Lib., London.

Rapi, Nina and Maya Chowdhry, eds. *Acts of Passion: Sexuality, Gender and Performance.* New York: Haworth Press, 1998.

Remnant, Mary, ed. *Plays by Women.* Vol. V. London: Methuen, 1986.

Remnant, Mary, ed. *Plays by Women.* Vol. VIII. London: Methuen 1990.

Ritchie, Aileen. *The Juju Girl.* London: Nick Hern Books, 1999.

River, Sol B. *Plays.* London: Oberon Books, 1997.

Rudet, Jacqueline. *God's Second in Command.* 1985 (2nd draft). Playscript ms 2824. British Lib., London.

Rudet, Jacqueline. 'Money to Live.' Mary Remnant, ed. *Plays by Women.* Vol. V. London: Methuen, 1986. 145–81.

Rudet, Jacqueline. 'Basin.' In Brewster 1987. 113–39.

Rudet, Jacqueline. *Take Back What's Yours.* 1989. Playscript ms 4163. British Lib., London.

Sengupta, Poile. 'Mangalam.' In Lakshmi 2000. 93–151.

Shange, Ntozake. *For colored girls who have considered suicide/when the rainbow is enuf.* San Lorenzo CA: Shameless Hussy Press, 1975. Rpt in *Shange. Plays One.* London: Methuen, 1992. 1–66.

Shapiro, Jacqui. *One of Us.* n.d. (1989?). Unpubl. ms, courtesy of the author.

Silas, Shelley. 'Calcutta Kosher.' In Nkrumah 2000. 176–235.

Smartt, Dorothea. 'Medusa? Medusa Black!' In Goodman 2000. 259–62.

Syal, Meera. 'My Sister-Wife.' In George 1993. 111–58.

Syal, Meera. *Bombay Dreams.* 2002. Playscript ms 10004. British Lib., London.

Visniec, Matei. 'The Body of a Woman as a Battlefield in the Bosnian War.' Gina Landor, intro. *Balkan Plots: Plays from Central and Eastern Europe.* London: Aurora Metro Press, 2000. 13–62.

Wandor, Michelene, ed. *Plays by Women.* Vol. IV. London: Methuen, 1985.

Wertenbaker, Timberlake. *Credible Witness.* London: Faber and Faber, 2001.

Wilson, Amrit. 'Chandralekha.' *Inqilab* 3/2 (Autumn/Winter 1994): 25–9. Publ. London: South Asia Solidarity Group.

Wilson, Amrit. *Survivors.* 1999. Unpubl. ms, courtesy of the author.

Yudd, Yazmine. *Unfinished Business.* 1999. Playscript ms 8831. British Lib., London.

Yudd, Yazmine. *Identity.* 2000. Playscript ms 9888. British Lib., London.

Zindika. *Paper and Stone.* 1989. Unpubl. ms, courtesy of the author.

Zindika. 'Leonora's Dance.' In George 1993. 76–110.

Zindika. *The Day Mother Took Us to the Seaside.* N.d. Unpubl. ms, courtesy of the author.

THEATRE THEORY AND CRITICISM

Archer-Straw, Petrine. *Negrophilia: Avant-Garde Paris and Black Culture in the 1920s.* London: Thames and Hudson, 2000.

Aston, Elaine. *An Introduction to Feminism and Theatre.* London: Routledge, 1995.

Aston, Elaine. *Feminist Theatre Voices.* Loughborough: Loughborough Theatre Texts, 1997.

Aston, Elaine and Janelle Reinelt, eds. *The Cambridge Companion to Modern British Women Playwrights*. Cambridge: Cambridge University Press, 2000.

Aston, Elaine and George Savona. *Theatre as Sign-System: A Semiotics of Text and Performance*. London: Routledge, 1991.

Austin, Gayle. *Feminist Theories for Dramatic Criticism*. Ann Arbor: University of Michigan Press, 1990.

Bayley, Clare. 'Review of *Mules*.' *Independent* 3 May 1996. In *London Theatre Record* 22 April–5 May 1996: 545.

Bharucha, Rustom. 'Somebody's Other.' In Pavis 1996. 196–216.

Bharucha, Rustom. *The Politics of Cultural Practice: Thinking Through Theatre in an Age of Globalization*. London: Athlone Press, 2000.

Billington, Michael. 'White Out.' *Guardian* 18 October 2000. *http://www.guardian.co.uk/arts/story*, 17 January 2002. 1–3.

Boon, Richard and Jane Plastow, eds. *Theatre Matters: Performance and Culture on the World Stage*. Cambridge: Cambridge University Press, 1998.

Brater, Enoch, ed. *Feminine Focus: The New Women Playwrights*. Oxford: Oxford University Press, 1989.

Brewer, Mary F. *Race, Sex, and Gender in Contemporary Women's Theatre*. Brighton: Sussex Academic Press, 1999.

Brewster, Yvonne (interviewed by Liz Goodman). 'Drawing the Black and White Line: Defining Black Women's Theatre.' *New Theatre Quarterly* 7/28 (1991): 361–8.

Case, Sue-Ellen. *Feminism and Theatre*. Houndsmill: Macmillan, 1998.

Chaudhuri, Una. 'The Future of the Hyphen: Interculturalism, Textuality, and the Difference Within.' Bonnie Marranca and Gautam Dasgupta, eds. *Interculturalism and Performance: Writings from PAJ*. New York: PAJ, 1991. 192–207.

Chowdhry, Maya. 'Living Performance.' In Rapi and Chowdhry 1998. 9–20.

Connor, Geraldine. *Carnival Messiah*. Programme notes. Leeds: West Yorkshire Playhouse, 2002.

Coren, Michael. *Theatre Royal: 100 Years of Stratford East*. London: Quartet Books, 1984.

Costa, Maddy. 'Review of "Sin Dykes".' *Time Out* 4 February 1998. In *London Theatre Record* 29 January–11 February 1998: 115.

Cousin, Geraldine. *Women in Dramatic Place and Time*. London: Routledge, 1996.

Croft, Susan. 'Black Women Playwrights in Britain.' T. R. Griffiths and M. Llewellyn-Jones, eds. *British and Irish Women Dramatists since 1958*. Buckingham: Open University Press, 1993. 84–98.

Croft, Susan. 'Bibliography.' In Nkrumah 2000. 310–19.

Croft, Susan. *She Also Wrote Plays*. London: Faber and Faber, 2001.

Curb, Rosemary. 'Core of the Apple: Mother-Daughter Fusion/ Separation in Three Recent Lesbian Plays.' Karla Jay and Joanne Glasgow, eds. *Lesbian Texts and Contexts*. New York: New York University Press, 1990. 355–76.

Curtis, Nick. 'Review of *Mules*.' *Evening Standard* 1 May 1996. In *London Theatre Record* 22 April–5 May 1996: 545.

Dahl, Mary Karen. 'Postcolonial British Theatre: Black Voices at the Center.' In Gainor 1995. 38–55.

Demastes, William W. *British Playwrights, 1956–1995: A Research and Production Source Book*. Westport, CT: Greenwood Press, 1996.

Diamond, Elin. *Unmaking Mimesis*. London: Routledge, 1997.

Dolan, Jill. *Presence and Desire: Essays on Gender, Sexuality, Performance*. Ann Arbor: University of Michigan Press, 1993.

Eyres, Harry. 'Review of "Talking in Tongues".' *The Times* 4 September 1991. In *London Theatre Record* 27 August–21 September 1991: 1044.

Feay, Suzy. 'Review of "Leonora's Dance".' *Time Out* 17 February 1993. In *London Theatre Record* 12–26 February 1993: 133.

Fischer-Lichte, Erika. 'Interculturalism in Contemporary Theatre.' In Pavis 1996. 27–40.

Fischer-Lichte, Erika. *The Show and the Gaze of Theatre: A European Perspective*. Iowa City: University of Iowa Press, 1997.

Gainor, J. Ellen, ed. *Imperialism and Theatre: Essays on World Theatre, Drama and Performance*. London: Routledge, 1995.

Gilbert, Helen and Joanne Tompkins. *Post-Colonial Drama: Theory, Practice, Politics*. London: Routledge, 1996.

Gilbert, Helen, ed. *(Post)Colonial Stages: Critical and Creative Views on Drama, Theatre and Performance*. Hebden Bridge: Dangaroo Press, 1999.

Giles, Freda Scott. 'Methexis vs. Mimesis: Poetics of Feminist and Womanist Drama.' In Zack 1997. 175–82.

Goodman, Lizbeth. *Contemporary Feminist Theatres: To Each Her Own*. London: Routledge, 1993.

Griffin, Gabriele. 'Exile and the Body.' Peter Wagstaff *et al.*, eds. Forthcoming Oxford: Berg, 2003.

Griffin, Gabriele. 'Violence, Abuse and Gender Relations in the Plays of Sarah Daniels.' In Aston and Reinelt 2000. 194–211.

Gross, John. 'Review of *Mules*.' *Sunday Telegraph* 5 May 1996. In *London Theatre Record* 22 April–5 May 1996: 546.

Gupta, Tanika. 'Interview.' In Stephenson and Langridge 1997. 115–21.

Hart, Lynda and Peggy Phelan, eds. *Acting Out: Feminist Performances*. Ann Arbor: University of Michigan Press, 1993.

Holledge, Julie and Joanne Tompkins. *Women's Intercultural Performance*. London: Routledge, 2000.

Jancovich, Ben. 'Review of "Leonora's Dance".' *City Limits* 18 January 1993. In *London Theatre Record* 12–26 February 1993: 133.

Joseph, May. 'Bodies Outside the State: Black British Women Playwrights and the Limits of Citizenship.' In Phelan and Lane 1998. 197–213.

Kingston, Jeremy. 'Candy Women.' *The Times* 2 May 1996: 33.

Lewis, Reina. 'Cross-Cultural Reiterations.' Amelia, Jones and Andrew Stephenson, eds. *Performing the Body, Performing the Text*. London: Routledge, 1999. 56–75.

Martin, Carol, ed. *A Sourcebook of Feminist Theatre and Performance*. London: Routledge, 1996.

Murray, David. 'Review of *Mules*.' *Financial Times* 2 May 1996. In *London Theatre Record* 22 April–5 May 1996: 546.

Nathan, David. 'Review of "Talking in Tongues".' *Jewish Chronicle* 13 September 1991. In *London Theatre Record* 27 August–21 September 1991: 1044.

Nightingale, Benedict. 'Review of "Leonora's Dance".' *The Times* 17 February 1993. In *London Theatre Record* 12–26 February 1993: 133.

Pavis, Patrice, ed. *The Intercultural Performance Reader*. London: Routledge, 1996.

Phelan, Peggy and Jill Lane, eds. *The Ends of Performance*. New York: New York University Press, 1998.

Pinnock, Winsome. 'Interview.' In Stephenson and Langridge 1997. 45–53.

Ponnuswami, Meenakshi. 'Feminist History in Contemporary British Theatre.' *Women and Performance* 14–15 (1995): 287–305.

Ponnuswami, Meenakshi. 'Small Island People: Black British Women Playwrights.' In Aston and Reinelt 2000. 217–34.

Rapi, Nina and Maya Chowdhry, eds. *Acts of Passion: Sexuality, Gender and Performance*. New York: Haworth Press, 1998.

Rose, Helen. 'Review of "Talking in Tongues".' *Time Out* 4 September 1991. In *London Theatre Record* 27 August–21 September 1991: 1044–5.

Rosenthal, Daniel. 'It's Time to Set the Clichés Free.' *Independent* ('Wednesday Review') 13 October 1999: 19.

Schechner, Richard. *Performance Theory*. 1977. Rpt London: Routledge, 1994.

Schechner, Richard. *Between Theater and Anthropology*. Philadelphia: University of Pennsylvania Press, 1985.

Schechner, Richard. 'Interculturalism and the Culture of Choice.' In Pavis 1996. 41–50.

Schneider, Rebecca. *The Explicit Body in Performance*. London: Routledge, 1997.

Shulman, Milton. 'Review of "Talking in Tongues".' *Evening Standard* 30 August 1991. In *London Theatre Record* 27 August–21 September 1991: 1044.

Stephenson, Heidi and Natasha Langridge. *Rage and Reason: Women Playwrights on Playwrighting*. London: Methuen, 1997.

Stone Peters, Julie. 'Intercultural Performance, Theatre Anthropology, and the Imperialist Critique.' In Gainor 1995. 199–213.

Turner, Victor. *Dramas, Fields and Metaphors: Symbolic Action in Human Society.* Ithaca NY: Cornell University Press, 1974.

Turner, Victor. *From Ritual to Theatre.* New York: PAJ Publications, 1982.

Turner, Victor. *The Anthropology of Performance.* New York: PAJ Publications, 1987.

Ugwu, Catherine, ed. *Let's Get It On: The Politics of Black Performance.* London: ICA, 1995.

Upton, Carole-Anne. 'The French-Speaking Caribbean: Journeying from the Native Land.' In Boon and Plastow 1998. 97–125.

Verma, Jatinder. 'Cultural Transformations.' Theodore Shank, ed. *Contemporary British Theatre.* London: Macmillan, 1994. 55–61.

Verma, Jatinder. '"Binglishing" the Stage: A Generation of Asian Theatre in England.' In Boon and Plastow 1998. 126–34.

Wandor, Michelene. 'The Impact of Feminism on Theatre.' *Feminist Review* 18 (Winter 1984): 76–92.

Woodis, Carole. 'Review of "Leonora's Dance".' *What's On* 17 February 1993. In *London Theatre Record* 12–26 February 1993: 133.

CONTEXTUAL MATERIAL

Afshar, Haleh. 'Muslim Women in West Yorkshire: Growing Up with Real and Imaginary Values amidst Conflicting Views of Self and Society.' In Afshar and Maynard 1994. 127–47.

Afshar, Haleh and Mary Maynard, eds. *The Dynamics of 'Race' and Gender.* London: Taylor and Francis, 1994.

Ahmad, Rukhsana. 'Interview.' 5 March 2001.

Ahmed, Sara. 'It's a Sun-Tan, Isn't It? – Auto-biography as an Identificatory Practice.' In Mirza 1997. 153–67.

Alibhai-Brown, Yasmin. *Mixed Feelings: The Complex Lives of Mixed-Race Britons.* London: Women's Press, 2001.

Alibhai-Brown, Yasmin and Anne Montague. *The Colour of Love.* London: Virago, 1992.

Allen, Sheila. 'Race, Ethnicity and Nationality: Some Questions of Identity.' H. Afshar and M. Maynard, eds. *The Dynamics of Race and Gender.* London: Taylor and Francis, 1994. 85–105.

Ang, Ien. *On Not Speaking Chinese.* London: Routledge, 2001.

Ang-Lygate, Magdalene. 'Charting the Spaces of (Un)location: On Theorizing Diaspora.' In Mirza 1997. 168–86.

Ardill, Susan and Sue O'Sullivan. 'Sex in the Summer of '88.' *Feminist Review* 31 (Spring 1989): 126–34.

Ashcroft, Bill, Griffiths, Gareth, and Helen Tiffin, eds. *The Empire Writes Back: Theory and Practice in Post-Colonial Literatures.* London: Routledge, 1989.

Aziz, Razia. 'Feminism and the Challenge of Racism: Deviance or Difference?' Helen Crowley and Susan Himmelweit, eds. *Knowing Women: Feminism and Knowledge.* Cambridge: Polity Press, 1992.

Baker Jr, Houston A., Diawara, Manthia, and Ruth H. Lindeborg, eds. *Black British Cultural Studies.* Chicago: University of Chicago Press, 1996.

Barkham, Patrick. 'Beginner's Guide to the Refugee Crisis.' *Guardian* 27 August 1999. *www.guardian.co.uk/Refugees_in_Britain/Story.*

Beale, Frances. 'Double Jeopardy: To Be Black and Female.' Toni Cade, ed. *The Black Woman: An Anthology.* New York: New American Library, 1970.

Blackstone, Tessa, Parekh, Bhikhu, and Peter Sanders, eds. *Race Relations in Britain.* London: Routledge, 1998.

Boyce Davies, Carole. 'Black British Women Writing the Anti-Imperialist Critique.' In Brinker-Gabler and Smith 1997. 100–17.

Brah, Avtar. 'Women of South Asian Origin in Britain.' In Braham *et al.* 1992. 64–78.

Brah, Avtar. *Cartographies of Diaspora: Contesting Identities.* London: Routledge, 1996.

Braham, Peter, Rattansi, Ali, and Richard Skellington, eds. *Racism and Antiracism: Inequalities, Opportunities and Policies.* London: Sage and The Open University, 1992.

Brinker-Gabler, Gisela and Sidonie Smith, eds. *Writing New Identities: Gender, Nation, and Immigration in Contemporary Europe.* Minneapolis: University of Minnesota Press, 1997.

Bryan, Beverley, Dadzie, Stella, and Susanne Scafe. *The Heart of the Race: Black Women's Lives in Britain.* London: Virago, 1985.

Butler, Judith. *Gender Trouble: Feminism and the Subversion of Identity*. London: Routledge, 1990.

Calhoun, Cheshire. 'The Gender Closet.' Martha Vicinus, ed. *Lesbian Subjects*. Bloomington: Indiana University Press, 1996. 209–32.

Cameron, Deborah and Elizabeth Frazer. *The Lust to Kill: A Feminist Investigation of Sexual Murder*. New York: New York University Press, 1987.

(charles), Helen. 'Whiteness – the Relevance of Politically Colouring "Non".' Hilary Hinds, Ann Phoenix, and Jackie Stacey, eds. *Working Out: New Directions for Women's Studies*. London: Falmer Press, 1992. 29–35.

Childs, Peter, ed. *Post-Colonial Theory and English Literature: A Reader*. Edinburgh: Edinburgh University Press, 1999.

Chowdhry, Maya. 'The Look Again Letters.' In Kendall 1994. 57–65.

Cixous, Hélène and Catherine Clément. *The Newly Born Woman*. 1975. Manchester: Manchester University Press, 1987.

Cixous, Hélène. *Rootprints: Memory and Life Writing*. 1994. London: Routledge, 1997.

Cliff, Michelle. *The Land of Look Behind*. Ithaca, NY: Firebrand Books, 1985.

Clifford, James. *Routes: Travel and Translation in the Late Twentieth Century*. Cambridge MA: Harvard University Press, 1997.

Creet, Julia. 'Daughter of the Movement: The Psychodynamics of Lesbian S/M Fantasy.' *Differences* 3 (Summer 1991): 135–59.

De Beauvoir, Simone. *The Second Sex*. 1949. Harmondsworth: Penguin, 1972.

Dhairyam, Sagri. 'Racing the Lesbian, Dodging White Critics.' Laura Doan, ed. *The Lesbian Postmodern*. New York: Columbia University Press, 1994. 25–46.

Dodd, Vikram. 'Dover, No Port in a Storm for Refugees.' *Guardian* 28 March 2000. *www.guardian.co.uk/uk_news/story*.

Donald, James and Ali Rattansi, eds. *'Race', Culture and Difference*. London: Sage, 1992.

Douglas, Mary. *Purity and Danger: An Analysis of the Concepts of Pollution and Taboo.* 1966. Rpt London: Routledge, 1995.

DuCille, Ann. *Skin Trade.* Cambridge MA: Harvard University Press, 1996.

Dunhill, Christina, ed. *The Boys in Blue: Women's Challenge to the Police.* London: Virago, 1989.

Dyer, Richard. *White.* London: Routledge, 1997.

Dyson, Ketaki Kushari. 'Interview.' 3 May 2001.

Farnham, Margot. 'Still Working against the Grain.' *Trouble and Strife* 23 (Spring 1992): 41–52.

Feminist Review 17 (Autumn 1984) Special issue *Many Voices, One Chant: Black Feminist Perspectives.*

Foner, Nancy. 'The Jamaicans: Cultural and Social Change among Migrants in Britain.' James L. Watson, ed. *Between Two Cultures: Migrants and Minorities in Britain.* Oxford: Basil Blackwell, 1977.

France, Marie. 'Sadomasochism and Feminism.' *Feminist Review* 16 (Summer 1984): 35–42.

Frankenberg, Ruth. *White Women, Race Matters: The Social Construction of Whiteness.* London: Routledge, 1993.

Garrett, Alexander. 'Safe. But is Asylum in Britain Sound?' *Guardian* 12 May 2002. *www.observer.co.uk/cash/story.*

Geertz, Clifford. *The Interpretation of Cultures.* New York: Basic Books, 1973.

Ghuman, Paul A. Singh. *Asian Adolescents in the West.* Leicester: British Psychological Society, 1999.

Gilman, Sander L. 'Black Bodies, White Bodies: Toward an Iconography of Female Sexuality in Late Nineteenth-Century Art, Medicine and Literature.' In Donald and Rattansi 1992. 171–97.

Gilroy, Paul. *There Ain't No Black in the Union Jack: The Cultural Politics of Race and Nation.* London: Unwin Hyman, 1987. Rpt London: Routledge, 1992.

Gilroy, Paul. *The Black Atlantic: Modernity and Double Consciousness.* London: Verso, 1993.

Griffin, Gabriele. 'The Struggle Continues – An Interview with Hannana Siddiqui of Southall Black Sisters.' Gabriele Griffin, ed.

Feminist Activism in the 1990s. London: Taylor and Francis, 1995. 79–89.

Hall, Stuart. 'The Question of Cultural Identity.' Stuart Hall, David Held, and Tony McGrew, eds. *Modernity and Its Futures.* Cambridge: Polity Press, 1992. 273–316.

Hammonds, Evelynn. 'Black (W)holes and the Geometry of Black Female Subjectivity.' *Differences* 6 (Summer–Fall 1994): 126–45.

Higginbotham, Evelyn Brooks. 'African-American Women's History and the Metalanguage of Race.' *Signs* 17/2 (Winter 1992): 251–74.

Hill, Mike, ed. *Whiteness: A Critical Reader.* New York: New York University Press, 1997.

hooks, bell. *Feminist Theory: From Margin to Center.* Boston MA: South End Press, 1984.

Hüchtker, D. 'Deconstruction of Gender and Women's Agency.' *Feminist Theory* 2/3 (December 2001): 328–48.

Hyde, Alan. 'The Racial Body.' *Bodies of Law.* Princeton: Princeton University Press, 1997. 222–40.

Ifekwunigwe, Jayne O. 'Diaspora's Daughters, Africa's Orphans? On Lineage, Authenticity and "Mixed Race" Identity.' In Mirza 1997. 127–52.

Ifekwunigwe, Jayne O. *Scattered Belongings: Cultural Paradoxes of "Race," Nation and Gender.* London: Routledge, 1999.

James, Selma, ed. *Strangers and Sisters: Women, Race and Immigration.* Bristol: Falling Wall Press, 1985.

Jeffreys, Sheila. *The Spinster and Her Enemies: Feminism and Sexuality 1880–1930.* London: Pandora Press, 1985.

Jenkins, Richard. 'Black Workers in the Labour Market: The Price of Recession.' In Braham *et al.* 1992. 148–63.

Johnson, Buzz. *I Think of My Mother: Notes on the Life and Times of Claudia Jones.* London: Karia Press, 1985.

Jones, Lisa. 'The Hair Trade.' In Shohat 1998. 119–30.

Karpf, Anne. 'We've Been Here Before.' *Guardian* 8 June 2002. www.guardian.co.uk/weekend/story.

Kay, Jackie. *The Adoption Papers.* Newcastle upon Tyne: Bloodaxe Books, 1991.

Kemp, S. and P. Bono, eds. *The Lonely Mirror: Italian Perspectives on Feminist Theory*. London: Routledge, 1993.

Kendall, Tina, ed. *Bad Reputation: Yorkshire Women, Politics and Power*. Castleford: Yorkshire Arts Circus, 1994.

Kristeva, Julia. *Desire in Language*. 1977. Ed. Leon Roudiez. Oxford: Basil Blackwell, 1980.

Kristeva, Julia. *Powers of Horror: An Essay on Abjection*. Trans. Leon S. Roudiez. New York: Columbia University Press, 1982.

Kristeva, Julia. *Revolution in Poetic Language*. 1974. Trans. Margaret Waller. New York: Columbia University Press, 1984.

Kristeva, Julia. 'Stabat Mater.' Toril Moi, ed. *The Kristeva Reader*. Oxford: Basil Blackwell, 1986. 160–86.

Kristeva, Julia. 'Women's Time.' Toril Moi, ed. *The Kristeva Reader*. Oxford: Basil Blackwell, 1986. 187–213.

Kristeva, Julia. *Strangers to Ourselves*. Trans. Leon S. Roudiez. London: Harvester Wheatsheaf, 1991.

Kureshi, Hanif. *Dreaming and Scheming: Reflections on Writing and Politics*. London: Faber and Faber, 2002.

Lewis, Reina. 'Dis-Graceful Images: Della Grace and Lesbian Sado-Masochism.' *Feminist Review* 46 (Spring 1994): 76–91.

Lively, Adam. *Masks: Blackness, Race and the Imagination*. London: Vintage, 1999.

Luthra, Mohan. *Britain's Black Population*. Aldershot: Arena/Ashgate, 1997.

MacKenzie, John M. *Propaganda and Empire: The Manipulation of British Public Opinion 1880–1960*. Manchester: Manchester University Press, 1984.

Mama, Amina. 'Black Women, the Economic Crisis and the British State.' *Feminist Review* 17 (Autumn 1984): 21–35. Excerpted Mirza 1997. 36–41.

Mama, Amina. *Beyond the Masks: Race, Gender and Subjectivity*. London: Routledge, 1995.

Mason-John, Valerie, ed. *Talking Black*. London: Cassell, 1995.

McDowell, Deborah E. 'Reading Family Matters.' Cheryl A. Wall, ed. *Changing Our Own Words: Essays on Criticism, Theory, and*

Writing by Black Women. 1989. Rpt London: Routledge, 1990. 75–97.

Mercer, Kobena. *Welcome to the Jungle: New Positions in Black Cultural Studies.* London: Routledge, 1994.

Milan Women's Bookstore Collective. *Sexual Difference: A Theory of Social-Symbolic Practice.* 1987. Trans. Patricia Cicogna and Teresa de Lauretis. Bloomington: Indiana University Press, 1990.

Mirza, Heidi, ed. *Black British Feminism.* London: Routledge, 1997.

Modood, Tariq. 'Ethnic Diversity and Racial Disadvantage in Employment.' In Blackstone *et al.* 1998. 53–73.

Modood, Tariq *et al. Ethnic Minorities in Britain: Diversity and Disadvantage.* London: Policy Studies Institute, 1997.

Morrison, Toni. *Playing in the Dark: Whiteness and the Literary Imagination.* London: Picador, 1993.

National Lesbian and Gay Survey. *What a Lesbian Looks Like: Writings by Lesbians on Their Lives and Lifestyles.* London: Routledge, 1992.

Ngcobo, Lauretta, ed. *Let It Be Told: Black Women Writers in Britain.* London: Virago, 1988.

Omosupe, Ekua. 'Black/Lesbian/Bulldagger.' *Differences* 3 (Summer 1991): 101–11.

Osborn, Andrew. 'Pygmy Show at Zoo Sparks Disgust.' *Observer* 11 August 2002: 19.

Osler, Audrey. *Speaking Out: Black Girls in Britain.* London: Virago Upstairs, 1989.

Owen, David. *Ethnic Minorities in Britain: Settlement Patterns.* 1991 Census Statistical Paper No. 1. University of Warwick: Centre for Research in Ethnic Relations, November 1992.

Owen, David. *Country of Birth: Settlement Patterns.* 1991 Census Statistical Paper No. 5. University of Warwick: Centre for Research in Ethnic Relations, December 1993.

Pahl, Jan. 'Refuges for Battered Women: Ideology and Action.' *Feminist Review* 19 (Spring 1985): 25–44.

Perverse Politics: Lesbian Issues. Special issue of *Feminist Review* 34 (Spring 1990).

Piper, Adrian. 'Passing for White, Passing for Black.' In Shohat 1998. 75–112.

Pizzey, Erin. *Scream Quietly or the Neighbours Will Hear.* Harmondsworth: Penguin, 1974.

Ponzanesi, Sandra. 'Diasporic Subjects and Migration.' Gabriele Griffin and Rosi Braidotti, eds. *Thinking Differently: A Reader in European Women's Studies.* London: Zed Books, 2002. 205–20.

Price, Lisa. 'Sexual Violence and Ethnic Cleansing: Attacking the Family.' Gabriele Griffin and Rosi Braidotti, eds. *Thinking Differently: A Reader in European Women's Studies.* London: Zed Books, 2002. 252–66.

Rajan, Gita. '(Con)figuring Identity: Cultural Space of the Indo-British Intellectual.' In Brinker-Gabler and Smith 1997. 78–99.

Rassool, Naz. 'Fractured or Flexible Identities? Life Histories of 'Black' Diasporic Women in Britain.' In Mirza 1997. 187–204.

Rich, Adrienne. 'Compulsory Heterosexuality and Lesbian Existence.' 1980. Rpt in *Blood, Bread and Poetry: Selected Prose 1979–1985.* London: Virago, 1986. 23–75.

Riley, Denise. *'Am I That Name?' Feminism and the Category of 'Women' in History.* Basingstoke: Macmillan, 1988.

Riley, Joan. *The Unbelonging.* London: Women's Press, 1985.

Root, Maria P. P. 'Mixed-Race Women.' In Zack 1997. 157–74.

Rose, Tricia. ' "Two Inches or a Yard": Silencing Black Women's Sexual Expression.' In Shohat 1998. 315–24.

Rowbotham, Sheila. *Women in Movement: Feminism and Social Action.* London: Routledge, 1992.

Ryan, Chris and C. Michael Hall. *Sex Tourism: Marginal People and Liminalities.* London: Routledge, 2001.

Sebestyen, Amanda, ed. *'68, '78, '88: From Women's Liberation to Feminism.* Bridport, Dorset: Prism Press, 1988.

Shaw, Carolyn Martin. 'The Poetics of Identity: Questioning Spiritualism in African American Contexts.' Elizabeth Abel, Barbara Christian, and Helene Moglen, eds. *Female Subjects in Black and White: Race, Psychoanalysis and Feminism.* Berkeley: University of California Press, 1997. 349–62.

Shohat, Ella, ed. *Talking Visions: Multicultural Feminism in a Transnational Age.* New York: MIT Press, 1998.

Shrage, Laurie. 'Passing Beyond the Other Race or Sex.' In Zack 1997. 183–90.

Silvera, Makeda. 'Man Royals and Sodomites: Some Thoughts on the Invisibility of Afro-Caribbean Lesbians.' Martha Vicinus, ed. *Lesbian Subjects.* Bloomington: Indiana University Press, 1996. 167–77.

Smith, Bonnie G., ed. *Global Feminisms since 1945.* London: Routledge, 2000.

Smyth, Cherry. *Lesbians Talk Queer Notions.* London: Scarlet Press, 1992.

Solomos, John. 'The Politics of Immigration since 1945.' In Braham *et al.* 1992. 7–29.

Solomos, John. *Race and Racism in Britain.* 1983. 2nd edn. Basingstoke: Macmillan, 1993.

Southall Black Sisters. 'Two Struggles: Challenging Male Violence and the Police.' Jill Radford and Dianna E. H. Russell, eds. *Femicide: The Politics of Woman Killing.* Buckingham: Open University Press, 1992.

Southall Black Sisters. *Domestic Violence and Asian Women.* Southall: Southall Black Sisters, 1997.

Stimpson, Catharine. 'Zero-Degree Deviancy: The Lesbian Novel in English.' *Critical Inquiry* 8 (Winter 1981): 363–79.

Stuttaford, Thomas. 'Paying the Ultimate Price.' *The Times* 12 November 1992: 19.

Sulter, Maud. *As a Blackwoman: Poems 1982–1985.* Hebden Bridge: Urban Fox Press, 1985.

Thiam, Awa. *Black Sisters, Speak Out: Feminism and Oppression in Black Africa.* 1978. London: Pluto, 1986.

Thomas, Elean. 'Claudia Jones, 1915–1964.' *Spare Rib* 202 (June 1989): 16–19.

Visram, Rozina. *Asians in Britain: 400 Years of History.* London: Pluto, 2002.

Walker, Alice. *In Search of Our Mothers' Gardens – Womanist Prose.* 1983. London: Women's Press, 1984.

Wall, Cheryl A., ed. *Changing Our Own Words: Essays on Criticism, Theory and Writing by Black Women.* 1989. Rpt London: Routledge, 1990.

Wallace, Michele. *Black Macho and the Myth of the Superwoman.* 1978. Rpt London: Verso, 1990.

Wambu, Onyekachi, ed. *Empire Windrush: Fifty Years of Writing about Black Britain.* London: Victor Gollancz, 1998.

Ward Jouve, Nicole. *'The Street Cleaner': The Yorkshire Ripper Case on Trial.* London: Marion Boyars, 1986.

Ware, Vron. *Beyond the Pale: White Women, Racism and History.* London: Verso, 1992.

Wilson, Amrit. *Finding a Voice: Asian Women in Britain.* London: Virago, 1978.

Wilson, Anna. 'Audre Lorde and the African-American Tradition: When the Family is not Enough.' Sally Munt, ed. *New Lesbian Criticism: Literary and Cultural Readings.* London: Harvester Wheatsheaf, 1992. 75–93.

Young, Robert J. C. *Colonial Desire: Hybridity in Theory, Culture and Race.* London: Routledge, 1995.

Zack, Naomi, ed. *Race/Sex: Their Sameness, Difference and Interplay.* London: Routledge, 1997.

Zindika. 'Interview.' 17 March 2001.

Zindika Kamauesi and Natalie Smith, eds. *When Will I See You Again!* London: Pen Press Publishers, 2002.

Index

Lightning Source UK Ltd.
Milton Keynes UK
UKOW02f1715050317
295892UK00001B/213/P